Home Cooking Parties for™

. . .Eight

by
John Perides

An easy to follow guide for friends to cook a restaurant style meal at home for half the cost

Home Cooking Parties Publishing
Medford, New Jersey

Library of Congress Control Number 2007931324
ISBN 978-0-615-15207-3
Copyright © 2007 by John Perides
All Rights Reserved Under International and
Pan-American Copyright Conventions
Published by Home Cooking Parties Publishing
Printed in the United States of America

Home Cooking Parties for™ . . . Eight

This easy to follow guide for home cooking parties includes everything you need to hold a cooking party for eight friends tonight. Best of all you share the cost and all of the work equally. You only need to invite them and tell them what to buy and bring. The rest is taken care of by this guide. So start the fun tonight. Included in this guide

Complete Menus for 15 Different International Meals

Shopping Lists for Each Friend

Recipes for Every Item

Preparation Plans Down to the Minute

Including . . . Who chops
. . . Who cooks
. . . Who plates and serves
. . . When to start
. . . When to serve
. . . Which pot or pan to use
. . . Which plate to use
. . . How to dress the plate

Contents

Introduction

…to Ma

When you are Greek, or in my case half Greek and half Italian with a Greek name, you grow up used to everyone mispronouncing your name. In fact in a mixed cultural setting like America, you eventually give up on correcting people and respond to whatever they call you…..

My dad, Steve, did not have a Greek accent; he was born in New York City and was only interested in being completely American. What was never lost in the Americanization of the Perides family was the love of food. All of my relatives were in the food business. My dad stayed away from the food business in his teens and 20s, but in 1946, when he returned from WWII, he trained as a butcher and then rented the meat counter in the back of his step dad's grocery store. I grew up behind that meat counter in the 1950s and in the independent butcher shop he opened around 1960 and retired from in 1973…..

Dad drilled it into my head that I was going to college and would work with my head – not my back – in my adult life. That happened because my parents wanted it to happen, but it doesn't change your name or your instincts…..

If you come from New York and New Jersey (after college), you can't help but notice that nearly every diner you walk into is owned by Greeks. That makes you stop and wonder if food should have been your adult way of life. So I ate it. I cooked it. I entertained with it. I built friendships around it. In short, it has been my avocation for over 40 years…..

For the last 10 years, I have been partying with friends over food in a special way, sharing everything. Buying it - Preparing it - Cooking it - Eating it…..“We are a family because we eat together” is even truer when you share the gathering and preparing of the food before eating it. The bonds of friendship, love and commitment grow stronger if you go those extra steps. Home Cooking Parties for Eight is a way to build those bonds within your family and within your friendships…..

Do not fear if you have a large family or a small kitchen. I have used these Home Cooking Parties for Eight plans for as many as 20 people at a single dinner and in the tiniest of kitchens. Just be sure you jimmy-up a big enough dining table and all sit down together to eat the meal…..

Now get to it. Pick a menu, invite your friends and share a great meal!

What is Home Cooking Parties for Eight?

Home Cooking Parties for Eight is an entertainment and relationship building book — not a cookbook. It shows how eight people can come together, share the expense and work of putting on a gourmet meal for themselves and have a wonderful time in the process. In this book there are detailed instructions for staging fifteen parties, but you are probably interested in the short version of how to get a fast start on one, so here it is. . . .

Getting a Fast Start

You can throw a Home Cooking Party for Eight tonight with almost no preparation. Do the following 5 easy steps and you are ready to start.

1. *Pick one of the menus in this book and make four copies of the Shopping List for that menu. Make at least one copy of the Preparation Plan and Recipes for that menu, too.*

2. *Ask 7 friends to come to a great dinner where you will all share the cost and fun of making the dinner.*

3. *Set up 4 teams of 2. Get a copy of the shopping list to each team and tell them their team number (the Host is always Team 4). On the list they will see what to buy and bring to the dinner. Tell them what time to be at your house with their groceries and that promptness is important. Each dinner is about a five hour experience from arrival to departure.*

4. *Shop for the items you don't have already on your part of the list and be home to welcome your friends.*

5. *When they are all there, open to the Preparation Schedule for the menu you selected and begin.*

You don't need to read anything else in this book to succeed. Enjoy the fun and the food!

Extra Quick Tips

You may want to make an extra copy of the Preparation Schedule to have around the kitchen and one extra set of Recipes to keep your originals clean. If you start at a different time than the 4:00 pm shown on each schedule, hand mark up your copies of the Preparation Schedule. Just add or subtract from each time to adjust the entire schedule. So if you start at 6:00 pm add 2 hours to every time shown in the schedule.

Stories, Menus, Shopping Lists, Prep Schedules & Recipes

Greek Style Dinner

Greek Style Dinner

Since my mother was Italian and my father was Greek, most of the food we ate was Italian. I would get the Greek food when we would visit the "Greek Side." My Grandma, aunts, uncles and cousins would set feasts of unusual foods before us each Greek Easter, during the Greek celebration of Christmas, the Epiphany, or on summer visits. On those days or at a big Greek wedding, the aromas and flavors would burst forward from an unusual array of appetizers, main courses and deserts. Wow!

Since I had this good fortune, I couldn't help but want to share a few of these great tastes with you. Believe me; you won't be hungry after this meal. Leftovers and doggie bags are okay. Good luck and stock up on the garlic!

When you visit a Greek diner there are so many meat dishes on the menu that most xenos (non-Greeks) believe that meat is the Greek staple. Not so fast. Greece and its islands have thousands of miles of coastline on the Mediterranean Sea where fish is the staple. Tonight's dinner has a nice, light entrée for our main course from those coastal regions with a twist. We will use salmon, a hearty cold water fish. If you are in Greece you would more likely find this dish served with sword fish, tuna, bream, sea bass or porgy. If you would like, any of these could be substituted for the salmon.

I am recommending ouzo with this meal for more authenticity as both an aperitif and as an after dinner drink. WARNING! If you don't like licorice, you will not like ouzo. Barring that oddity, you can drink ouzo straight up in shots or as a mixed drink. Try it over cracked ice; try it mixed with water or club soda (it turns milky white); or mix it with vodka and orange juice for a new twist on the screwdriver. If you become really interested in ouzo, there are dozens if not hundreds of bar recipes on the internet. The key to drinking ouzo is to eat snacks known as mezedes. These keep the effects of the alcohol from overwhelming you and enable you to sit and drink slowly for hours in a profoundly calm state of mind where all is beautiful and life is fine. In the villages of Greece where life is slow people can be found in the tavernas drinking ouzo day or night. Sunday afternoons after church the tavernas fill up with lively voices and singing. Sometimes the village priest even shows up to sing (and drink). Men do much of the cooking and serving in the tavernas, but when it is done by a woman, she typically acts as a den mother to the old men who come around each day. She knows their likes and dislikes, favorite seats and personal history.

You can get close to this feeling of "taverna" right in your own home by sharing this meal and its preparation with friends you know a lot about. For fun, throw in a few people you don't know that well. After a few ouzos, who cares? You will come to know them all as close friends.

Greek Style Dinner

5:00 p.m.   **Cocktails**

Ouzo
Wine, Beer, Mixed Drinks

        Mezedes

Crackers with Yogurt/Onion Dip
Chopped Green Olives and Pimientos on Baguette
Feta Cheese
Manouri Cheese (substitute: Kasseri)
Celery and Kalamata Olives

6:30 p.m.   **Dinner**

    Beverages   Water, Wine, Beer and Soda

    Soup   Avgolemono Soup with Peloponnesian Dolmades

    Salad   Classic Greek Salad

    Entree   Olive Crusted Salmon

        Accompanied by

Spanakorizo

    Dessert   Cousin Frannie's Baklava
Aunt Stasa's Finikia
Café and Tea
Liqueur - Ouzo

Greek Style Dinner Shopping Lists

Shopper 1

1 lb. ground beef
½ cup dry mint
32 lg grape leaves (64 sm) (fresh or jarred)
**In lieu of the above three items, buy 32
pre-made dolmades with meat or rice in
cans packed in oil.**

1 lb sweet, unsalted butter
2 lbs butter
10 cups chicken broth
1 pint plain yogurt
1 package dried onion soup/dip mix
1 box stone ground wheat crackers
5 cups uncooked white rice
1 large jar honey
4 packages of frozen, chopped spinach;

Shopper 2

2 large heads Romaine lettuce
3 small red onions
8 small/medium or 4 large white onions
2 bunches scallions
1 green bell pepper
1 red bell pepper
3 large tomatoes
2 small or one large cucumber (small ones
have fewer seeds)
3 full heads of garlic
1 bunch fresh thyme
1 bunch fresh oregano
1 bunch fresh dill
1 bunch fresh parsley
8 celery stalks
1 (16 ounce) package phyllo dough
2 lb Kalamata black olives

Shopper 3

2 loaves of French baguette bread
4 pieces of pita bread
1 lb chunk of Feta cheese
1 lb chunk of Manouri cheese (substitute:
Kasseri cheese)
1 cup crumbled feta cheese(w/extra spices)
1 medium jar green olives with pimientos
1 small jar pimientos (packed in oil)
1 small jar of small capers
2-½ lbs walnuts nuts) (pieces okay)
10 lemons

Shopper 4 (Host)

8 six-ounce salmon fillets
salt
ground black pepper
3 tsp dried oregano
½ tsp garlic salt
1 TBSP dried dill
1 TBSP corn starch
2 tsp baking powder
3 tsp ground cinnamon
½ tsp rosewater (or vanilla extract)
6 cups sugar
2 eggs
1-½ quarts olive oil
1 cup corn oil
1 cup orange juice
4 cups sifted flour
1 cup unseasoned bread crumbs

Preparation Schedule – Greek Style Dinner

Teams
1/
2/
3/
4/Hosts

4:00 pm	**1, 2, & 3**- Arrive at **4**'s. Put on chef's aprons. Unpack and stack groceries in a central location. Put fish and meat in refrigerator. Leave cheese, phyllo, spinach at room temperature. Have a cocktail. **1**- Start Mezedes Platter 1 recipe and serve with first cocktails. **4**- Serve cocktails. Start Avgolemono Soup and Dolmades recipe, while enjoying a cocktail and mezedes with guests.
4:15 pm	**1**- Start Finikia Cookie recipe and complete. **2**- Start Mezedes Platter 2 recipe and serve, immediately. **3**- Start Mezedes Platter 3 recipe and serve, immediately. **4**- Continue soup prep. At the same time, set table and continue serving drinks.
4:30 pm	**4**- Continue soup prep until dolmades are formed and simmering in the chicken stock. At the same time, pan roast/sauté 2 heads of garlic according to Instructions in Olive Crusted Salmon.
5:00 pm	**1, 2, 3 & 4**- Eat mezedes and drink cocktails as they are ready, while you merrily work on your other food preparations. **2**- Pre-heat oven to 350°. Start Baklava recipe. Continue until complete. Baklava should be in the oven no later than 5:45 pm. **3**- Chop ingredients and assemble according to Greek Salad recipe. Refrigerate to marinate until ready to serve. **4**- Dolmades should be simmering in chicken stock by now. Soup prep for serving will be completed by **1**. Start Olive Crusted Salmon recipe. Continue until crust is complete and on salmon. Cover salmon with plastic wrap and place pan in refrigerator.
5:15 pm	**1**- Pick up soup prep and cooking where **4** left off.
5:45 pm.	**1**- Plate Avgolemono and Dolmades Soup and serve. **2**- Latest time to put Baklava in oven. If it is in ahead of time, good. Complete prep of syrup for Baklava. **3**- Help **1** plate, garnish and serve soup.
6:00 pm	**Eat Soup in Dining Room** **At 6:15 everyone helps clear soup dishes to the kitchen.**

6:15 pm	**1-** Pick up Greek Salad recipe where **3** left off. Chop lettuce and complete assembly and dressing. Plate and serve. **2-** Watch the Baklava to be sure it does not burn. Remove the Baklava when it is browned properly. Complete soaking with syrup. **3-** Cut pita bread into quarters. Help **1** plate and serve salad. Add quartered pita to salads. **4-** Start Spanakorizo recipe. Complete and serve at 7:30 pm.
6:30 pm	**Eat Salad in Dining Room** **At 6:45 everyone helps clear salad dishes to the kitchen.**
6:45 pm	**1-** Put salmon in oven at 350°. Watch the salmon so the crust does not burn and the fish remains moist and tender. Use broiler as shown in recipe if crust needs more browning. **2-** Baklava should be out of the oven and soaking in syrup by now.
7:00 pm	**3-** Warm dinner plates. Put butter for bread on dinner table.
7:15 pm	**1-** Plate salmon. Work with **4** in plating entrée. Follow plating and garnishing directions in salmon recipe. **3-** Slice 1 baguette into 12 pieces. Heat bread for 5 minutes in oven. Place in basket, cover with a cloth napkin and set on table. **4-** Plate Spanakorizo. Follow plating directions in salmon recipe, and pass to **1** for plating salmon.
7:30 pm	**Eat Entree in Dining Room** **At 8:00 everyone helps clear dishes to the kitchen.**
8:00 pm	**1-** Prepare syrup for dipping Finikia cookies. While syrup comes to a boil, prepare cookie topping. Dip cookies for 2 or 3 seconds when syrup boils, set on non-stick baking sheet or parchment, and add topping to warm cookies.
8:15 pm	**1-** Plate Finikia (2). Decorate dessert plate with honey. **2-** Cut and plate Baklava. Work with **1** on plating dessert. **3-** Brew coffee and tea. Set out ouzo for after dinner drink. **4-** Set up coffee cups, dessert plates, spoons and forks for service.
8:30 pm	**Eat Dessert and Have Coffee in Dining Room** **Relax! Job Well Done!**

Mezedes

Remember, the idea is to get these out fast to go with the cocktails.

Ingredients:

Platter 1:
1 pint plain yogurt
1 package dried onion soup/dip mix
1 box stone ground wheat crackers

Platter 2:
1 medium jar green olives with pimientos
1 small jar pimientos (packed in oil)
6 small capers
½ tsp garlic salt
½ lemon; juiced
1 TBSP olive oil
ground black pepper
1 loaf of French baguette bread

Platter3:
½ lb chunk of Feta cheese
½ lb chunk of Manouri cheese (substitute: Kasseri cheese)
½ lb Kalamata black olives
8 celery stalks
2 TBSP olive oil
1 tsp dried oregano

Instructions:

Platter 1: Mix one package of dry onion soup mix with a pint of plain yogurt. Place yogurt dip into medium bowl. Place bowl in the center of a serving platter. Place wheat crackers around the yogurt and onion dip and serve with first cocktails.

Platter 2: Finely chop the green olives with pimientos with extra pimientos and a few capers, garlic salt, ground pepper, the juice of ½ lemon and 1 TBSP of olive oil into a tapenade. This can be done by pulsing in a food processor to the consistency of a lumpy mix (do not puree into a paste. It's okay if you accidentally do. Cut baguette into thin slices and top with olive and pimiento tapenade; plate and serve as mezedes, immediately.

Platter 3: Chunk ½ lb each of Feta and Manouri cheeses for mezedes; wash and cut 8 celery stalks. Plate cheeses and celery stalks together. Sprinkle on a few Kalamata olives. Drizzle olive oil and then sprinkle dried oregano over the olives, cheeses and stalks. When you sprinkle the oregano get it on the borders of the platter, too. Serve these mezedes, immediately.

Plating:

Plate all items on serving platters and serve family style while everyone works. Provide small plates, napkins and toothpicks along with these finger foods.

Avgolemono Soup with Greek Dolmades

This recipe contains meat and is from Southern Greece (The Peloponysos). There is also a Greek Dolmades recipe from Asia Minor (Constantinople) which was 80% Greek-populated until 1920 when ethnic cleansing by the Turks began in earnest. My family came from Constantinople and Smyrna in Asia Minor and was directly impacted by that cleansing with some aunts, uncles and cousins paying with their lives. My grandparents left Turkey at separate times over a decade earlier and were introduced to each other in America. The Constantinople Greek Dolmades recipe is meatless, essentially seasoned rice wrapped with grape leaves and marinated.

Grape leaves are best picked from Grape Vines in the spring, while they are still tender. They can be washed and frozen between layers of waxed paper and will keep for a year. They are also available in jars from some fruit markets or specialty stores that carry Greek or Italian imported foods. Your goal is to find grape leaves that have very thin veins, which will make the taste less stringy.

A tremendous shortcut for this recipe is to buy pre-made dolmades packed in oil, but that wouldn't be as much fun, would it? Pre-made is more expensive. Use your discretion on this point. I give the option on the shopping list of taking the shortcut. If you choose pre-made, drop down to Cooking Dolmades and Soup Base.

The **dolmades** are made first, then the soup.

Dolmades Ingredients:
1 lb. ground beef
1 large white onion; minced
½ cup uncooked white rice
1 egg
½ cup dry mint
1 TBSP butter; softened
½ bunch fresh parsley
3-½ TBSP lemon juice
salt
pepper
Up to 4 TBSP of water, if needed
32 large grape leaves (64 small) (fresh or jarred)

In lieu of all of the above, buy 32 pre-made dolmades with meat in cans packed in oil.

Dolmades Instructions:

Put a large pot of water on the stove to boil grape leaves.

While waiting for water to boil, thoroughly mix all ingredients except chicken broth and grape leaves in a bowl. If the consistency is too hard, add water, one tablespoon at a time (up to 4 tablespoons). The proper consistency will be slightly sticky, similar to an uncooked meatball.

Depending on the size of the leaves, you will need approximately 32 grape leaves (Fila - pronounced fee'-lah). Small leaves tend to be more tender, but you may need more small leaves to make the 32 dolmades. If packed in a jar, drop the grape leaves into boiling water without separating. When the water returns to the boil turn off the heat. Cover and let the pot stand for 10 minutes until the leaves are softened, but not so tender that they fall apart when you handle them. If fresh grape leaves are used, drop them into boiling water and continue to boil for one minute. Remove from heat and drain immediately.

Fold grape leaves around a tablespoon of meat mixture, sealing completely.

Soup Base Ingredients:
32 dolmades (from above)
½ stick butter
6 cups chicken broth

Cooking Dolmades and Soup Base: If you start with pre-made, canned dolmades, this step is your starting point and cut the simmering time in half. In a large pot, preferably one with a large surface area on the bottom, melt ½ stick (4 tablespoons) butter. Arrange rolled dolmades on top of the melted butter. Do this all at once, not as you roll them. Pour 6 cups of chicken broth over dolmades, cover pot, and simmer for 1 hour. This broth will also become the soup base after the simmering is complete (see below).

Final Avgolemono Soup Ingredients:
Hot soup base from cooking dolmades (above)
1 egg
1 tsp water
3 TBSP lemon juice
1 TBSP corn starch
1 TBSP dill; dried
Zest of lemon

Final Avgolemono Soup Steps Done Just Before Plating the Soup:

Zest one lemon for garnish. Squeeze one to two lemons to obtain 3 tablespoons of juice.

Separate egg. Whisk egg white mixed with 1 teaspoon water in a large bowl until frothy. Add yolk and mix.

Add corn starch to lemon juice and stir; whisk while pouring into egg mixture.

Skim a cup of hot broth off of the dolmades. It is now a chicken/beef broth, due to simmering with the ground beef inside of dolmades, and should be reduced if you started with uncooked rice inside of the dolmades. Add 1 tablespoon of the soup at a time to the egg mixture while whisking well. Egg mixture should thicken. Do not pour the cup of broth into the whisked egg or vice versa, since that will just cook the egg.

Plating:

Remove all dolmades from the broth pot. Arrange 3 to 5 dolmades (depending upon appetite) into each soup bowl for serving. Mix remaining broth into the thickened egg-lemon mixture. Stir well and ladle into soup bowls over dolmades. Garnish with a pinch of dried dill and a bit of lemon zest. Serve and enjoy!

Classic Greek Salad

Greeks like to eat their salad at the end of the meal, but before dessert. You might try this sometime, it helps with digestion. For this meal we will keep it before the entrée for all of your non-Greek (i.e. xeno) guests. Rinse and dry the lettuce in advance and allow it to dry completely so it will be crispy. Assemble the non-lettuce ingredients and the dressing, well in advance to allow them to marinate in the refrigerator. Use half of the dressing in the marinating ingredients. Save half of the dressing to add fresh when you chop and toss in the lettuce, just before serving.

Salad Ingredients:

2 large heads Romaine lettuce; rinse and dry leaves; reserve 8 whole leaves from the head for use on the plate to hold tossed salad; chop the rest of the 2 heads just before serving
1 small red onion; very thinly sliced
8 ounces cracked and pitted black olives; preferably Kalamata
1 green bell pepper; chopped
1 red bell pepper; chopped
3 large tomatoes; chopped
2 small or one large cucumber; sliced (small ones have fewer seeds)
1 cup crumbled feta cheese (ready crumbled with extra spices already added is okay)
4 pieces of pita bread; quartered

Dressing Ingredients:

¾ cup olive oil
1-½ tsp dried oregano
3 lemons; juiced
ground black pepper to taste

Instructions:

Slice onion and cucumbers. Chop peppers and tomatoes. In a large bowl, combine the sliced onion, pitted olives, bell peppers, tomatoes, cucumber, and feta cheese.

In a separate bowl, whisk together the olive oil, oregano, lemon juice and black pepper. Pour half of the dressing on the chopped ingredients, toss, cover and place bowl in refrigerator to marinate until ready to complete and serve salad. Reserve other half of dressing at room temperature until just before serving.

When ready to serve, reserve 8 whole pieces of lettuce for plate garnish. Chop the rest of the Romaine lettuce and place in a large salad bowl with other marinated ingredients. Be sure the bowl is large enough to toss the salad well after the rest of the dressing is added. Re-whisk the remaining dressing and pour over salad; toss thoroughly and plate.

Plating:

For plate presentation, place one large romaine lettuce leaf on a salad plate (trim to provide just a slight overlapping of the plate. Place a serving of the dressed, tossed salad onto the trimmed leaf and serve with pita bread cut into quarters.

Olive Crusted Salmon

No matter which fish you select for this dish, watch your baking time. The top of your crust should be medium brown and crisp while the fish is moist and tender.

Ingredients:

8 six-ounce salmon fillets (or other fish as desired)
1 cup unseasoned bread crumbs
16 ounces cracked, pitted and sliced Kalamata black olives

Topping Ingredients:

½ lb Manouri cheese; cut into small cubes (substitute: Kasseri cheese)
½ lb feta cheese; cut into small cubes
1 large or 2 small red onions; chopped
4 TBSP chopped fresh thyme
4 TBSP chopped fresh oregano
4 TBSP chopped roasted garlic
2 TBSP chopped capers
½ bunch fresh parsley

Instructions:

Peel 2 heads of garlic and slice cloves lengthwise in half. Heat oil in a pan at moderate to medium heat and add the garlic. Watch the pan and stir to make sure the garlic does not burn. As pieces of garlic turn golden brown on all sides remove them from the oil and place them on a paper towel to drain until all of the garlic is done. This pan roasted garlic will be used as part of the topping ingredients and as a plating garnish.

Pre-heat the oven to 350 degrees. Chop, cube and combine all of the topping ingredients (except bread crumbs and olives). Remember to keep some garlic, capers and herbs in reserve for the garnish. Slice most of the olives and reserve for assembling salmon topping. Save 16 whole olives for plate garnish.

Assembling topping on salmon: Grease a large baking pan and equally space the 8 salmon fillets in the pan. Equally divide the topping into eight portions and pat each portion onto each fillet. Sprinkle the sliced olives onto the topping, and then sprinkle the bread crumbs onto the olives. Lightly press down the bread crumbs and olives. The topped salmon can be covered and stored in the refrigerator ahead of time and brought out when it is time to cook in the oven.

Bake the fillets for 15 to 20 minutes at 350°. While the bread crumbs should be a golden brown in 20 minutes, you want to be sure that the fish is not overcooked. If the crust does not brown in 20 minutes and to preserve the moistness and tenderness of the fish, you may lightly brown the top crust under a broiler for 1 minute or less rather than continuing baking it in the oven longer than 20 minutes.

Plating:

Plate the fillet over the Spanakorizo. Place two generous piles of Spanakorizo, slightly separated, in the center of the plate. Place the salmon between the two piles of Spanakorizo. Garnish the edges of each plate with olives, capers, roasted garlic, freshly chopped thyme and oregano and a sprig or two of parsley.

Spanakorizo

After you eat this, you will never eat plain boiled spinach again!

Ingredients:

6 small/medium or 3 large white onions; chopped fine
8 cloves garlic; chopped fine
2 bunches scallions; thinly sliced
4 cups uncooked white rice; rinsed
4 packages of frozen, chopped spinach; thawed, thoroughly squeezed and drained
1 bunches fresh dill; chopped (substitute: 2 TBSP of dried dill)
4 cups olive oil
4 cups chicken stock
salt (to taste)
pepper (to taste)
1 lemon; juice (to taste)

Instructions:

Thaw, squeeze and drain spinach. Chop onions and garlic. Slice scallions. Rinse rice.

Heat half of the olive oil over medium heat in the widest pot you have with a cover. Add onions, garlic and scallions and sauté until soft and translucent. Do not brown! Add uncooked, rinsed rice and stir thoroughly to coat. Add thawed and drained spinach and stir in until all has been added and thoroughly coated with oil. Add 4 cups of chicken stock. Bring to a boil, cover and cook over low heat until rice is tender, approximately 20 minutes. Stir occasionally while cooking. Nearly all of the stock should be absorbed by the rice in the mix. Test the rice to be sure it is cooked. If the Spanakorizo is too wet, cook a bit longer to reduce excess liquid. Keep warm until ready to serve.

Just before serving chop fresh dill. Mix chopped dill and lemon juice into the Spanakorizo. Add salt and pepper to taste. Add only enough additional oil and stir in well to make the entire dish glisten, but it should not be overly runny with oil or broth. You don't want oil or broth running all over the dish when you plate this under the fish. If the Spanakorizo is too wet, use a slotted spoon when plating to drain off excess liquid.

Plating:

See plating instructions for fish.

Cousin Frannie's Baklava

My cousin Frances is half Italian and half Irish. So what's she doing making Baklava? She married Victor, a Syrian, and so began her love of Middle Eastern cooking. Baklava is so delicious that it is claimed by nearly all of the countries bordering on the Eastern Mediterranean. I can't blame them. An important difference of this recipe, compared to the restaurant style Baklavas which I don't care for, is my Italian mother's change (she learned from my Greek Grandma) of using fewer sheets of phyllo on the top and bottom. It makes the finished pastry easier to cut and eat with a fork without exploding all of the walnuts all over the plate and tabletop.

Baklava Ingredients:
1 (16 oz) package phyllo dough; thawed if frozen.
2 lbs (more if you like!) walnuts nuts; chopped fine
1-½ lbs butter; clarified (Yes, that's a lot of butter!)
2 tsp ground cinnamon
2 cups sugar

Syrup Ingredients:
1 cup water
2 cups white sugar
½ lemon; juiced
½ tsp rosewater (or vanilla extract)

Topping: Honey to drizzle over cut Baklava and for plate decoration just before serving

Baklava Directions:

In a food processor, pulse-grind 2 lbs of walnuts to a chunky texture. Avoid pulverizing the walnuts into dust! Put ground walnuts into a large bowl with 2 cups of sugar and cinnamon; mix well.

Melt the 1-½ lbs of butter in a pot and take off the white foam that rises to the top. Then skim the resulting clear yellow liquid off of the white stuff that is at the bottom of the pot. You will be using the clear yellow liquid. This is liquid is clarified butter and has a higher burn point than butter with that white stuff. By the way, you don't have to throw away all of the white stuff which will be 20 to 25% of the original butter. It is the highly flavorful milk solids and proteins from the butter and can be used in non-cooking applications.

If the phyllo is still frozen, stop! If it is thawed completely, open the phyllo and gently spread the pile of sheets flat. Keep the sheets stacked after you have unfolded the pile, and keep the pile of sheets covered with a damp cloth to keep them from drying out while you assemble the Baklava.

Use a 9" x 13" x 3" high pan. Brush the bottom and walls well with liquid butter.

Place a layer of phyllo in the bottom of pan. If you have the extra large sheets of phyllo, fold them or cut them in half and count each large sheet as 2 layers. Brush every layer of phyllo with liquid butter (yes, every layer).

Place 2 more layers of sheets in the bottom of pan and brush each with more butter. Spread a thin layer of walnut mix on the phyllo across the whole pan. This is a thin to medium thin layer. Just be sure to use up all of the walnut mix by the end of layering.

Place another layer of phyllo over the layer of walnuts. Brush generously (yes, generously) with liquid butter.

Repeat the layers of walnut mix, phyllo and brushed liquid butter until you reach the top of the pan. Be sure to use up all of the walnut mix. Save some liquid butter for basting halfway through the baking.

The top layer should be 2 layers of phyllo with butter brushed after each layer and generously on the top. Put pan into refrigerator for 15 minutes to harden the butter.

Preheat oven to 350°.

Remove Baklava from refrigerator after 15 minutes, and using a sharp knife, cut the chilled Baklava into squares or triangles. Both are traditional. The pieces should be about 3" x 3" square. Cut a few squares into triangles for those wishing a smaller piece, but do not remove any pieces from the pan as you cut. You will have leftovers of this. Be sure to cut cleanly all the way to the bottom of the pan and through the bottom layers of phyllo. This will allow the syrup to be applied later to circulate to all layers of the Baklava. Return the pan to the refrigerator briefly until the oven is properly preheated to 350°.

Put cut Baklava into oven and bake for 45 minutes or until top is golden brown. At the halfway point brush the top of the Baklava again with liquid butter.

While Baklava is baking make syrup. In a pot, pour in 2 cups of sugar and 1 cup of water. Add the juice of half a lemon. This is twice as thick as standard simple syrup, and the lemon helps keep the sugar in solution when the syrup is cooling to room temperature. Boil and keep stirring with a wooden spoon until the syrup lightly coats the spoon. It must remain liquidy. When the syrup reaches the boil add a ½ teaspoon of rosewater (or vanilla) into the syrup and stir. Boil for 10 more minutes, and then remove from the heat. Allow the syrup to cool slightly at room temperature until Baklava is ready, but do not chill.

When the Baklava is done, remove it from the oven and pour the syrup over the cut pieces in the pan. The syrup must be poured over the cut pieces while they are still in the pan to allow for soaking into the layers. Get some down the insides of the pan, too. If the baklava is hot, as is recommended here – fresh from the oven - the syrup can be warm (room temperature), but not cold. If you were to wait and the baklava cools then the syrup should be hot. One way or the other, this is a must or the Baklava will not soak up the syrup. This is light syrup and it has a subtle taste. Pour it on and let it soak in. Do not use the honey until you are ready to plate the Baklava.

Plating:

When you are ready for dessert, plate the piece of Baklava onto one side of a salad/dessert plate or a dinner plate. Place 2 Finikia cookies on the other side of the plate. Do not crowd these desserts onto a small plate. Drizzle a line or two of honey between the two desserts. Drizzle a generous zigzag line of honey over each dessert. Then serve.

Finikia Cookies

This recipe came from my Aunt Stasa. She escaped from Turkey in 1922 at the age of 5 or 6 with relatives and her infant sister. Her parents did not. Throughout the 1950s and 1960s we would have gala celebrations at her house in Brooklyn every Greek holiday. I couldn't wait for dessert, but if I got caught sneaking a cookie off the table before dinner….well, oh boy!

Cookie Dough Ingredients:

1 lb sweet, unsalted butter
¾ cup sugar
1 cup corn oil
2 level tsp baking powder
1 cup orange juice
½ tsp cinnamon
sifted flour (around 3 to 4 cups) (Use only as much as needed to form soft, pliable dough that does not stick to your hands.)

Dough Method and Baking:

Preheat the oven to 350°. Mix butter, sugar and oil until smooth. Add orange juice, baking powder and cinnamon; work well. Add as much flour, at ½ cup at a time, as needed to make a soft, pliable dough that does not stick to hands. Knead slightly. Pinch off pieces of dough the size of a large walnut and form into slightly flattened (3/4" high) oval shapes with slightly tapered (pinched) ends. Place on an ungreased cookie sheet. Bake at 350° until cooked through. Test a cookie at 20 minutes to see if it is cooked through. If not try again at 25 minutes. Cool cookies on rack.

Syrup Ingredients:

1 medium jar honey
1 cup sugar
1 cup water
1 lemon; juiced

Boil water, sugar and honey and add juice of one lemon and make a syrup.

Topping Ingredients:

8 ounces shelled walnuts (pieces are okay); chopped fine
½ tsp cinnamon
1 TBSP sugar
Some extra honey to drizzle on top

Topping Instructions: Mix chopped walnuts, cinnamon and sugar, well. Dip cooled Finikia cookies for 2 to 3 seconds into slowly boiling syrup and place on rack over a platter (these will drip). While the cookies are still wet and warm, sprinkle tops with the topping mixture of walnuts, cinnamon and sugar. Allow to cool on a rack before serving.

Plating:

See Baklava recipe for plating suggestion.

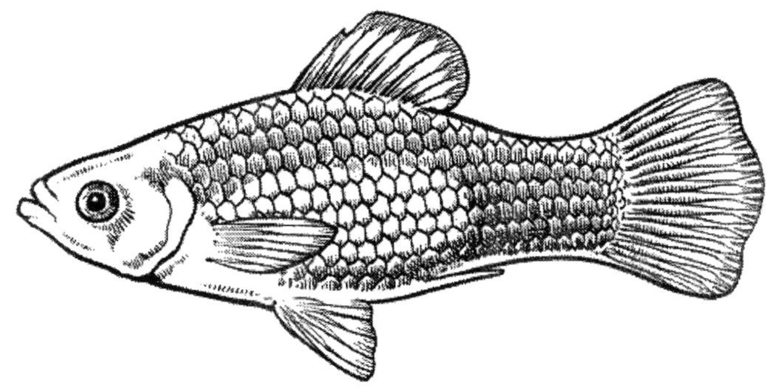

Greek Style Dinner with Meat

Greek Style Dinner with Meat

My dad, Steve Perides, had an Italian butcher shop (he was 100% Greek) on Rockaway Parkway in Canarsie (Brooklyn) for over 25 years. I grew up working in that store from the age of 8 and serving the wonderful assortment of customers and characters that came into the shop. Let me tell you about Caramello. That wasn't his real name. Few people went by their real names in the neighborhood. He was Caramello because he liked to chew on those soft Kraft caramels. He had one in his mouth all the time and was only too happy to show it to you through a toothy grin. He was an old Italian guy with a hat, no matter the season, who walked up and down the street of stores like he was the Mayor of Rockaway Parkway. At least once a day he would come into the store and all the butchers would shout out, "Hey, Caramello, what's up?" Caramello never came more than two steps into the store. He would lean against the wall near the door, silently looking at the yelling butchers out of the corner of his eyes and then, always with a sneer on his face and wave of his arm, say the same thing, "I no say nothin'." He would spend another minute in the air-conditioning and disappear out the door, never to be seen again until the next day when all would be repeated. He has a permanent place in my heart and mind, and he no said nothing!

It would be a major omission if I had only a Greek fish dinner in this book. I grew to a significant size, out — not up, unfortunately, from the concentrated protein and portions that came from my dad's store and from my mom's cooking. We would each get a full ribeye or sirloin steak for dinner and there was always an extra one for the meat platter, just in case anyone was still hungry. So here you are, a Greek meal with a generous helping of meat and respect for those delicious ribeyes. Once again, stock up on the garlic and ouzo!

The Tzatziki you will have tonight is a classic Greek appetizer dip, and if you choose, it can be used as a condiment with the main meal. This appeared occasionally on my Aunt Stasa's appetizer table but it did not burn into my soul until I sat in a taverna in the Plaka during a visit to Athens. The Tzatziki was served with simple slices of bread and pieces of cold cucumber. Maybe I was extra hungry that day, but it was instant love. When I came home a friend who had been in the taverna with me that day, begged me to make it for her party. So I did, and I almost killed everyone at the party. I had a slight miscue. I started by straining and draining regular plain yogurt like it said in the directions and wound up with only half the amount yogurt I had when I started. This was new to me, but it seems strained yogurt has been doing this for centuries. The recipe gave the amount of yogurt after straining. Only I didn't know this was important. That meant that the garlic I put in was twice as much as it should have been for the amount of yogurt I had. It turned into an unintended health food that burned everyone's lips, tongues and sensibilities! When you strain your yogurt overnight to remove the excess liquid, it will reduce almost in half. Keep this in mind. The recipe for this dinner takes this into account with a lot of warnings, so you should be able to taste the rest of the meal.

The dessert, Galatoboureko is a creamy sensation found at Greek festivals and pastry shops, but not readily in restaurants or at our family gatherings. So it took until my middle age to finally experience this at the St. Thomas Greek Orthodox Church Festival in Cherry Hill, New Jersey. I immediately went home and foraged for this recipe in a 50+ year old cookbook my Greek grandma had given to my Italian mother (…you know, for ideas…). Mom never made it. She never was big on cookbooks or measuring cups. Well it took over 50 years for this beauty to make it to the table. You will be glad it is on your dinner party table.

Greek Style Dinner with Meat

5:00 p.m.   **Cocktails**

        Ouzo
        Wine, Beer, Mixed Drinks

    Mezedes (Appetizers)
        Tzatziki with Cucumber Slices and Breadsticks
        Spetzofai with Pita Bread

6:00 p.m.   **Dinner**

Beverages   Water, Wine, Beer and Soda

Soup   Youvarlakia in Tomato Orzo Soup

Salad   Feta and Tomato Salad

Entree   Ribeye Steak Greek Style

    Accompanied by
        Cousin Frannie's Spanakopita
        Sautéed Vegetables

Dessert   Galatoboureko (Crème Pie)
        Kourabiedes (Butter Cookies)
        Café and Tea
        Liqueur - Ouzo

Greek Style Dinner with Meat Shopping Lists

Shopper 1

8 beef ribeye steaks, 1" thick, bone-in

Dry Rub for Steak:
- 1/3 cup garlic powder
- 1/3 cup dried oregano
- 1/3 cup dried basil
- 3 teaspoon salt
- 1 teaspoon pepper

Dry rub both sides of all of the steaks the night before the big dinner. Wrap each one individually in plastic wrap and refrigerate overnight.

Shopper 2

1-½ lbs Italian sweet sausage
1-½ lbs lean chopped meat, beef or veal
1 quart of extra virgin olive oil
5 lbs pre-sifted flour
1 lb 10X powdered sugar
5 lbs sugar
Honey with squeeze top lid, if possible
3 lbs salted butter
2 lbs sweet butter
8 cups whole milk

16 ounces strained plain low fat or regular yogurt; or 32 ounces of plain yogurt that you will strain overnight before the big dinner.

Shopper 3

8 fresh mint leaves
12 garlic cloves
1 bunch fresh dill
2 bunches fresh parsley
7 lemons
2 large seedless cucumbers
2 red bell peppers
8 medium carrots
4 yellow squash
3 medium white onions
6 small onions or 3 more medium whites
3 lbs fresh large ripe tomatoes
8 cups vegetable stock or broth
12 hearts of artichoke, preferably in jar packed in oil
7 packages chopped frozen spinach
1 package of thin, crisp bread sticks
8 slices pita bread

Shopper 4 (Host)

Salt
Pepper
2 lbs cottage cheese
16 ounces olives, preferably Kalamata
4 lbs feta cheese
2 - 16 ounce packages phyllo dough
¼ cup plain bread crumbs
1 tsp whole cloves
¼ cup red wine
3 TBS brandy
3 TBSP vanilla extract
3 TBSP of uncooked rice
2 tsp cornstarch
½ tsp red wine vinegar
1 level tsp baking powder
½ cup orzo pasta
1 dozen eggs
1-1/2 cups farina

Preparation Schedule – Greek Style Dinner with Meat

Teams
1/
2/
3/
4/Hosts

4:00 pm   **1, 2, & 3-** Arrive at **4**'s kitchen. Put on chef's aprons. Unpack and stack all groceries in a central location. Put meat, milk and cheese in refrigerator. Leave butter and phyllo on counter. Have a cocktail.
1- Start Tzatziki recipe immediately. Serve when ready.
2- Start Spetzofai recipe immediately. Serve when ready.
4- Serve cocktails; dry rub preparation of ribeye steaks, if not done the night before, and place in refrigerator to marinate, while enjoying a cocktail and mezedes with guests.

4:15 pm   **3-** Start Spanakopita recipe.
4- Set table with sharp steak knives and continue serving drinks.

4:30 pm   **4-** Start Tomato Orzo soup recipe and work on it right through plating. Continue serving cocktails.

5:00 pm   **1, 2, 3 & 4-** Eat mezedes and drink cocktails as they are ready, while you merrily work on your other food preparations.
1- Start Galatoboureko recipe. Continue until it is placed in the refrigerator to chill the basted butter prior to baking. Turn on oven and preheat to 350°. Do not place tray of Galatoboureko in oven until Spanakopita is removed (see 6:15 pm).
2- Cut and refrigerate all ingredients for Feta Tomato Salad. Do not plate or dress the ingredients.

5:15 pm   **2-** Prepare dough for Kourabiedes cookies. Form and place cookies on greased baking sheet, cover and aside at room temperature.

5:30 pm.   **3-** Put tray of Spanakopita in oven to bake.

5:45 pm.   **4-** Plate soup, garnish and serve.
4- Help **4** plate, garnish and serve soup. Baste top of Spanakopita with more butter just before sitting down to eat soup.

6:00 pm   **Eat Soup in Dining Room**
At 6:15 everyone helps clear soup dishes to the kitchen.

6:15 pm	**1-** Remove Galatoboureko from refrigerator and place in preheated oven on middle rack as soon as **3** removes Spanakopita from oven.
	2- Plate Feta Tomato Salad. Dress and serve.
	3- Remove Spanakopita from oven and set on top of stove until ready to serve. Cut 4 pieces of pita bread into quarters. Help **2** plate and serve salad. Add quartered pita to salads.
	4- Put Kourabiedes cookies into 350° oven on lower rack just before sitting down to eat salad. Check cookies for doneness in 15 minutes (right after eating salad). It is okay that the cookies and Galatoboureko are in the oven at the same time.
6:30 pm	**Eat Salad in Dining Room**
	At 6:45 everyone helps clear salad dishes to the kitchen.
6:45 pm	**1-** Remove marinated ribeye steaks from refrigerator and cook.
	2- Start Sautéed Vegetable recipe and remain with it until plating for the main course takes place.
	3- Remove Galatoboureko from oven and brush top with butter. Return to oven. Prepare syrup for Galatoboureko.
	4- Remove Kourabiedes cookies from oven and place on rack to cool. Pit and chop Kalamata olives for steak recipe. Prepare olive and Feta topping for steak recipe. Set aside at room temperature.
7:00 pm	**3-** Remove Galatoboureko from oven and pour on syrup. Set on counter to cool.
	4- Warm dinner plates.
7:15 pm	**1-** Plate steaks. Work with **2** in plating steak and vegetables.
	2- Plate Sautéed Vegetables with **1**. Serve immediately.
	3- Slice Spanakopita, plate and serve on the side.
7:30 pm	**Eat Entree in Dining Room**
	At 8:00 everyone helps clear dishes to the kitchen.
8:00 pm	**3-** Add powdered sugar to tops of Kourabiedes cookies.
	4- Set up coffee cups, dessert plates, spoons and forks for service.
8:15 pm	**2-** Plate Kourabiedes (2). Decorate dessert plate with honey.
	3- Cut and plate Galatoboureko. Work with **2** on plating dessert.
	4- Brew coffee and tea. Set out ouzo for after dinner drink.
8:30 pm	**Eat Dessert and Have Coffee in Dining Room**
	Relax! Job Well Done!

Tzatziki

Remember, when you make this, you must either buy nearly twice the amount of regular plain yogurt and strain it overnight or buy already strained yogurt in the amount shown below. After straining, yogurt has a phenomenally rich, creamy texture that is pure reward for the palate.

Ingredients:

1 container (16 ounces) strained plain low fat or regular yogurt; or 32 ounces of plain yogurt that you will strain overnight before the big dinner
2 large seedless cucumbers; not peeled, 1 finely chopped and the other cut into medium slices
2 tsp salt
4 garlic cloves; smashed and chopped finely
2 TBSP chopped fresh dill plus additional sprigs for garnish
1 TBSP extra virgin olive oil
½ tsp red wine vinegar
a generous dash of ground black pepper (to taste)
1 package of thin crisp bread sticks

Instructions:

On the night before you make the Tzatziki, place the yogurt, if not strained, into a sieve or fine mesh strainer set over a bowl; cover and refrigerate overnight. Discard drained liquid. Place strained yogurt in medium bowl or food processor.

Do not peel the cucumbers. Cut medium slices from the first. Cover and refrigerate the slices. Slice open the remaining cucumber and diligently remove any seeds and shave away any very wet parts, leaving only relatively dry cucumber meat. Discard the wet stuff and seeds. Chop the remaining dry cucumber finely with skin on and place in a colander over a bowl. Add 1 teaspoon of salt and toss. Allow to sit for 15 minutes at room temperature. While the salted cucumber is sitting at room temperature, chop the fresh dill. With the flat side of chef's knife, mash the garlic to a paste with ½ teaspoon of salt. Set aside. After the 15 minutes of sitting, wrap chopped cucumber in kitchen towel and squeeze to remove as much liquid as possible. Pat dry with paper towels, then add to the bowl of strained yogurt. For easy mixing, the yogurt and cucumber can be in a food processor (pulse to leave small chunks of the cucumber in the Tzatziki. Add mashed garlic, chopped dill, oil, vinegar and pepper to yogurt. Stir thoroughly or mix in food processor to combine. Taste and add more salt as you require. Cover and refrigerate for a short while.

Plating:

Place Tzatziki dip in a medium bowl topped with cucumber slices and dill sprigs. Put the bread sticks on the side of the bowl upright in a tall glass.

Spetzofai

This is a wonderful mix of country sausage, peppers and tomatoes. To please all of the palates at your party use sweet red bell peppers. For the more adventurous, this dish can be made with hot peppers. Just be sure to strip out the seeds from the hot pepper, or it will turn into a five-alarm dish. The sausage can be plain country sausage, but since I am half Italian, I am recommending Italian sweet sausage for the extra wonderful spices that are typically in that variety. This is a quick cooking (stir fried) treat good for a fast start hot appetizer.

Ingredients:

1-½ lbs Italian sweet sausage
2 medium white onions
2 red bell peppers
1 large ripe tomato; finely chopped
2 cloves of garlic; sliced
1 tsp dried oregano
¼ cup red wine
3 TBSP of olive oil
4 slices pita bread cut in quarters

Instructions:

Peel onions and cut into chunks.

In a heavy-bottomed frying pan, skillet or wok, sauté the onion in the olive oil over medium heat until translucent, about 5 to 8 minutes stirring constantly with a wooden spoon.

While onions are cooking, cut sausage into medium to thin slices. It is okay if the slices fall apart during cooking. Trim peppers and remove seeds. Cut into chunks.

When onions are translucent, increase heat to high and add sausage, peppers, chopped tomato, oregano and garlic. Stir to mix all ingredients well. Stir constantly until sausage browns, garlic becomes clear (browning can't hurt the flavor of this dish) and tomato starts to break down (about 5 to 10 minutes). Stir in red wine. Continue stirring until wine and other loose liquids are boiling off and reduced by about two-thirds. You do not want a runny sauce.

Plating:

Serve warm in small soup or dessert bowls with cut slices of pita bread laid atop the Spetzofai.

Youvarlakia in Tomato Orzo Soup

At Greek Easter, one of the treats was walking into Aunt Stasa's kitchen and there on the table were magnificent Keftethes. These fried meatballs had crispy exteriors, wonderful spices and in her version, a little bit of rice sprinkled throughout. These were on a toothpick and ready for popping into the mouth. I have taken the boiled little cousin of the Keftethes, Youvarlakia (small meatball) for this recipe and put it into a tomato based vegetable soup. The cooking of the Youvarlakia in the tomato soup adds the extra flavor of the beef and spices to the soup. The lemon juice adds tang. The rice, orzo and cornstarch thicken the soup. The orzo adds one more texture for the palate. In the end and although it is red, this is not the tomato soup of your childhood.

Youvarlakia Ingredients:

1-½ lbs lean chopped meat; beef or veal
1 medium onion; chopped finely
8 fresh mint leaves; chopped coarsely
3 TBSP of uncooked rice
¼ tsp salt
¼ tsp pepper
2 eggs; separated
¼ cup flour

Youvarlakia Instructions:

Separate the eggs. Reserve the yolks for the soup. Chop onion and mint. Knead the meat, onion, mint, rice, egg white, salt and pepper. Shape small round meatballs about the diameter of a quarter. Lightly dust meatballs with flour. Boil in soup for 35 minutes (see below).

Tomato Soup Ingredients:

2 TBSP salted butter
2 tsp cornstarch
¼ cup fresh parsley; chopped coarsely
1 lemon; juiced
2 egg yolks (reserved from Youvarlakia recipe)

1 medium onion; chopped
3 TBSP olive oil
8 cups vegetable stock or broth
1 lb fresh tomatoes, seeded and diced
½ tsp salt
½ tsp pepper
½ cup orzo pasta

Soup Instructions:

Chop onion. Sauté chopped onion over medium-high heat in olive oil until deep brown. While onions brown, seed and chop tomatoes. When onions are browned, add vegetable stock/broth and seeded, diced tomatoes. Add salt and pepper. Boil about 15 minutes or until tomatoes start breaking down. You can accelerate this by carefully mashing the tomatoes as they cook. Add Youvarlakia and boil. After 30 minutes more, add orzo and boil for an additional 5 minutes. While orzo is boiling in the soup, beat the egg yolks with ¼ cup cold water, lemon juice and cornstarch. After the orzo has boiled its 5 minutes, turn the soup down to low and strain out the Youvarlakia. Divide them among the soup plates. Some of the orzo will come out with the Youvarlakia. That's okay. While whisking the soup, slowly pour the egg yolk, cornstarch, lemon juice, water mix into the soup. When it is fully dispersed, add the butter to the soup and return the soup to the boil. As soon as the soup boils again, turn off the heat and serve.

Plating:

Arrange the Youvarlakia (3 to 6, depending upon appetite) into each individual soup bowl for serving. Ladle soup into bowls over Youvarlakia. Garnish with chopped parsley. Serve and enjoy!

Feta and Tomato Salad

Salad Ingredients:

6 medium to large tomatoes
8 ounces cracked and pitted black olives (preferably Kalamata)
1-½ lbs block of feta cheese
4 pieces of pita bread; quartered
8 sprigs of parsley

Dressing Ingredients: (Note the dressing is not mixed and then applied, rather it is applied to the salad as individual ingredients and layers of flavor.)

12 TBSP olive oil
2 tsp dried oregano
2 lemons; quartered

ground black pepper to taste at the table

Crack and pit Kalamata olives.

Instructions:

Slice the feta cheese block in half and in half again until you have 8 long flat slabs of feta of approximately the same size. This can be done with a good knife or a cheese wire. If the slabs happen to break, that's okay.

Trim tomato tops and bottoms off. Slice each of the 6 tomatoes into 4 equal thick slices.

Plating:

For plate presentation, arrange 3 slices of tomato on each flat salad plate. Squeeze half of the lemon juice directly onto the tomatoes. Sprinkle a small amount of the dried oregano on the tomatoes. Lay the slab of feta cheese on top of the tomatoes. Sprinkle a few olives on each plate. Dress with 2 quarters of pita bread and serve. Liberally pour the olive oil over the cheese, olives, tomatoes and pita. Add one last squeeze of lemon juice over all. Dust the entire plate with more dried oregano. Lay on a fresh sprig of parsley.

Ribeye Steak Greek Style

Dry Rub Ingredients:
1/3 cup garlic powder
1/3 cup dried oregano
1/3 cup dried basil
3 tsp salt
1 tsp pepper

8 beef rib-eye steaks (1 inch thick)
½ cup olive oil

Steak Toppers:
2 lemons; quartered
1 cup crumbled feta cheese
1 cup pitted and sliced ripe Kalamata olives
1 bunch fresh parsley
¼ tsp salt
¼ tsp pepper

Dry Rub Instructions:

In a small bowl, combine and mix the first five dry ingredients; rub onto both sides of steaks. Allow the dry rub to marinate the steaks in the refrigerator for at least 30 minutes and up to several hours before cooking (overnight, even better).

While steaks marinate, pit and slice Kalamata olives. Crumble feta cheese. Toss together with salt and pepper. Set aside at room temperature.

Grilling or Broiling Steaks: Use high heat with either method until desired doneness is reached. Plate with Spanakopita and sautéed vegetables.

Use a meat thermometer to judge doneness and to get each person the perfect steak.

For 1" thick steaks:
Rare 120 - 125 (4 to 5 minutes per side)
Medium-Rare 130 - 135 (6 to 7 minutes per side)
Medium 140 - 145 (8 to 9 minutes per side)
Medium-Well 150 – 155 (9 to 10 minutes per side)
Well Done 160 and above (10 to 12 minutes per side)

Skillet and Oven Cooking: If you do not have a grill, the cooking can be accomplished in a large skillet over high heat, sear 2 steaks at a time in oil on each side for 4 minutes and 4 minutes. Using two skillets at once, each with 2 steaks, this step will take about 20 minutes. Transfer the steaks to a 350° oven while others are being seared. This will continue to cook the steaks to the desired doneness. If no one in your party wants well-done or medium well done steaks, hold the steaks out of the oven until the last steaks are seared and put them in the preheated oven all at once for approximately 5 to 8 more minutes for rare to medium rare and longer for more doneness. Use a meat thermometer to judge doneness and to get each person the perfect steak.

Plating:

Plating the steaks with the side dishes and serving should take enough time for the steak "to sit" (about 5 minutes) before they are cut into. This will allow the steak to be cut and eaten without the juices running all over the plate.

Plate each steak with the eye of the steak slightly off-center. It is okay if the end of the rib bone protrudes slightly off of the plate. Place the sautéed vegetables in the largest available opening after the steak is placed. Give one last squeeze of lemon juice over each steak and the sautéed vegetables. Sprinkle the cheese and olives onto the eye of the steak. Use a few sprigs of fresh parsley to garnish the plate. Preferably the parsley will sit at the plate edge along side of the eye of the steak, but it can go on top of the cheese and olives on the eye of the steak if there is no other room on the plate. Serve immediately. Use sharp steak knives.

Cousin Frannie's Spanakopita

She's not Greek, she's not Turkish, but Frannie is a great cook. This version of Spanakopita is so much better than any you may have had at a Greek diner or wedding that you may find yourself making it just for yourself for dinner. Her use of cottage cheese is a stroke of genius because it extends the tang normally attributed to feta cheese but is higher in moisture content. This makes the entire finished dish moister than the restaurant and classic recipe versions. Your palate will appreciate the difference. This original recipe is for a 9" x 13" x 3" high pan. It will yield 12 full-sized servings of 3" x 3" x 3" Spanakopita. You may want to cut back on the ingredients by one-third and use a 9" x 9" x 3" high pan (if you can find one). I prefer not to mess with perfection, and believe it is far better to have leftovers for the coming week, so here it is in its full glory.

Ingredients:

7 packages of chopped frozen spinach
2 lbs feta cheese
2 lbs cottage cheese
6 small onions
16 ounces phyllo dough
2 lbs butter for sautéing and brushing
¼ cup plain bread crumbs

Instructions:

Defrost spinach in microwave, open packages and put into a colander to drain. Squeeze all excess moisture out of spinach before you begin combining ingredients. You can use alternate means of defrosting quickly such as warm water, just don't cook the spinach. It will get too soft.

Use a 9" x 13" x 3" high baking/roasting pan.

While spinach is defrosting, chop the onions finely and sauté in butter in a large frying pan. After it is sautéed put in a handful of bread crumbs, plain. This soaks up the moisture and the pie will hold tight. Then put in the thoroughly drained and squeezed spinach, crumbled feta cheese and cottage cheese. Toss over the heat a couple of times for one minute to combine and remove from stove.

Melt the rest of the 2 lbs of butter in a pot and take the white foam that rises to the top off. Then skim the resulting clear yellow liquid off of the white stuff that is at the bottom of the pot. You will be using the clear yellow liquid. This is clarified butter and has a higher burn point than butter with that white stuff. By the way, you don't have to throw away all of the white stuff which will be 20 to 25% of the original butter. It is the highly flavorful milk solids and proteins from the butter and can be used in non-cooking applications.

Brush the inside of the baking pan very well with the clarified butter. Place 2 layers of the phyllo in the bottom of the pan and brush well with clarified butter. Repeat by adding 2 more layers of the phyllo and brushing with clarified butter until you have used up ½ of the package (8 ounces) of phyllo. This has a thicker bottom than the Baklava recipe because there is far more residual moisture in the cheeses and spinach than there is in walnuts.

Put in a layer of the cheese and spinach mixture and cover this layer with 2 sheets of phyllo. Brush generously with clarified butter. Repeat these layers of cheese and spinach mix, two layers of phyllo and clarified butter until you reach the top of the pan. Finish off with a phyllo layer and most of the rest of your clarified butter. Save a couple of ounces of clarified butter for one more basting of the top halfway through the baking time.

Put the baking pan into the refrigerator for 15 minutes until the butter on the top becomes hard again. Preheat the oven to 350°.

Remove the pan from the refrigerator and cut the Spanakopita into 3" x 3" pieces. Cut all the way down to the bottom of the pan. For smaller appetites, cut a few of the 3" x 3" pieces on the diagonal to create half-pieces. Leave all of the cut pieces in the pan. You will have leftovers of this.

Bake on the middle rack of the oven at 350° for 45 minutes or until the dough is golden on top. Half way through the cooking, brush butter on the top again. Use a generous amount of the liquid butter.

At end of cooking time, remove from oven and allow at least 15 minutes of standing time before you recut the pieces and remove them from the pan.

Plating:

Use a butter plate. Plate slice of Spanakopita on butter plate and serve on the side of the steak and vegetables.

Sautéed Vegetables

Ingredients:

8 carrots; cut to 3" lengths and julienned
4 yellow squash; cut into 3/4" length rounds
12 hearts of artichoke; drained if packed in water and sliced in half
1 lemon; juiced
6 garlic cloves; smashed and minced
4 TBSP olive oil
4 pats salted butter
salt; to taste
pepper; to taste

Instructions:

Wash, cut the vegetables as shown above.

Sauté smashed garlic in olive oil over medium heat until clear. Do not brown.

Push garlic to edge of pan and add julienned carrots and cook until tender. Stir frequently. Test one after about 5 minutes. It should crunch a little bit as you bite.

Push carrots and garlic to edges of the pan. Add cut squash and cook over high heat until tender (approximately 3 minutes). Stir constantly.

Push squash to edge of pan. Add cut artichoke hearts and heat until warmed through. Reduce heat to low. Toss in 4 pats of salted butter. Then mix all of the vegetables in the pan. Salt and pepper to taste.

Plating:

Plate with steak and Spanakopita. See steak recipe for plating instructions.

Galatoboureko

Galatoboureko Ingredients:

1 (16 ounce) package phyllo dough; thawed if frozen. You may have some left over.
1 cup sweet clarified liquid butter (Start with 3 sticks of butter)
8 cups whole milk
2 cups sugar
1-½ cups farina
7 eggs; beaten
1 TBSP vanilla extract

Syrup Ingredients:

3 cups water
1-½ lbs sugar
½ lemon; juiced
1 tsp vanilla extract

Topping Ingredients:

Pure honey to drizzle over cut Galatoboureko and for plate decoration just before serving. Get one of those plastic bottles with the squeeze top lid. It is great for drizzling and plate decoration.

Filling Instructions:

The first team member makes the filling. Heat milk in a large saucepan. Just before the hot milk boils add 2 cups sugar and 1 TBSP vanilla extract. Stir to dissolve all of the sugar. When the milk is nearly boiling, gradually add the farina, stirring constantly with a wooden spoon to make the cooked filling smooth. When all of the farina has been added and stirred in, remove from the heat and stir occasionally to prevent the formation of a crust. Continue stirring to hasten cooling to room temperature. When the farina cools to lukewarm, beat eggs and add in a little at a time stirring constantly until all eggs have been added and mixed in evenly.

Assembly Instructions:

The second team member works on these assembly instructions while the filling is being made. Melt the 3 sticks of sweet butter in a pot and take the white foam that rises to the top off. Then skim the resulting clear yellow liquid off of the white stuff that is at the bottom of the pot. You will be using the 1+ cup of clear yellow liquid. This is liquid or clarified butter and has a higher burn point than butter with that white stuff. By the way, you don't have to throw away all of the white stuff which will be 20 to 25% of the original butter. It is the highly flavorful milk solids and proteins from the butter and can be used in non-cooking applications.

Open phyllo and gently spread the pile of sheets flat. Keep the sheets stacked after you have unfolded the pile, and keep the pile of sheets covered with a damp cloth to keep them from drying out while you assemble the Galatoboureko.

Use a 9" x 13" x 3" high pan. You will not fill this pan to the top. Brush the bottom and walls well with liquid butter. Place 7 layers of phyllo sheets in bottom of pan to form the bottom crust of the Galatoboureko. If you have the extra large sheets of phyllo, fold them or cut them in half and count each large sheet as 2 layers. Brush every sheet of phyllo generously with liquid butter as you add it to the bottom of the pan (yes, every sheet). Allow the phyllo to overlap to the outside of the pan. At the end you will trim and wet these ends so they will seal during cooking.

Spread all of the lukewarm creamy farina filling evenly onto the bottom crust.

Place 7 layers of phyllo sheets on top to form the top crust of the Galatoboureko. Brush every sheet of phyllo generously with liquid butter as you add it to the top (yes, every sheet). Allow the phyllo to overlap to the outside of the pan.

When 6 of the 7 layers are on top of the filling, brush the top again with liquid butter, then trim all of the edges even with each other. Brush the trimmed edges with water so they will seal during cooking. You may place all of the trimmed phyllo evenly on the top of the sixth layer and brush again with liquid butter. Add the seventh and final layer of phyllo on top of the trim pieces and butter the top of the seventh layer. Trim its edges even with the other trimmed wet edges and pinch together. Put pan into refrigerator for 15 minutes to harden the butter.

Preheat oven to 350°.

Remove Galatoboureko from refrigerator after 15 minutes, and using a sharp knife, score the top crust into squares or triangles. Do not cut all the way through to the bottom. Stop at the farina filling. The pieces should be about 3" x 3" square. Score a few squares into triangles for those wishing a smaller piece, but do not remove any pieces from the pan as you cut. You will have leftovers of this. Return the pan to the refrigerator until the oven is properly preheated.

Put scored Galatoboureko into oven and bake for 45 minutes or until top is golden brown. Halfway through the baking basted the top again with liquid butter.

While Galatoboureko is baking make syrup. In a pot, pour in 1-½ lbs of sugar and 3 cups of water. Add the juice of half a lemon. This is twice as thick as standard simple syrup, and the lemon helps keep the sugar in solution when the syrup is cooling to room temperature. Boil and keep stirring with a wooden spoon until the syrup lightly coats the spoon. It must remain liquidy. Add a 1 teaspoon of vanilla into the syrup and stir. Boil for 10 more minutes, and then remove from the heat. Keep hot.

When the Galatoboureko is done remove it from the oven and pour the hot syrup over the scored pieces using a basting spoon. The syrup must be poured over the Galatoboureko while it is still hot in the pan to allow for soaking into the layers. Get some down the insides of the pan, too. Pour it on and let it soak in.

Plating:

Do not use the honey until you are ready to plate the Galatoboureko. When you are ready for dessert, plate the piece of Galatoboureko onto one side of a salad/dessert plate or a dinner plate. Place 2 Kourabiedes cookies on the other side of the plate. Do not crowd these desserts onto a small plate. Drizzle a line or two of honey between the two desserts. Drizzle a medium zigzag line of honey on the Galatoboureko only, not on the cookies. Then serve.

Kourabiedes Cookies

This recipe came from my Aunt Stasa. These cookies could not be sneaked off the table at the Epiphany, because the white powdered sugar would leave a tell tail trail on the floor and marks on your hands, face and clothes. Beyond that the nervousness induced by sneaking one of these cookies would cause you to breathe funny which would cause you to inhale some of the loose sugar. That would send you into an immediate coughing fit and the whole family knew what you did. Take my hard earned experience as advice, leave these until everyone sits down for dessert. You will love eating them honestly (notice, no comma between them and honestly).

Cookie Dough Ingredients:

1 lb sweet butter; softened
½ cup sugar
2 egg yolks
1 level tsp baking powder
1 tsp vanilla
3 TBSP brandy
2 lbs sifted flour (around 3 to 4 cups). (Use only as much as needed to form a stiff dough.)
1 tsp whole cloves (1 per cookie)
1 lb 10X powdered sugar

Dough Preparation Instructions and Baking:

Preheat the oven to 350 degrees.

Keep butter at room temperature for 30 minutes to an hour before using in this recipe. Do not refrigerate the butter when you arrive at the host's kitchen.

Cream softened butter and sugar until smooth in a large bowl. Beat egg yolks and add to creamed butter. Add sifted flour, brandy, baking powder and vanilla; work well. Add as much flour, at ½ cup at a time, as needed to make a stiff dough that is just moist enough to stay together. Knead well by hand. If dough is too dry that it is falling apart, add a little bit more of brandy (not water) until stiff texture is reached.

Grease cookie sheet. Pinch off pieces of dough the size of a large walnut and form into flattened (1/4" high) crescent shapes. Place on greased cookie sheet. Insert a whole clove in the center of each cookie. Bake at 350 degrees until cooked through. Test a cookie at 15 minutes to see if it is cooked through. If not try again at 20 minutes. Cool cookies on rack.

When the cookies are at room temperature (NOT HOT), top each cookie with a thick layer of confectioner's sugar. Be patient at this step. You want a lot of confectioner's sugar on the top of each cookie, at least 1/8" and as much as ¼". You only live once! When the sugar is on, gently poke through to the top to the clove so it can be seen. The cloves should not be eaten. They are tough to chew and bitter, but they give the cookies an aroma and flavor that is descended from Mt. Olympus.

Plating:

See Galatoboureko recipe for plating suggestion.

Italian Family Favorites

Italian Family Favorites

Since I told you about the Greek side of my family, I thought I would share a few of the special Italian memories and tastes of my childhood. We had a big family on the Italian side, seven aunts, seven uncles, fifteen cousins and my grandparents. Add to that the once-removed cousins from around the corner, godmothers and godfathers, and just close family friends and you can see how a Sunday dinner could escalate quickly into feeding the entire Italian population of Brooklyn!

Antipasto and cocktails made up an important event during our family gatherings. On holidays or any Sunday my mother would set out chunks of Italian cheeses, ham, salami, capicola, olives, pickles and canapés on the built-in bar in our knotty pine basement. Between 1 and 2 pm aunts, uncles, cousins and friends would gather 'round that small feast for an hour or two before dinner was served. Everyone was hungry by that time, and so many laughs and good moments were shared during the antipasto and dinners in our house that fifty years later we still seek each other out to relive those moments of closeness and have some good things to eat together.

Soup wasn't always served, usually it was a bowl of macaroni or baked macaroni, but the soup I offer in this meal is so good, I couldn't pass up sharing it. Veal was served on special occasions and was always a family favorite. Those tender morsels of meat just melted in your mouth and provide a lasting memory. My mother liked preparing them in advance, usually Milanese style. Tonight you will cook medallions of veal and eat them as soon as they are ready. Veal against a backdrop of fresh vegetables and risotto will give you the classic makings of the Italian family Sunday meal.

We never finished a meal quickly and dashed off. Sunday was for taking pause in the company of people you took great comfort in being around. Spending a few hours around the table was not uncommon. The main course was always followed by fruit and nuts. Oranges, pears and apples were peeled right at the table with steak knives while toasted almonds and walnuts were opened with nut crackers with the shells being collected all over the table cloth, to be swept away later. Hot castagnes (pronounced cas-ta-nyas) (chestnuts) were served, too, when in season. I always had the job of stabbing the castagnes with a fork before they were toasted in the oven, so they wouldn't explode. After some time had passed over fruit and nuts, the pies and cakes would come to the table with coffee. For this meal we will have one of the classic desserts our family had so often and never tired of, ricotta pie. In fact, we had ricotta desserts in pie form, cakes, and pastries. If it was someone's birthday there was always an Italian cassata cream (cannoli cream) cake and a big box of pastries from Napoli's Bakery on Rockaway Parkway in Canarsie. Fortunately for all of us, it was almost always someone's birthday! Enjoy the good tastes from my family!

Italian Family Favorites

5:00 p.m.   Cocktails

         Wine, Beer, Mixed Drinks

     Antipasto   Egg Florentine on Garlic Baguette
           Provolone Cheese
           Black Olives
           Pimientos in Olive Oil
           Italian Bread

6:00 p.m.   Dinner

     Beverages   Water, Wine, Beer and Soda

     Soup   Spiced Sausage and Potato Soup

     Salad   Spinach Salad
           With Hot Balsamic Bacon and Mushroom Dressing
           Italian Bread and Butter

     Entree   Sautéed Medallions of Veal, Lemon Butter Sauce

       Accompanied by

           Zucchini
           Risotto Parmesan with Porcini Mushrooms

     After Dinner   Fruit and Nuts

     Dessert   Ricotta Pie
           Café and Tea
           Liqueur

Italian Family Favorites Shopping Lists

Shopper 1

1 baguette
1 loaf of crusty Italian bread
1-½ lbs Italian sweet sausage
16 veal medallions, leg or tenderloin cuts;
each approx. 2 oz. and pounded to 1/4-inch
thick
4 naval oranges
4 pears; Anjou or Bartlett
4 apples; Gala (sweet) or Granny Smith
(tart)
3 lemons

Shopper 2

1 lb chunk of aged, imported provolone
1-½ cups grated Parmesan-Reggiano
½ lb Italian black olives, Ligurian/Gaeta,
1 jar pimientos packed in olive oil
2 med or 1 lg bag fresh baby leaf spinach
1 small jar candied dried fruit
8 oz bag toasted, shelled pecans
8 oz walnuts; in shells
8 oz almonds; in shells

Shopper 3

2 quarts of mushroom (preferred) or
vegetable stock
2 quarts of chicken broth
24 very small zucchini (or 4 very large)
1 large white onion
4 large starchy potatoes
½ lb sliced white mushrooms
4 oz dried porcini mushrooms or 8 oz fresh
Portabella mushrooms
6 cloves of garlic
2 shallots
1 bunch fresh chives
1 bunch fresh thyme
2 bunches fresh parsley

Shopper 4 (Host)

Salt
Ground black pepper
1 cup flour; all purpose
1 cup white sugar
1 box 10X powdered sugar
2 TBSP vanilla extract
2 TBSP garlic salt
¼ tsp crushed red pepper
2 cups balsamic vinegar
1 quart extra virgin olive oil
½ cup ditalini pasta (Use any other pastina
in place of the ditalini)
2 cups Arborio rice
¼ lb sliced bacon
1 lb butter
1 quart heavy cream
1-½ lbs ricotta cheese
1 doz eggs
½ cup dry sherry
¾ cup white wine

Preparation Schedule – Italian Family Favorites

Teams
1/
2/
3/
4/Hosts

4:00 pm	**1, 2, & 3**- Arrive at **4**'s kitchen. Put on chef's aprons. Unpack and stack all groceries in a central location. Put meats, cream, eggs and ricotta in refrigerator. Leave butter, olive, pimientos and provolone cheese at room temperature. Have a cocktail. **4**- Put a pot of water on to boil for pastina for Italian Ricotta Pie.
4:15 pm	**1**- Start Italian Ricotta Pie recipe. Boil pastina in water started by **4**. Place pie in oven by 4:30 pm. **2**- Start Antipasto Platter recipe. Serve when ready. **3**- Pre-heat oven to 400°. Start Egg Florentine recipe. Serve when ready. Turn oven down to 325° as soon as baguette is toasted. **4**- Set table with steak knives for veal course. Serve cocktails.
4:30 pm	**1**- Put ricotta pie in oven for 2 hours at 325° as soon as ready. **4**- Prepare sausage soup recipe. Serve at 6 pm.
5:00 pm	**1, 2, 3 & 4**- Eat Antipasto in the kitchen, and drink cocktails while you merrily work on your other food preparations.
5:15 pm	**1**- Chop chives for sauce for veal. Cover and reserve. **2**- Wash and dry spinach for salad recipe. Reserve. **3**- Peel and slice zucchini for entrée. Cover and refrigerate. **4**- Chop shallots for risotto recipe. Cover and reserve.
5:45 pm	**1**- Help **4** plate and serve soup. **2**- Prepare salad dressing recipe. Turn off heat when ready. **3**- Heat stock and mushrooms for risotto recipe. Cover. Keep warm. **4**- Plate soup and serve with help from **1** at 6 pm.
6:00 pm.	**Eat Soup in Dining Room** **At 6:15 everyone helps clear soup dishes to the kitchen.**
6:15 pm	**1**- Check on doneness of ricotta pie. A fork stuck in the pie should come out clean (may be a slight bit damp) with no ingredient chunks on the tines of the fork. If it is not done check it every 10 minutes until it is done. Remove the pie from oven when top is firm and slightly brown and set aside to cool to room temperature.

         48

2- Re-heat salad dressing over medium heat. Complete assembly and plating of salad. Dress and serve salads with help from **4**.
3- Strain out mushrooms and chop for risotto recipe. Reserve.
4- Cut ½ loaf of Italian bread. Place on table with butter for salad course. Help **2** serve salads.

6:30 pm   **Eat Salad in Dining Room**
At 6:45 everyone helps clear salad dishes to the kitchen.

6:45 pm   **3-** Heat up stock and simmer for risotto. Start skillet portion of preparing risotto recipe. Continue until ready to serve at 7:30 pm.

7:00 pm   **1-** Prepare veal portion of veal recipe. Serve at 7:30 pm.
2- Sauté zucchini and keep warm for serving at 7:30 pm.
4- Warm dinner plates. Prepare lemon butter sauce for veal recipe.

7:15 pm   **1-** Help **3** plate and serve entrée.
2- Pre-heat oven to 400°.
3- Plate entrée with **1 and 4**.
4- Help **3** plate and serve entrée.

7:30 pm   **Eat Entree in Dining Room**
At 8:00 everyone helps clear dishes to the kitchen.

8:00 pm   **1-** Chop nuts and dried fruit for dessert pie. Top pie with fruit, nuts and 10X powdered sugar according to recipe.
2- Toast nuts for 6 minutes in oven, and place in basket on table.
3- Wash fruit, and place in bowl on table.
4- Place Sambucca and glasses on table, if available.

8:15 pm   **1, 2, 3 & 4-** Return to table and relax for a half-hour with good conversation, fruit and nuts.

8:45 pm   **1-** Cut and plate Ricotta Pie. Serve with help from **2** when ready.
2- Help **1** plate and serve the Ricotta Pie. Serve when ready.
3- Work with **4** on coffee and tea service.
4- Set up coffee cups, teaspoons and tablespoons for dessert service. Brew coffee and tea. Serve coffee and tea when ready.

9:00 pm   **Eat Dessert and Have Coffee and Tea in Dining Room**
Relax! Job Well Done!

Egg Florentine on Garlic Baguette

This wasn't a Sunday dinner item, but Aunt Margaret made it, and it tastes so good, it's worth your time to make as a special appetizer tonight.

Ingredients:

1 baguette
6 oz fresh spinach
¼ cup olive oil
4 cloves of garlic, sliccd
8 eggs
garlic salt
salt
ground black pepper
parmesan
fresh parsley, chopped

Instructions:

Pre-heat oven to 400°.

Cut stems off of spinach leaving only leaves. Slice garlic into fine slices. Chop fresh parsley for garnish.

Cut ends off of baguette. Slice baguette lengthwise once and crosswise into fours making eight open-face pieces. Brush or spray each piece with olive oil on all sides. Sprinkle garlic salt on open faces of all pieces. Toast in 400° oven for 5 minutes. Remove when golden brown.

In a large skillet, heat olive oil. Briefly sauté spinach in oil. Wilt spinach, do not cook until soft. Add sliced garlic, sauté for an additional minute. Spread garlic throughout pan. Add eggs, sunny side up and spread as evenly throughout pan as possible. Season with salt and pepper. Cover pan and cook until eggs are white on top and cooked firm, but not hard and not runny.

Remove pan from heat and immediately cut eggs and spinach into eight servings with a full yolk on each serving.

Plating:

Plate toasted baguettes on one end of a large platter. Place a bit of spinach and an egg on each piece of baguette. Sprinkle with parmesan and fresh chopped parsley. Complete plating of provolone, black olives, pimientos and Italian bread. Serve as finger food with cocktails.

Antipasto Platter
Provolone
Black Olives
Pimientos in Olive Oil
Italian Bread

Ingredients:

1 lb chunk of aged, imported provolone cheese
½ lb Italian black olives, Options: Ligurian, Gaeta,
1 jar pimientos packed in olive oil
½ loaf of crusty Italian bread (use half now and half with salad course)

Directions:

Cut provolone into small cubes, ¾" on a side.

Drain any liquid from the olives.

Cut ½ of the loaf of Italian bread into ½"slices.

Transfer the pimientos and oil to a small bowl that will fit on the end of the large platter. Use a sharp knife to slice the pimientos in the bowl into ½"strips. If you can only find pimientos packed in vinegar and water, drain them and slice them. Add your own olive oil when you put the sliced pimientos in the bowl. Feel free to jazz the oil up a bit with a sprinkling of dried basil, oregano, thyme, rosemary, or for that matter all of them.

Plating:

Plate all items on the same large platter. Place the Egg Florentine on Garlic Baguette on one half of the platter and the bowl of pimientos on the other end. Place the Italian bread slices in the center of the platter. Sprinkle the chunks of provolone and the olives around the bowl of pimientos. Place a teaspoon in the bowl with the pimientos and olive oil. Provide small plates and toothpicks along with these finger foods. When you eat this, dip the sliced Italian bread in the excess oil in the pimiento bowl.

     51

Spiced Sausage and Potato Soup

The crushed red pepper gives this some zip, but I can assure you it will not be too spicy, just nice and memorable. If you must - forego adding the crushed red pepper.

Ingredients:

1 tsp salt
1 tsp pepper
1 large white onion; finely chopped
4 large starchy potatoes; peeled and medium diced
2 quarts of chicken broth
1 TBSP vanilla
¾ cup fresh parsley; chopped
1-½ lbs Italian sweet sausage; use just the meat, remove the sausage casings
¼ tsp crushed red pepper
3 TBSP balsamic vinegar
½ stick butter; Softened and cut into chunks
1 TBSP flour
1 quart heavy cream
½ cup grated Parmesan-Reggiano

Instructions:

Peel and dice potatoes. Chop onion and parsley. Remove sausage meat from casing.

In a large stockpot add potatoes, onion, chicken broth and half of the parsley (save some parsley for use as garnish). On high heat, bring to a boil and then reduce heat to simmer. Season with salt and pepper and ¼ teaspoon of crushed red pepper. Simmer 15 to 20 minutes or until all vegetables become tender but not soft.

While the vegetables cook in stockpot, in a separate sauté pan, over medium-low heat, slowly cook the sausage meat. Drain the fat away a few times during the cooking to allow some good brown caramelized sausage bits to form on the bottom of the pan.

When the vegetables are tender, drain the fat away from the sausage one more time and add the sausage to soup. Scrape the brown bits into the soup too. You can even deglaze the pan with some of the heated stock and pour that into the soup.

In a separate bowl mix cream and flour well so all of the flour is dissolved. Add it to the soup and sausage mixture and cook until soup thickens. Then stir in the butter, vanilla and balsamic vinegar. Simmer soup another 10 minutes. Taste. Add more salt to taste.

Plating:

Plate in large soup bowls. When you ladle the soup, dig down in the pot to get sausage and vegetables in each bowl. Then go back and top off each bowl with more soup. Garnish with grated parmesan cheese and fresh parsley. Serve hot!

Spinach Salad with Hot Balsamic Bacon and Mushroom Dressing

Ingredients:

2 medium or one large bag fresh baby leaf spinach (you used some for the Egg Florentine)
2 garlic cloves; smashed and minced
¼ lb sliced bacon, cut into 1" lengths
½ lb sliced white mushrooms
1 cup balsamic vinegar
½ cup extra virgin olive oil
2 lemons, juiced

½ loaf Italian bread; sliced

Instructions:

Cut bacon to 1" pieces. Slice mushrooms about (¼" slices). Smash and mince garlic.

Sauté bacon over medium heat until well cooked but not crispy. Drain off fat. Spread bacon to edges of pan. Add olive oil. Heat the oil. Sauté minced garlic for 2 minutes. Add sliced mushrooms. Heat mushrooms thoroughly but leave firm. Add balsamic vinegar and juice of 2 lemons. Heat mixture thoroughly, mixing bacon and all other ingredients.

Plating:

While bacon cooks, wash the spinach with cold water. Drain and dry leaves. Cut stems off of spinach.

When the dressing is complete, arrange dried leaves onto eight large salad plates. Spoon hot dressing and bacon over spinach. This should partially wilt the top leaves of spinach, but there will be some crisp leaves remaining underneath. Serve hot.

Sautéed Medallions of Veal and Lemon Butter Sauce

Ingredients:

2 lb (16 pieces) veal medallions, leg cut is fine and less expensive compared to tenderloin cut; each approx. 2 oz. and pounded to ¼ inch thick
ground black pepper
salt
flour; all purpose
4 TBSP olive oil

Sauce:
6 TBSP butter
¾ cup white wine
4 TBSP chopped fresh chives (2 TBSP for sauce and 2 TBSP for garnish)
salt
ground black pepper
1 lemons

Instructions:

Veal: If the cutlets in your butcher's case are cut large and are fewer than 8 pieces to the pound, you will have to cut them and pound them yourself. You want 16 thin pieces from your 2 pounds of veal. Pound the cutlets to approximately ¼" between 2 sheets of clear plastic wrap. Heat olive oil in a sauté pan over medium-high heat. Salt and pepper the veal, then dredge each piece in flour. Sauté the veal slices in hot oil 2 minutes on the first side (turn only once) and less than 2 minutes on second side. Don't over cook them. They will only be slightly brown on the edges. Drain on a plate on a paper towel and pat any excess oil off the top side with another paper towel. Cover with foil to maintain heat. When all veal is done, turn off the heat and pour off excess oil from pan. Restack cooked veal back in pan and cover to maintain heat while completing zucchini and risotto.

Sauce: Chop chives. In a sauté pan over medium-low heat, melt butter, gently. Skim off curds. Add chives and wine to clarified butter. Stir until warm. Add juice of one lemon, salt and pepper seasoning. Stir until warm. Reserve for plating.

Plating:

If you have very large bowls over 10" diameter, they will be ideal for this presentation. Otherwise, use flat dinner plates. Evenly divide the risotto among the eight plates. Fill the center of plate with creamy risotto. Pile it high and leave a minimum of a 1" border around the outside of plate. More border is better. Plate two slices of veal on the sides of risotto just touching at the top of the pile. Place 6 pieces of zucchini in a messy crisscross pile on top of veal. The zucchini may be soft, don't worry if the slices are bent in odd directions. Divide the remaining mushroom pieces evenly among the 8 plates. Spoon several tablespoons of warm wine-butter-chive sauce over the veal, mushrooms and zucchini. Garnish entire plate with a wild sprinkle of fresh chopped chives. Get some on the some on the outside border of the plate. Serve immediately.

Sautéed Zucchini

If you are forced to buy large (long) zucchini instead of small ones, buy 4 zucchini, peel them, cut them in half and then cut each one lengthwise into long skinny strips like Texas steak fries to make the 48 pieces.

Ingredients:

24 very small zucchini; peel skin off and cut lengthwise into 48 long pieces
5 TBSP olive oil
salt

Instructions:

Peel zucchini. Cut into 48 long strips.

In sauté pan, heat the oil. Sauté zucchini about 2 minutes stirring frequently.

Drain oil off zucchini on a plate with a paper towel, add a pinch of salt and ground pepper over the zucchini. When sautéing is complete, turn off heat, drain oil from pan and return all cooked zucchini to the warm pan. Cover pan.

Plating:

Plate with veal and risotto. See plating instruction in veal recipe.

Risotto Parmesan with Porcini Mushrooms

Mushroom stock and vegetable stock are now available on the soup aisle of your market in 1-quart paper containers. They are both rich and deep in color. These stocks are necessary for the preparation of this dish.

Ingredients:

2 (1-quart) containers of mushroom (preferred) or vegetable stock
4 oz dried porcinis (look for these in produce department, Portabella can be substituted)
1 TBSP extra-virgin olive oil
1 TBSP butter
2 shallot, finely chopped
2 cups Arborio rice
½ cup dry Sherry
4 sprigs fresh thyme; leaves chopped
4 sprigs fresh thyme; for garnish
½ cup grated Parmesan-Reggiano
Salt
Ground black pepper

Instructions:

If Portabella mushrooms are substituted, wash them well. Place mushrooms and stock or broth in a saucepan and bring stock to a boil. Reduce heat to low and leave simmering. Strain mushrooms from stock, cover the saucepan and continue simmering the stock.

Coarsely chop half of the porcinis (Portabella) and reserve. They will be added back to the rice later. Chop the other half into larger pieces and reserve. The other half will be a garnish over the squash and veal.

Chop the shallots.

On a burner right next to the simmering stock, use a large skillet to heat oil and butter over medium-high heat. Add chopped shallots and sauté 2 minutes. Add Arborio rice. Stir rice well to coat with oil and butter. Sauté, 2 minutes more. Add sherry and cook until the liquid is completely absorbed. Add several ladles of hot stock (no mushrooms at this time) and reduce heat to medium. Simmer uncovered, stirring frequently until liquid is absorbed.

As soon as the liquid is absorbed, ladle half of the remaining hot stock into the rice. Repeat this step of adding half of the remaining stock each time after the liquid is absorbed by the rice. Stir mixture each time you add broth and remove from heat when the rice is cooked to al dente. Taste it to be sure the rice is firm to the bite but not hard. There may be some unused stock left over. Cool and store any remaining liquids if there are any. The ideal total cooking time for perfect risotto once you put the rice in the pan is 22 minutes. The consistency should be creamy.

Chop the leaves from 4 sprigs of fresh thyme and stir into rice with ½ cup of grated cheese and the chopped mushrooms. Season risotto with salt and pepper to taste.

Plating:

Plate with veal and zucchini. See plating instruction in veal recipe.

Fruit and Nut Preparation

We are really just warming the nuts in their shells for this part of the meal. True toasted nuts are shelled before toasting and then usually toasted about 8 minutes. You can buy toasted nuts in bags and put them out for people to eat by the handful, but why? They are already full from dinner. Our purpose in the Italian meal is to provide a warm nut as a conversation piece. The cracking of the nut or peeling of the fruit is part of the social aspect of being at the table between the main course and the dessert. More than eating, they both represent something to do with your hands as you engage in lively conversation to keep from falling asleep. My Uncle Pat on the Greek side would always go into the living room right after a big holiday meal and fall deeply asleep - complete with loud snoring. Since there was no wall between the dining room and his chair, he always woke up in time for dessert.

Sometimes it is also good to put out a bottle of Sambucca at this point in the meal with tiny liqueur glasses.

Ingredients:

4 naval oranges
4 pears; Anjou or Bartlett
4 apples; Gala (sweet) or Granny Smith (tart)
8 oz walnuts; in shells
8 oz almonds; in shells

Instructions:

Pre-heat oven to 400°.

Wash fruit and dry.

Spread all nuts in shells on a cookie sheet. Toast in pre-heated oven for 6 minutes.

Plating:

Stack fruit high in a medium size bowl. Provide small plates and knives for peeling fruit.

Pour mixed hot nuts into a basket lined with a cloth napkin. Place 3 or 4 nut crackers in the basket.

Place bowl, basket, plates and knives on table family style.

Italian Ricotta Pie

My Aunt Tessie made this pie all the time in the traditional Neapolitan style with barley or wheatberries. It was great, but we don't have time to soak the grain for hours and hours so we will use the recipe without the barley. You will love it. Also, it doesn't matter if the cut pieces are square, this is still pie!

Ingredients:

½ cup ditalini pasta   (Use any other pastina in place of the ditalini)
1-½ lbs ricotta cheese
1 cup white sugar
3 eggs; beaten
¾ tsp vanilla extract
1 small jar candied dried fruit; for topping
8 oz bag toasted, shelled pecans; for topping
10X powdered sugar; for dusting

Instructions:

Preheat oven to 325°.

Grease a 9x9 inch baking dish.

Bring a large pot of lightly salted water to a boil. Add pasta and cook for 8 to 10 minutes or until al dente; drain well.

While waiting for water to boil and pastina to cook, beat eggs. In a large bowl, mix together ricotta, sugar, beaten eggs and vanilla. As soon as pastina is rinsed in cold water and drained, add 1 cup of the cooked pastina to the bowl and mix well. Pour mixture into greased baking dish.

Bake for 2 hours, or until top is firm. Let cool before adding toppings.

Chop pecans and candied fruit, coarsely.

Top the pie with a sprinkling of chopped candied fruits and chopped nuts. Lightly dust top of pie with 10X powdered sugar.

Plating:

Cut the pie into nine 3" squares. Serve all outside pieces to assure everyone gets some crusty edge (sweeter from caramelizing). Plate on flat dessert plates. If you have flat white paper doilies, put them on the plate before plating the pie. Serve warm or at room temperature.

Parsley
Sage
Rosemary
And
Garlic

Parsley, Sage, Rosemary and Garlic

All sorts of things can happen when you try to put a gathering together like Home Cooking Parties for Eight. With over one month of advanced notice, one of our couples failed to show up. In two years of doing these dinner parties, this was the first time this had ever happened. After waiting an extra half-hour for their arrival, I couldn't wait anymore. I drove to their house, and it was dark. No one was home! I don't know what happened to them, but we recovered quickly. My friend Kenny went on an emergency supermarket run, right after we checked our host couple's cupboard for the missing ingredients. It was also a good thing Kenny had a cell phone with him, because after he left, we had to call him to say we forgot to put the sour cream on the emergency list. That is a critical part of the fabulous Honey-Thyme Glazed Ricotta Tart dessert! We got through to him before he had returned all the way home. He circled back and made the buy. This experience convinced me that you have to connect and confirm with everyone a day or two before one of these dinners.

The others in our merry group of cooks were working from the Home Cooking Parties for Eight Preparation Schedule even before I returned with the report that our fourth couple was definitely a no-show. Once Kenny returned with the missing goodies, we had no trouble covering the prep and cooking that was supposed to be done by the missing couple. Our first course of Turkish Lentil Soup with Mint Infused Sizzling Butter went on the table right on schedule. The whole group was completely won over before that. When Diane whipped the Toasted Baguettes with Sweet Peppers and Parmesan out of the oven for an opening snack, they were all whooping it up!

Missing cooks did not keep us from our plan of overeating that night. As we sipped Drambuie and Cognac and munched chocolate mint wafers at the end, this group was ready for another celebration from Home Cooking Parties for Eight, but we all agreed for waistline control it should be a few months down the road. Kenny immediately ran into his den and came out with the grilling cookbook that came with his new Weber Gas Grill, and asked if I could fashion a cooking party from the grill recipes. "No problem," I said. I relished the idea. "Oh boy, this could be fun," I thought, and so was born the Grilling from Beginning to End menu in this book.

Another very important lesson I learned from this night was that while we are organized in 2-person teams, one member of each team can handle most if not all of the workload. So if you wind up missing people or you have some dinner attendees that are just duds in the kitchen, it should not impact your ability to put each course on the table at the right time. For now, I hope you enjoy this scrumptious indoor meal flavored with so many delicious herbs and spices!

Parsley, Sage, Rosemary and Garlic

5:00 p.m.   Cocktails

        Wine, Beer, Mixed Drinks

      Snacks

        Monterey Jack Cheese
        Spanish Olives and Wheat Crackers
        Sweet Red Pepper on Toasted Baguette

6:00 p.m.   Dinner

    Beverages   Water, Wine, Beer and Soda

    Soup   Turkish Lentil Soup with Mint-Infused Butter

    Salad   Escarole Salad with Creamy Garlic Dijon Dressing and
        Garlic Croutons

    Entree   Pan-Seared Beef Tenderloin with Herb-Mustard Coating
        and Red Wine-Mustard Reduction Sauce

      Accompanied by

        Caramelized-Onion Risotto Parmesan with Bacon

        Deep-Fried Carrots and Portabella Mushrooms

    Dessert   Ricotta Tart with Honey-Thyme Glaze and Pine-Nut
    Crust

        Café and Tea
        Liqueur

Parsley, Sage, Rosemary and Garlic Shopping Lists

Shopper 1

1 baguette
1 large jar of Spanish Olives w/Pimientos
½ lb unsalted butter
1 qt beef stock
2 qts chicken stock
1 large jar Dijon mustard
½ lb chunk or thickly sliced Canadian bacon
8 oz honey
1 box After Eight® chocolate dinner mints
1 can Reddi Wip
1 box garlic croutons
1 cup red wine

Shopper 2

1 lb Monterey Jack Cheese
1 box Wheat Crackers
1 can (3 TBSP) tomato paste
1 can Goya® lentils (12 to 16 oz)
1 jar sweet red peppers
1 10" pre-baked pie crust
1 lb Arborio rice
1 cup grated Parmesan
¼ cup pine nuts
1 pint extra virgin olive oil
1 qt canola oil
1 pint sour cream

Shopper 3

4 large white onions
1 large head fresh escarole
1 bag baby carrots
3 large fresh lemons
12 garlic cloves
1 tsp dried spearmint
2 bunches fresh parsley
1 bunch fresh thyme
dried sage leaves
1 bunch fresh basil
16 oz portabella mushrooms
1 cup fresh ricotta cheese
8 oz cream cheese
½ cup mascarpone cheese

Shopper 4 (Host)

8 - 1" thick beef tenderloin steaks
salt
ground black pepper
crushed dried red pepper
1 bag pre-sifted white flour
1 cup granulated sugar
1 bottle pure vanilla extract
3 TBSP garlic salt
1 doz large eggs
1 small bottle red wine vinegar

Preparation Schedule – Parsley, Sage, Rosemary and Garlic

Teams
1/
2/
3/
4/Hosts

4:00 pm   **1, 2, & 3**- Arrive at **4**'s kitchen. Put on chef's aprons. Unpack and stack all groceries in a central location. Put Reddi Wip, steak, bacon, eggs, ricotta and sour cream in refrigerator. Leave butter and other cheeses at room temperature. Have a cocktail.

4:15 pm   **1**- Preheat oven to 400°. Prepare Baguette Recipe. Serve when ready. Reduce oven to 350° for ricotta tart.
2- Start Ricotta Tart recipe. Put pie in oven by 5 pm.
3- Start Monterey Jack Cheese/Olive Platter recipe. Serve when ready.
4- Start Lentil Soup recipe. Continue until ready to serve at 6:00 pm.

5:00 pm   **1, 2, 3 & 4**- Eat appetizers in the kitchen as they are ready, and drink cocktails while you merrily work on your other food preparations.
1- For Deep Fried Vegetable recipe: cut baby carrots in half along the length (julienne style) and chop portabella mushrooms into large bite-sized pieces. Refrigerate for later completion of vegetable recipe.
2- Bake Pie at 350° on middle oven rack for 30 minutes until top is firm.
3- Chop and thoroughly mix garnishes in a deep bowl for tenderloin steaks. Set aside.
4- Cook bacon for risotto recipe while soup is simmering. Chop or crumble and set aside.

5:30 pm   **1**- Mix oil and mustard for steaks. Help **3** coat the edges of steaks.
2- Remove ricotta tart from oven. Set on wire rack to cool. Turn off oven. Wash escarole and dry leaves well. Tear escarole leaves into bite size pieces. Keep leaves at room temperature separate from dressing until ready to toss and serve. Prepare the dressing and salad at 6:15 pm.
3- Cut tenderloin into 1" steaks. Work with **3** to coat edges with mustard and mixed garnish. Carefully plate to avoid knocking off the garnish. Cover and refrigerate coated steaks.

5:45 pm   **4**- Prepare mint butter for soup. Plate soup. Infuse with mint butter. Serve at 6:00 pm.

6:00 pm   **Eat Soup in Dining Room**
At 6:15 everyone helps clear soup dishes to the kitchen.

6:15 pm.   **2-** Complete assembly and plating of salad. Dress and serve salads at 6:30 pm with help from **3**.
3- Help **2** serve salads. Find out how done everyone wants their steak.
4- Cook onions and garlic for risotto recipe. Put the chicken stock on to simmer. Turn heat off under onions and stock when it is time to for the salad course. Return afterward.

6:30 pm   **Eat Salad in Dining Room**
At 6:45 everyone helps clear salad dishes to the kitchen.

6:45 pm   **1-** Set up flour and vegetables according to preparation plan in vegetable recipe. Wait until 7:00 pm to start coating and cooking steps.
2- Prepare honey-thyme glaze. Glaze ricotta pie and refrigerate to chill.
3- Prepare to pan-sear steaks by placing steaks and ingredients for sauce next to stove and heating pan(s). Follow instructions in recipe for searing steaks to correct doneness. When steaks are done, prepare sauce in same pan(s). Plate just at 7:30 pm with **1 and 4**.
4- After the salad course, warm dinner plates. Turn the heat on under the onions and garlic and the stock, and complete the risotto recipe. Carefully follow recipe instructions on adding liquids and stirring rice constantly to create creamy texture. Plate risotto using cup, according to plating instructions in steak recipe with **1 and 3** just before 7:30 pm.

7:00 pm   **1-** Complete Deep Fried Vegetable recipe. Heat oil in fry pan. Follow directions to coat and deep fry vegetables. Place fried vegetables on paper towels to drain excess oil. Keep warm until serving with entree. Plate with **3 and 4** just before 7:30 pm.

7:30 pm   **Eat Entree in Dining Room**
At 8:00 everyone helps clear dishes to the kitchen.

8:15 pm   **1-** Help **2** plate and serve Ricotta Pie at 8:30 pm.
2- Cut and plate Ricotta Pie. Garnish with Reddi Wip whipped cream on the side. Serve with help from **1** at 8:30 pm.
3- Help **4** set up cups and flatware for dessert.
4- Brew coffee and tea. Set up coffee cups, teaspoons and tablespoons for dessert service. Brew coffee and tea. Serve at 8:30 pm.

8:30 pm   **Eat Dessert and Have Coffee and Tea in Dining Room**
Relax! Job Well Done!

Monterey Jack Cheese, Spanish Olives and Crackers

Ingredients:

1 lb block of Monterey Jack cheese
1 box wheat crackers
1 large jar of Spanish olives with pimientos
1 bunch fresh parsley

Instructions:

Drain olives well.

Cut Monterey Jack into ¾" cubes.

Plating:

Arrange the cheese neatly in a fun configuration of your choosing on one end of a platter.

Place a medium size bowl on the other end of the platter. Pour the drained olives into the bowl.

Add wheat crackers to center of platter between the cheese and olives.

Garnish the edges of platter with a generous amount of whole parsley.

Serve family style. Put out some napkins and toothpicks next to the platter.

Garlic Baguette with Sweet Red Pepper and Parmesan

Ingredients:

1 baguette
12 to 16 oz jar of sweet red peppers
¼ cup olive oil
Garlic salt
Grated Parmesan
Fresh chopped parsley

Instructions:

Pre-heat oven to 400°.

Chop fresh parsley for garnish.

Cut ends off of baguette. Slice baguette diagonally into ½" slices 2-½" to 3" long. Place cut pieces onto a cookie sheet. Brush or spray each piece with olive oil on all sides. Sprinkle garlic salt and Parmesan on open faces of all pieces.

(If you want the sweet peppers heated, you can add them to the baguette before placing in the oven. The baguettes will be soft and chewy rather than toasty. Your choice, but I recommend putting the sweet peppers on after toasting in the oven so you keep the crunch.)

Toast in 400° oven for 5 minutes.

Plating:

Plate toasted baguettes on a serving platter.

Place sweet pepper onto each baguette.

Garnish generously with chopped fresh parsley and a bit more parmesan.

Serve family style as finger food.

Turkish Lentil Soup with Mint-Infused Butter

The first time I made this it was Turkish Red Lentil Soup. It is now just Turkish Lentil Soup. Turns out red lentils can only be purchased dry and must be soaked overnight - BAAHH!! Too much time! We switched to Goya Canned Lentils on the advice of a lentil expert. Yes, there are lentil experts. The amount of crushed red pepper from the original recipe (4 teaspoons) must be cut back significantly. It made the soup nostril burning spicy. In fact, it was a real WOW! I have cut the recipe back to a single teaspoon. The plain soup with no crushed red pepper was excellent on its own.

Ingredients:

8 TBSP unsalted butter
1 cup white onion; grated
2 garlic cloves; smashed and minced
10 cups water
4 cups beef stock
1 can Goya® lentils (12 to 16 oz)
4 TBSP Arborio rice
3 TBSP tomato paste
Salt
Freshly ground pepper
4 TBSP all-purpose flour
1 tsp crushed red pepper (you could add more if you want a really spicy soup)
2 tsp dried spearmint (or dry fresh mint in oven at 350° 10 to 12 minutes)

Instructions:

Grate (or mince) onion. Smash and mince garlic.

Melt 2 tablespoons of butter in a large saucepan. Add the onion and garlic, and cook 5 minutes over medium heat, stirring until softened. Add the water, stock, lentils, rice and tomato paste. Cover and bring to a boil. Skim the soup if any debris forms on the top, then cover and cook over medium-low heat approximately 45 minutes, stirring occasionally, until the lentils have dissolved. Pass or press the soup through a fine disk, sieve or food mill removing any remaining bean husks or chunks; season with salt and pepper. Return the pureed soup to the saucepan and bring to a simmer over low heat.

In a small skillet, melt 4 tablespoons of the butter. Stir in the flour whisking constantly and cook over moderate heat until a smooth brown roux forms with the aroma of hazelnuts. Be patient, it will brown up and smell like hazelnuts. Gradually whisk the brown roux into the simmering soup and simmer for 5 minutes. Wipe out the roux skillet (don't wash!). While the soup simmers and thickens slightly, re-heat the wiped out skillet, while working the crushed red pepper and spearmint through a sieve into the hot skillet. Toss out any husks or stems that won't go through the sieve. Add 2 tablespoons of butter and heat just until sizzling.

Plating:

Plate into the largest soup bowls you have, drizzle some of the mint-pepper infused butter into each bowl of soup and serve hot.

Escarole Salad with Creamy Garlic Dijon Dressing

Ingredients:

4 garlic cloves; smashed and minced
2 TBSP red wine vinegar
2 TBSP Dijon mustard
½ cup extra-virgin olive oil
salt
ground black pepper
1 large or two small heads of escarole (12 cups packed)

Instructions:

Thoroughly wash or soak the escarole in cold water. Get all of the sand off. Dry the leaves well.

Smash and mince garlic.

In a large bowl, mix the minced garlic with the vinegar, mustard and olive oil until blended. Season the dressing mixture with salt and pepper.

Tear the dry escarole leaves into bite-sized pieces. Add the escarole to the bowl and toss until all leaves are well coated.

Plating:

Plate the tossed salad onto flat salad plates. Garnish each salad with garlic croutons. Serve.

Pan-Seared Tenderloin with Mustard and Herb Coating

I have led groups where this steak dish was prepared by complete amateurs for eight people and twenty people and each time it came out to rave reviews. So don't worry if you have no steak preparation or cooking experience. Everything will work out great!

Ingredients:
8 beef tenderloin steaks (each about 1-inch thick)
salt and ground black pepper (to taste)
½ cup finely chopped parsley
2 TBSP dried sage leaves
½ cup fresh chopped basil leaves
4 minced garlic cloves
2 TBSP finely chopped fresh Rosemary, main stems removed
6 large dollops of Dijon mustard slightly thinned with extra-virgin olive oil

Sauce:
2 TBSP Butter
1 cup red wine
2 large dollops of Dijon mustard
salt and pepper seasoning

Instructions:
Garnish: Chop and thoroughly mix the parsley, sage, rosemary, basil and minced garlic on a large chopping board. Place slightly thinned Dijon mustard in a bowl. Lightly salt and pepper the raw beef. Coat the edge of a steak all the way around in mustard (slightly thinned with oil) and then roll its edges in the chopped, minced garnish. Set aside onto a plate until all eight steaks have had their edges coated. Cover and refrigerate until ready to cook.

Cooking Beef: Over medium-high heat, dry heat (no oil) one or two skillets large enough to fit all eight tenderloin steaks at the same time. Quickly place all eight steaks into the hot pan(s) and sear them one side one for four minutes. Turn once. Sear on second side for four minutes. Remove all from pan and set aside on a fresh plate. Juices will collect on the plate and will be used in the sauce. These steaks will be rare to medium rare when served. If anyone requires a medium steak, increase the cooking time for each side by 1 minute (5 minutes/side). If anyone requires a well-done steak, throw them out of the party – no, just kidding – increase the cooking time for each side by 1-½ minutes (5-½ minutes/side).

Sauce: Continuing on medium-high heat and in the same skillet(s), deglaze the pan(s) with the cup of red wine. Scrape pan(s) with a wooden spoon to hasten deglazing. If 2 pans were used, combine the contents into one pan. Reduce the volume of the wine by 50%, add two large dollops of mustard. Pour back any juices that have come off of the steaks and collected on the plate. Whisk to mix thoroughly. Add butter, gently. Stir until warm. Add salt and pepper seasoning. Stir until warm.

Plating:
Plate one filet on a large flat dinner plate. Place 8 to10 pieces of vegetables next to and on top of filet. Plate risotto by forming in a cup (size: 1-cup); press down slightly; invert cup onto diner plate next to filet; and remove the cup leaving the well-formed mound of risotto. Garnish risotto with parmesan. Spoon two tablespoons of warm sauce over the filet. Garnish entire plate with a wild sprinkle of fresh chopped parsley. Serve immediately.

Deep Fried Carrots and Portabella Mushrooms

I know you never heard of doing your veggies this way, but it has been a big hit each time I have included carrots and mushrooms prepared in a deep-fry fashion. This is a takeoff on Konkani cooking from the west of India in the tiny state of Goa. All my friends love them. I think you will agree.

Ingredients:

1 bag of baby carrots (preferred) or carrots cut to baby carrot size
16 oz portabella mushrooms
1 quart canola cooking oil for deep-frying
garlic powder
coarse salt (kosher, sea, etc)
ground black pepper
pre-sifted flour

Instructions:

Cut all vegetables to large bite size pieces. If baby carrots are not available, cut thick carrot pieces in half, lengthwise to simulate the thickness of baby carrots.

In a deep frying pan heat 1 quart of cooking oil to 350°.

Pre-heat oven to 250°.

In a large bag (with no holes in bag) (plastic or paper) place 1 cup of flour, 1 tablespoon of coarse salt, 1 teaspoon of ground pepper and 1 tablespoon of garlic powder. Shake bag briefly to mix dry ingredients.

Place all of the cut vegetables into a large strainer to dampen. Thoroughly wet the vegetables and allow them to drain briefly. While they are still damp, throw a handful of them into the bag and shake vigorously coating all of the vegetables. Remove the vegetables from the bag leaving the excess flour in the bag. Repeat until all vegetables are coated. Throw bag away.

When the oil gets up to temperature, place the coated vegetables into the hot oil and fry for six (6) to eight (8) minutes. Test a carrot at six minutes. Depending upon the size of your fryer, you may have to do several batches.

Drain the cooked vegetables on paper towels to absorb the excess oil. Lightly sprinkle with coarse salt. Do not allow the vegetables to get cold. Line a large ovenproof dish with fresh paper towels. Transfer the drained vegetables to the large ovenproof dish and keep in a warming oven at 250° until ready to plate.

Plating:

See plating instructions for Pan-Seared Tenderloin.

Caramelized-Onion Risotto with Bacon

Typically to make risotto onions are sautéed until translucent before being cooked with raw rice. In this recipe the onions are browned and caramelized separately. At the end of the risotto cooking, they are stirred into the finished risotto to keep their flavor distinct.

Ingredients:

½ lb thickly sliced meaty bacon (or Pancetta or Canadian bacon)
½ cup extra-virgin olive oil
2 large onions; halved lengthwise and thinly sliced crosswise
2 quarts chicken stock (or low sodium broth)
2 garlic cloves; smashed and minced
2 cups Arborio rice
1 tsp coarsely chopped thyme (plus some extra chopped leaves for garnish)
1 cup freshly grated Parmesan cheese, ½ cup for risotto cooking and ½ cup for garnish
Salt and freshly ground pepper

Instructions:

In a large skillet, cook the bacon over medium heat until well warmed (Canadian) or crisp (for regular bacon), about 8 minutes. Transfer to paper towels to drain, then crumble (or chop).

Bring the 2 quarts of chicken stock to a boil in a medium saucepan. Reduce heat to simmer, cover and keep hot over low heat.

In large saucepan, heat 3 tablespoons of the olive oil. Add the onions and cook over medium-high heat until lightly browned, about 4 minutes. Reduce heat to medium and continue to cook the onions, stirring occasionally, until they are soft and well-browned, about 15 more minutes. Add the minced garlic and cook over medium heat until fragrant (about 1 minute). Remove onions and garlic to a bowl and keep aside. Leave as much oil in the pan as possible. Pour back any oil that accumulates in the bowl. Add 2 additional tablespoons of oil to the pan and heat. Add the raw rice and cook, stirring, for 2 minutes over medium heat. Then add enough stock to just cover the rice (about 1-½ cups), and stir constantly over medium heat until the stock has been absorbed. Continue adding stock, about 1-½ cups at a time, and cook, stirring constantly until the stock has been completely absorbed before adding more stock. The rice is done when the grains are just tender and the sauce is creamy. **This takes 22 minutes from when you add the first stock to the rice, but taste the rice to be sure it is firm but not hard.**

Remove the pan from the heat and stir in the onions, bacon, chopped thyme and ½ cup of Parmesan cheese. Taste and season with salt and pepper, as needed.

Plating:

Serve generous portions with steaks. Garnish with extra Parmesan cheese and a light sprinkling of chopped thyme (leaves only). See plating instructions for Pan-Seared Tenderloins.

Ricotta Tart with Honey-Thyme Glaze and a Pine-Nut Crust

Trust me on this one. Use a pre-baked 10" or 11" pie crust for this pie. It will save you much needed time. Graham crust is okay.

Ingredients:

Pastry: USE PRE-BAKED PIE CRUST
1 Keebler® Pre-Baked Graham Cracker Crust (10")
¼ cup pine nuts

Filling:
1 cup fresh ricotta cheese
8 oz cream cheese, softened
1 tsp pure vanilla extract
½ cup mascarpone cheese
½ cup sour cream
¼ cup sugar
¼ cup honey
3 large eggs
1 tsp minced thyme
½ tsp finely grated lemon zest
a pinch of salt

Glaze:
½ cup honey
½ tsp thyme leaves
¼ tsp finely grated lemon zest

Instructions:

Pastry: Toast pine nuts in a dry pan over medium heat. Watch them carefully, so they don't burn. Crack toasted pine nuts and press into pre-baked pie shell. Sprinkle pie shell with two teaspoons of vanilla extract.

Filling: In a bowl, using an electric mixer beat the ricotta, cream cheese, vanilla, mascarpone and sour cream at moderate speed until smooth. Beat in the sugar and honey. Add the eggs, 1 at a time; beat well after each addition. Beat in the minced thyme, lemon zest and a pinch of salt. Pour the filling into the tart shell and bake at 350° for 30 minutes, or until just set and a little wobbly. Transfer to a rack to cool completely, minimum 1 hour.

Glaze: In a saucepan, bring the honey to a boil over moderately high heat. Remove from the heat and let cool down to warm, about 10 minutes. Stir in the thyme and lemon zest, then pour the glaze over the tart. Chill uncovered in refrigerator. Serve chilled.

Plating:

Cut pie into 8 equal servings. Use large flat dessert or salad plates. Place a slice of pie on plate and put a generous amount of whipped cream (Reddi Wip) on the side of the pie. Serve.

Chinese without the WOK

Chinese without the WOK

My dad was a big fan of Chinese food. After eating steaks, chops and broiled chicken all week in his butcher shop, he enjoyed going out on Sunday to the local Chinese restaurant for the family style dinners – one from Column A, two from Column B and one from Column C. One of the items always had to be his favorite, Moo Goo Gai Pan. I think he just used to like saying the Moo Goo part of the name. We always ate Chinese food at the restaurant – no take out, with the lone exception being the occasional heating of a can of Chun King Chow Mein by my mother for my sister and me. We never owned a wok.

My sister-in-law, Kathy, gave me a wok as a Christmas gift about 10 years ago – Instant Love. I cook everything in it, including Italian cuisine! Yesterday, I used it to make up syrup to glaze a peach pie. I love the fact that you can push cooked items up the sides to stay warm while you sauté new items in the hot flat bottom. What a great gift, but alas, I know not everyone has one of these miracle pans, so I have chosen Chinese foods that can be prepared by your dinner party chefs without the wok. If by some stroke of luck, you have a wok, use it where I call for pan stir frying, sautéing or deep frying. Otherwise, any pan will do.

On my visits to China, I have had the rare pleasure of eating snake, bugs (unwittingly) and all sorts of strange animals. One restaurant I visited in the Jiangsu Provence had a wall of cages with live animals to select from to assure freshness. Kind of like picking your own live lobster out of a tank at a pricey US restaurant, only these were furry little creatures. Fortunately there was Becks® beer to wash down the bad feelings. There will be neither snakes nor bugs in this meal, but we will draw from the world famous Cantonese cuisine of Guangzhou, China and other Chinese provinces. We will even have some items, not Chinese, but popular in Chinese restaurants in the USA today.

Enjoy!

Chinese without the WOK

5:15 p.m.   Cocktails

Wine, Beer, Mixed Drinks

Snacks

Crab Rangoon

6:00 p.m.   Dinner

Beverages   Water, Wine, Beer and Soda

Appetizer   Stuffed Black Chinese Mushrooms

Soup   Cantonese Seafood Soup

Salad   Cold Asparagus with Soy and Sesame

Entree   Imperial Chicken with Plum Sauce Glaze

Accompanied by

Garlic Snow Peas with Water Chestnuts
Fluffy White Rice

Dessert   Mandarin Orange Cake and Pudding
Café and Tea
Chinese Lychee Liqueur

Chinese without the WOK Shopping Lists

Shopper 1

4 oz cream cheese, softened
4 oz fresh crab meat or canned crab meat, drained and flaked
1 red onion
3 white onions
1 green onion
1 head garlic
1 red bell pepper
2 lbs asparagus spears (min. 32 spears)
1-½ cups sesame oil
1 jar sweet and sour sauce
1 jar Chinese hot mustard
1 can evaporated milk
1 box Duncan Hines® Moist Deluxe Butter Recipe Golden Cake Mix

Shopper 2

1-½ cups lean ground pork
4 TBSP Chinese rice wine or dry sherry
24 Chinese dried black mushrooms; 1-½" to 2" diameter caps
4 cups fresh snow peas
3 eight-ounce cans water chestnuts
4 cups rice, medium or long grain
¼ ounce stick agar agar (or powder)
1 cup soy sauce
4 Mandarin oranges
1 package won ton wrappers (use 24)
3 cups oriental plum sauce

Shopper 3

4 sole fillets (ask fish monger to give you the bones and trimmings from fish)
1 lb very large shrimp; 16 count/lb
1 large carrot
16 button mushrooms
5 lemons
1 package fresh baby spinach leaves
bean sprouts, for garnish
8 half (split) chicken breasts; boned, but with skin on

Shopper 4 (Host)

Fresh ground black pepper
Salt
2 cups sugar
2 chicken bouillon cubes
1 cup dry white wine
4 TBSP cornstarch
1 can of spray vegetable oil
1 TBSP Chinese Five-Spice
½ gal canola oil
½ tsp lemon extract
1 tsp dry mustard
3 tsp ground ginger
½ tsp Tabasco® sauce
½ tsp fennel seeds
4 eggs
1 stick of butter
3 cans mandarin orange slices
1 bottle Maraschino cherries
¼ tsp Worcestershire sauce

Preparation Schedule – Chinese without the WOK

Teams
1/
2/
3/
4/Hosts

4:00 pm **1, 2, & 3**- Arrive at **4**'s kitchen. Put on chef's aprons. Unpack and stack all groceries in a central location. Put fish, fish trimmings, pork and chicken in refrigerator. Leave cream cheese and butter at room temperature. Have a cocktail.

4:15 pm **1**- Start Cantonese Seafood Soup recipe. Serve at 6:30 pm.
2- Start Crab Rangoon recipe. Serve when ready.
3- Start Chinese Mushroom recipe. Serve at 6 pm.
4- Set table and continue serving drinks. Start Asparagus Salad recipe and prepare to point of marinating and chilling in refrigerator.

5:15 pm **1, 2, 3 & 4**- Eat Crab Rangoon in the kitchen, and drink cocktails while you merrily work on your other food preparations.
2- Serve Crab Rangoon.
3- Preheat broiler to 500°.
4- Prepare Chicken with Plum Sauce recipe up to point where ready for oven. Cover and place in refrigerator

5:30 pm **2**- Simultaneously prepare Mandarin Orange Pudding recipe and Mandarin Orange Cake recipe. Refrigerate pudding to chill.

5:45 pm **2**- When Chinese Mushrooms are out of the broiler, turn the oven to bake and reduce heat to 365°.
3- Plate Chinese Mushroom appetizer with help from **4** at 6 pm.
4- Help **3** plate and serve appetizer.

6:00 pm. **Eat Appetizer in Dining Room**
At 6:15 everyone helps clear dishes to the kitchen.

6:15 pm. **1**- Plate soup with garnish and serve at 6:30 pm.
2- Place Mandarin Orange Cake in oven on lowest rack to bake.
3- Prepare rice recipe. Start 18-minute simmering step of rice with pot covered just before sitting down for soup course.
4- Remove chicken from refrigerator and lightly baste with more plum sauce mixture. Put Chicken in oven on top rack for first 15 minutes at 6:30 pm, just before sitting down for soup course.

6:30 pm   **Eat Soup in Dining Room**
At 6:45 everyone helps clear soup dishes to the kitchen.

6:45 pm   **1-** Trim snow peas, slice water chestnuts and mince garlic according to Garlic Snow Peas and Water Chestnuts recipe. Stir fry will take place after salad course is eaten.
2- Remove marinating asparagus from refrigerator. Complete assembly and plating of salad. Dress and serve salads.
3- Remove rice from heat after 18 minutes of cooking are complete, and set aside covered to allow liquid to absorb.
4- Remove Chicken from oven and baste with plum sauce mixture. Return Chicken to oven top rack a few minutes before sitting down for salad course. Put final cup of plum sauce in a covered sauce pan over very low heat to warm while eating salad course.

7:00 pm   **Eat Salad in Dining Room**
At 7:15 everyone helps clear salad dishes to the kitchen.

7:15 pm   **1-** Stir fry Garlic Snow Peas and Water Chestnuts and plate with **4**.
2- Remove Mandarin Orange Cake from oven, if done. Allow to cool for at least 15 minutes before removing from pan.
3- Complete fluffing of rice just before serving. Plate Rice, Chicken, and Snow Peas and Water Chestnuts with **4**.
4- Remove chicken from oven and final baste with warm plum sauce. Work with **3** to plate and serve entree.

7:30 pm   **Eat Entree in Dining Room**
At 8:00 everyone helps clear dishes to the kitchen.

8:00 pm   **4-** Brew coffee and tea.
2- Remove Mandarin Orange Cake from pan and set aside to cool.

8:15 pm   **1-** Help **2** in plating dessert. Cut pudding and plate with cake. Garnish with Maraschino cherries and Mandarin orange slices.
2- Final preparation of dessert. Slice cake, plate with pudding, garnish and serve with help from **1**. Serve when ready.
3- Work with **4** on coffee and tea service.
4- Set up coffee cups, teaspoons and tablespoons for dessert service. Serve coffee and tea when ready.

8:30 pm   **Eat Dessert and Have Coffee and Tea in Dining Room**
Relax! Job Well Done!

Crab Rangoon

This extremely popular item is sold in many Chinese restaurants in the United States. Oddly enough, it is not Chinese in origin. As far back as the 1950s, the first well-know restaurant to serve this item was Trader Vic's, a Polynesian restaurant in New York City. In fact, Rangoon is not even in China; it is the capital of Myanmar, formerly Burma; and it is not certain that they know Crab Rangoon there. I can attest. I've been there, albeit for an hour for a plane refueling, and when we landed they did not serve us Crab Rangoon. All they did was guard the plane with riflemen far away from the terminal and get us back off the ground as quickly as possible. None-the-less, you will love this ubiquitous Chinese restaurant snack.

Ingredients:

4 oz cream cheese; softened
4 oz fresh crab meat or canned crab meat; drained and flaked
½ tsp red onion; chopped fine
¼ tsp Worcestershire sauce
¼ tsp soy sauce
freshly ground black pepper; to taste
½ green onion; finely sliced
1 clove garlic; smashed and finely minced

1 package won ton wrappers (use 24)
4 cups canola oil for deep-frying
1 jar sweet and sour sauce
1 jar Chinese hot mustard

Instructions:

Chop and slice the vegetables, as called for in the ingredients. Combine the softened cream cheese and crab meat. Mix in the remaining six filling ingredients one at a time.

On a flat surface, lay out a won ton wrapper in front of you so that it forms 2 triangles (not a square). Wet the edges of the won ton. Add 1 teaspoon of filling to the middle, and spread it out toward the left and right points of the wrapper so that it forms a log or rectangular shape (otherwise the wrapper may break in the middle during deep-frying). Fold over the edges of the wrapper to make a triangle. Wet the edges with water and press together to seal. Keep the completed Crab Rangoon covered with a damp towel or paper towel to keep them from drying out while preparing the remainder.

Heat a pan and add oil for deep-frying. (My apologies, but a wok or a deep fryer is much better for this purpose.) When oil is ready (temperature between 360° - 375°), carefully slide in the Crab Rangoon triangles, taking care not to overcrowd the pan. Deep-fry until they are golden brown, about 3 minutes, turning once. Remove with a slotted spoon and drain on a paper towel or brown bag.

Plating:

Place two dipping bowls centered on a large platter with Sweet hand Sour Sauce and Chinese Hot Mustard. Serve the Crab Rangoon, family-style, hot and piled high on the platter.

Stuffed Black Chinese Mushrooms

I recommend that you use authentic Chinese dried black mushrooms instead of fresh button mushrooms. You may also substitute dried shiitake mushrooms if the Chinese black prove too hard to find. In either case, do not discard the mushroom soaking water or the stems. It has fine flavor and will be used in the sauce for this dish and in the soup.

Pork Filling Ingredients:
1-½ cups lean ground pork
3 tsps Chinese rice wine or dry sherry
3 tsps soy sauce
½ tsp sugar
1 tsp sesame oil
1 tsp cornstarch
½ red bell pepper; deseeded and chopped
2 whole water chestnuts; finely chopped
2 tsps minced ginger
4 TBSP green onion; finely chopped and halved
1 egg white

24 Chinese dried black mushrooms; 1-½" to 2" diameter
1 can of spray vegetable oil
Cornstarch for dusting
1 TBSP Chinese Five-Spice

Sauce Ingredients:
1 cup water from soaking mushrooms (stock)
1 clove garlic; smashed and minced
Half of the chopped stems from soaked mushrooms
1 TBSP soy sauce
1 TBSP sesame oil
1 TBSP Chinese rice wine or dry sherry
2 tsps cornstarch
2 additional TBSP water from soaking mushrooms (stock)

Instructions:

Mushroom and Vegetable Prep: Soak the dried mushrooms in 1-½ quarts of hot water for 30 minutes to soften.

While the mushrooms are being soaked, chop and mince the vegetables as called for in the ingredients. Keep each vegetable separate, since some will be used in the sauce. Split the chopped green onion into 2 portions. Half will be in the filling and half will be a garnish.

After the 30-minute soak, remove any stems from caps. Place the caps in a steamer, and chop the stems finely. Toss the chopped stems back in the soaking water. Save the water for both the sauce recipe, below, and the soup recipe.

Steam the mushroom caps for 30 minutes over boiling water.

Pork Filling Instructions: While the mushrooms are being steamed, in a medium bowl combine the pork with the rice wine or dry sherry, soy sauce, sugar, sesame oil and

                    81

cornstarch. Add the egg white, knead to mix the ingredients. Gradually add the vegetables, using your fingers to knead all the ingredients together. Cover the bowl and marinate the pork filling in the refrigerator for 15 minutes.

After the 30-minute steaming, remove mushroom caps from heat and place bottom side (insides) down on a paper towel to wick off excess moisture. Cover with a second paper towel and gently press down to wick off excess moisture. Spray the tops with a light coating of vegetable oil. Lightly dust the oiled tops with Chinese Five Spice. These are ready for filling.

Pre-heat oven broiler to 500°. Spray a light coating of vegetable oil on broiling pan.

Turn the mushroom caps over and dust the bottoms (insides) of the mushrooms with cornstarch (this will help the filling stick). Stuff each cap with 1 tablespoon of the seasoned pork mixture, making a mound in the cavity and press down slightly. Place on broiling pan. When all caps are filled and on broiling pan, spray a light coating of vegetable oil on the filled caps.

Broil at 500° for 8 minutes. Keep an eye on the broiling to be sure they don't burn. The tops should be crisp. If you must, rotate the caps a bit to ensure all caps broil evenly. Remove from oven when tops are crisp, and place on stovetop to sit while the sauce is made.

Sauce Prep: When the mushroom fillings are crisp, and you have removed the caps from the broiler, heat a pan over high heat. When hot, add the tablespoon of sesame oil, and swirl. Add the minced garlic and half of the chopped mushroom stems and cook for 1 minute stirring frequently. Add the cup of mushroom stock, soy sauce, and rice wine/sherry. Bring to a boil, then reduce the heat and simmer for 1 minute. Combine the cornstarch with 2 additional tablespoons of mushroom soaking water, stir or shake well to mix and add to the wok, and simmer for a few minutes, until thickened slightly. Taste the sauce, add a drop or two of soy and ground black pepper to taste. Stir well. Serve.

Plating:

On a flat salad or dessert size plate, spoon 2 tablespoons of sauce in the center. Place three mushroom caps close together on the sauce. Sprinkle a few chopped green onion pieces on the sides of the plate. Serve.

Cantonese Seafood Soup

Ingredients:

4 sole fillets

For broth:
(ask fish monger to save bones and trimmings from fish)
2 white onions; sliced
1 large carrot; chopped fine
2 chicken bouillon cubes
leftover mushroom stock and stems from Chinese Stuffed Mushroom Recipe

16 button mushrooms; halved
2 TBSP canola oil
1 lb very large shrimp; 16 count/lb
1 cup dry white wine
4 TBSP lemon juice -- or juice of 2 lemons
salt
1 package fresh baby spinach leaves

bean sprouts, for garnish

Instructions:

Chop and slice the vegetables, as called for in the ingredients. Place the fish bones and trimmings together with the sliced onion, chopped carrot and chicken stock cubes in 4 pints of water. Bring to a boil and then simmer for 30 minutes. Strain out the solids and save the broth. Add the mushroom stock and half of chopped mushroom stems saved from Chinese Stuffed Mushroom recipe. Return to boiling point and then turn off heat.

Cut 4 fillets of sole in half by slicing lengthwise. Tie each of the 8 fillet pieces loosely into a loose knot and poach in heated stock until tender. Remove filets an hold aside.

Heat canola oil in pan to high temperature. Stir fry the mushrooms in the oil until tender, add the prawns and stir fry for 2 more minutes. Season with a pinch of salt. Add the dry white wine and lemon to the pan, stir and remove from the heat. Add the spinach to the pan and cover to wilt.

Bring the stock again to the boil and turn off heat.

Plating:

Use the largest soup bowls you have. Place one poached sole filet knot in each soup bowl. Add two shrimp, several mushroom pieces and spinach to each bowl. Ladle the broth into each bowl. Garnish the tops with bean sprouts. Serve while still steaming.

Cold Asparagus with Soy and Sesame Dressing

Try to get tender, thin spears of asparagus, not those ones that look like baseball bats! If you get stuck with baseball bats only use the top half of each spear.

Ingredients:

2 lbs asparagus spears (or a minimum of 32 spears)
pinch of salt for boiling water

¼ cup soy sauce
¼ cup sesame seed oil
½ tsp sugar
2 cloves garlic; smashed and minced fine

1 lemon for zesting

Instructions:

Cut or break tough ends off bottoms of stalks. If you break by hand, gently grasp the asparagus on both ends about 1" to 2" in. Gently bend the asparagus and it will break at the best point on its own. Discard the tough end.

Bring 6 cups water with a pinch of salt to boil in saucepan. While waiting for water to boil, prepare the dressing. Mix the soy sauce, sesame oil, sugar and minced garlic in a bowl. Stir and reserve.

When water boils, drop in asparagus. Boil 1 minute. Drain. Rinse with cold water. Drain again and place cooked asparagus on a paper towel to wick remaining water away.

Arrange the cooked asparagus in a flat-bottomed pan so all pieces are laying flat. Pour the dressing over the asparagus. Cover pan and refrigerate for 30 minutes to marinate and chill asparagus.

Plating:

Divide the marinated asparagus evenly among 8 flat salad plates. Line the asparagus up side by side with the tips all facing in the same direction. Top with a small amount of lemon zest. On each plate, thinly drizzle a tablespoon of the marinade/dressing in a zig zag over the asparagus and extending out onto the bare plate. Serve.

Imperial Chicken with Plum Sauce Glaze

It is a good bet that the plum became a sauce and met the chicken in China about 3000 years ago during the Zhou Imperial Dynasty. The Zhou period of rule saw great advances in culinary technique with the use of sophisticated combinations of fruits, vegetables, meats and spices. Naturally, this was largely enjoyed by the nobility who are just like our friends.

Take my advice, find a Chinese grocery and buy the plum sauce. Making your own will take too long. I am recommending that you start with chicken breasts with skin. The skin on will help retain moisture in the meat during the roasting. Let each dinner party guest decide if they want to remove the skin when the entrees are served. If anyone votes for skin-off, remove the skin and do the final basting of the skinned chicken with the warmed plum sauce.

Ingredients:

½ tsp lemon extract
8 half (split) chicken breasts; boned, but with skin on
1 tsp dry mustard
1 tsp ground ginger
½ tsp Tabasco® sauce
3 cups oriental plum sauce
½ tsp ground black pepper
½ cup onion; minced
½ tsp fennel seeds; crushed
4 TBSP lemon juice
2 TBSP soy sauce
spray oil for baking pan (PAM® or other)

Instructions:

Spray a 9" x 13" roasting pan with oil spray. If you have a rack for the pan, use it. Rinse chicken; pat dry and place in the roasting dish, skin side up.

In a bowl, mix together 2 cups of plum sauce with all of the other ingredients. Pour and brush on about half of the mix over the chicken, top and bottom. Lift the skin partially away from each breast a bit and brush some of the sauce under the skin. Replace the skin and brush some sauce on top of the skin. Roast the chicken, uncovered, on the top rack in a 365° degree oven for about 15 minutes. Remove from oven. Pour and brush the breasts with the second half of the mix. Roast the chicken for another 15 minutes on the top rack at 365° degrees, until meat is no longer pink in its thickest part.

While chicken is roasting for the final 15 minutes, warm the remaining cup of plum sauce in a microwave oven or over very low heat. When roasting is done, remove chicken from the oven and baste the skin with the remaining cup of warm plum sauce. Allow to sit for 5 minutes on top of stove before plating.

Plating Rice, Chicken and Vegetables:

Spread a cup of white rice onto 2/3 of the plate to the edge. Place chicken breast on rice. Plate water chestnuts and snow peas on the open side of the plate. Dab a bit of warm plum sauce on top of the breasts just before serving. Serve.

Garlic Snow Peas and Water Chestnuts

Ingredients:

4 cups fresh snow peas
2 eight-ounce cans water chestnuts; sliced
2 cloves of garlic; smashed and minced
4 tsp canola oil
2 tsp Sesame oil
Salt; to taste
Ground black pepper; to taste

Instructions:

Wash and drain snow peas. Trim ends and strings off.

Rinse and drain water chestnuts. Dry with a paper towel. Slice into ¼" slices.

Smash garlic cloves and mince.

In a large non-stick skillet or a wok, heat canola oil over high heat. Add garlic and stir fry for 2 minutes. Add snow peas and stir-fry for 2 minutes. Add sliced water chestnuts and stir-fry 1 minute. Add 2 teaspoons of sesame oil. Stir-fry 1 more minute. Season with a pinch of salt and pepper.

Plating:

Plate according to instructions in chicken recipe.

Fluffy White Rice

When the Chinese eat white rice, they don't fool around with it. It is plain white rice with no fragrances. Of course the fried rice many of us order in Chinese restaurants is loaded with flavor. That invention of the Yangzhou province historically was to make a main course out of the odds and ends left over from previous meals. Only in America do we eat it as a side dish. Leave it to us to maximize the number of calories we can fit on one plate!

For our side dish we will have the traditional plain fluffy white rice, and it will serve as a field of white on which to place our chicken. We do not want to steer too much attention away from the plum sauce flavors.

Ingredients:

4 cups rice
6 cups water

Nothing else. The Chinese do not normally eat fragrant rice.

Instructions:

Most American-grown rice is fortified with vitamins and minerals in the form of a powder coating, and should not be rinsed before cooking. If you use imported rice, remove dust and impurities by rinsing rice in a couple of changes of water. Run your fingers through the rice as you rinse. Drain.

Place rice into a flat, heavy bottomed pot with a tight fitting lid.

Add the 6 cups of water. Without the lid, bring to a boil on a medium heat. Stir well.

Place the lid on pot, and simmer on a very low heat for about 18 minutes. Turn off the heat and allow the rice to rest for 15 minutes to complete the water absorption process.

Mix the rice to fluff it up just prior to serving.

Notes: Cooking time may vary depending on rice type. In general long grain rice needs a bit more water than short. Never toss in oil, butter or salt, or any other additive. Do not remove the lid from the pot until the rice is ready to serve. Do not wash rice after cooking.

Plating:

Normally, the Chinese serve their white rice in separate bowls and eat it directly from the bowl with chopsticks. Not us! We will use it for food and for decorative purposes, as well. See the plating directions in the chicken recipe.

Mandarin Orange Butter Cake and Pudding

The Mandarin orange is a sweet gift of oriental foods introduced to Europe and the USA in the nineteenth century. They flourish now in Florida and California. In this case we mingle two uses of the orange into a sweet finish to our Chinese meal.

Cake Ingredients:

1 box Duncan Hines® Moist Deluxe Butter Recipe Golden Cake Mix
3 eggs
1 stick of butter; softened
1 can mandarin orange slices; juice and all pulp

2 cans mandarin orange slices; drained for garnish
1 bottle Maraschino cherries; drained for garnish

Cake Instructions:

Heat oven to 365°.

Mix the cake mix, eggs, softened butter and 1 can of mandarin orange slices (juice and all) together with an electric mixer until well blended.

Pour mixture into greased, metal bundt cake pan.

Bake at 365° on lowest rack of the oven for time indicated on the cake mix box. When done a toothpick of fork pierced into the cake should come out clean. If not, bake the cake a few more minutes, but watch carefully.

Allow cake to cool in pan at least 15 minutes before removing. Then allow cake to continue cooling to room temperature (i.e. not warm to the touch).

Plating Cake and Pudding:

Slice cake into 24 equal slices. For each serving, place 2 slices laying flat on a dessert large plate with the tapered edges facing each other and overlapped about 1". Place one square of Mandarin Orange pudding centered on the 2 cake slices. Garnish top of pudding with a Maraschino cherry and the sides of the plate with a few Mandarin orange slices. Serve.

Mandarin Orange Pudding

This lightly sweet crème dessert makes a colorful and delicious pairing for the orange cake.

The agar agar called for below is a gelling agent made from a combination of algae from the species gelidium. The name, agar agar, is Malaysian in origin, and the harvest of the long red and purple fronds goes back hundreds of years. The fronds are freeze dried and dehydrated naturally, producing colorless sheets which are shaped into bars. Agar is available in the traditional bars, flakes, and powder, all of which can be used interchangeably for gelling purposes. This recipe presumes you will find it in a bar or stick form. One agar bar is equal to four tablespoons of flakes or two teaspoons of powder. Unlike gelatin, all forms of agar need to simmer for a while to dissolve, and letting them soak in the liquid for a while gives you a head start. You may simplify things and shorten you preparation time if you find the flake or powder form of this gelling agent.

Pudding Ingredients:

¼ ounce stick agar agar
2/3 cup sugar
2 cups warm water; to soak agar agar
¼ cup evaporated milk
4 cups water; additional to original 2 cups
3 cans Mandarin orange slices; pulp only – drain juice

Pudding Instructions:

Soak agar agar stick in a medium bowl with 2 cups warm water for 30 minutes. This amount of time can be reduced to a few minutes if agar agar is in flake or powder form.

Transfer agar agar and water to a large saucepan. Add 4 cups of water. Bring to a boil over medium heat and cook until agar agar is completely dissolved.

While agar agar is soaking and then boiling, drain the mandarin orange slices. Chop the pulp into small pieces.

Remove the saucepan from heat and add sugar, evaporated milk and chopped Mandarin orange pulp. Stir until the sugar is totally dissolved.

Pour into a 9" x 9" cake pan. Let stand until cool.

Refrigerate until pudding is chilled and firm, about 15 min. The chilled pudding can remain in the refrigerator for a longer period of time.

Plating:

Cut the gelled pudding into 3" x 3" squares. Plate with mandarin orange cake and garnish according to plating instructions in cake recipe.

Tropical Pig Roast

Tropical Pig Roast

The day we did this dinner at our friend's house there was no full pig in sight. We just had a pork roast, but we all agreed it would be fun to call it a pig roast anyway. The last time I was involved with a true pig roast done at home was about 20 years ago. That pig, ready for the spit, was about 75 pounds! If you got a truly BIG porker, you could easily double that size. Needless to say, this would be a bit much for eight people. In fact, the real pig roast party eventually fed about 40 with plenty of leftovers. We also found that the pig had to be cooked overnight to be ready in time for an afternoon party. The spit had to be kept running and the fire had to be fed. The one staying up all night to baby sit the piggy wound up in no shape for a party the next day. In all this turned out to be a massive commitment, and with Home Cooking Parties for Eight, we are all about reducing the burden on any one person. Division of labor and division of cost is what it is all about from getting the groceries right through to the final cup of coffee. So here we are with a very manageable pork butt roast that will bubble away in exotic juices for several hours and put a smile on your face. (See the early marinating tip I give to the Host in the roast recipe.)

This meal is a bit different because I recommend a special punch to start the festivities. This is a cool breeze vanilla and citrus punch that is reminiscent of the great Creamsicle® from the Good Humor® trucks. When I was a kid, the Creamsicle® was a wonderful summertime treat and a breath of fresh air in the heat of the afternoon. Fortunately for us, the ingredients of this punch are so simple; you may already have them in your pantry. You just never thought of bringing them together in the same glass. Here you will get the chance to set the tropical mood right from the start of your dinner experience. Maybe you have some of those little umbrellas for the glasses to start everyone off with a laugh.

The mangos and pineapples in our meal encourage our minds to drift to the tropics as we prepare and eat. The wild mango originated in Southeast Asia, Burma to be exact. It has become well-known in the USA because it was transplanted to California, Mexico and Florida over 100 years ago. My mother had a beauty of a mango tree in her backyard in Fort Lauderdale. When that tree came to maturity, she would ship boxes full of mangos to us "up north." We loved to see the UPS truck pull up in front of our house. She used to say that she wanted to spread a little bit of Florida sunshine. Little did she know she was really sending us Burmese sunshine. I have sprinkled this delectable fruit into your salad and the scrumptious upside-down tropical cake that tops off your meal. The pineapple is also a well-traveled fruit. I'll bet you think it originated in Hawaii. Nope. Brazil. Pineapple didn't make it to Hawaii until 1813. From Brazil it spread throughout the Caribbean. Our Columbian

Exchange friend, Christopher Columbus was responsible for introducing it to Europe where it became the rarest of sweet treats for the wealthy and was enjoyed 300 years before the first Hawaiian tasted the fruit. Lucky for us it is available everywhere thanks to companies like Dole and Del Monte, so we can include it in our punch, appetizer and dessert.

When you look at the menu, you may question the Zucchini, Potato and Parmesan Soup. Tropical? Well, yes. Columbus at work again. The zucchini seeds, originally from South and Central America, found their way to the Mediterranean thanks to our intrepid friend. Even those big 3 foot-long Italian cucuzza (often pronounced "Gagoots") originally came from the tropics.

So this truly is a tropical meal in every respect. Best of all you will share the great tastes with friends. Enjoy!

Tropical Pig Roast

5:00 p.m.   Cocktails

Tropical Breeze Punch
Wine, Beer, Mixed Drinks

Snacks

Puna Goat Cheese Spread
Pineapple and Summer Sausage
Stone Ground Wheat Crackers

6:00 p.m.   Dinner

Beverages   Water, Wine, Beer and Soda

Soup   Zucchini, Potato and Parmesan Soup

Salad   Light Summer Salad Greens with Mango, Raspberry
Vinaigrette Dressing and Croutons
Warm Baguette and Butter

Entree   Tropical Pork Roast with Black Beans

Accompanied by

Baked Zucchini with Herbs and Tomatoes

Dessert   Tropical Upside-Down Cake with Vanilla Ice Cream
and Toasted Pecans
Café and Tea
Liqueur

Tropical Pig Roast Shopping Lists

Shopper 1

½ gallon of vanilla ice cream
1 baguette
½ cup grated parmesan cheese
1lb Puna goat cheese or
   ½ lb crumbled plain feta cheese and
   ½ cream cheese
1 box stone ground wheat crackers
1 box unflavored croutons
3 cans pineapple chunks
1 can evaporated milk
3 cans (15 oz) Goya® black beans
1 box light brown sugar
1 bottle raspberry vinaigrette dressing

Shopper 2

1 large can pineapple juice
6 lemons
3 mangos
1 large bottle ginger ale
1 cup toasted chopped pecans (pieces ok)
1 lb salted butter
½ lb unsalted butter
1 pint whole milk
1 cup extra virgin olive oil
1 bottle pure vanilla extract
1 half gallon orange juice
1 quart chicken broth

Shopper 3

1 stick summer sausage
2 medium Yukon gold potatoes
8 medium zucchini
3 large sweet onions
1 bunch celery
2 green bell peppers
1 bunch scallions
1 bunch fresh thyme
1 bunch fresh parsley
1 bunch fresh basil
6 plum tomatoes
2 pkgs spring mix salad (mesclun greens)

Shopper 4 (Host)

5 lb boneless pork butt roast
oven cooking bag
4 seedless navel oranges
14 cloves garlic
12 limes
1 cup orange juice
coarse salt (kosher, sea, etc)
ground black pepper
1 bottle cumin seed
ground ginger
dried oregano
baking powder
3 cups all-purpose flour
1 cup sugar
2 large eggs
dark rum (for cake and punch)

Preparation Schedule – Tropical Pig Roast

Teams
1/
2/
3/
4/Hosts

SPECIAL NOTE: At least 2 hours before the start, 4 makes marinade and marinates pork roast in refrigerator (overnight is even better).

4:00 pm   **1, 2, & 3**- Arrive at **4**'s kitchen. Put on chef's aprons. Unpack and stack all groceries in a central location. Put milk, ginger ale and juices in refrigerator. Put ice cream in freezer. Leave 2 eggs, butter and cheeses at room temperature. Have a cocktail.

4:15 pm   **1**- Make Tropical Breeze Punch and refrigerate until ready to serve.
2 - Chop vegetables for soup. Reserve.
3- Start cake recipe. Chop 3 cups of mangos for salad and cake. Refrigerate 1 cup of chopped mangos for salad. Chop 1 cup of toasted pecans, reserve half for garnish. Continue fruit cooking and batter preparation portions of the cake recipe. Place cake in oven on bottom rack by 5:00 pm.
4- Turn oven on and set to 350°. Place marinated roast and marinade into oven bag and into oven immediately in a covered roasting pan. Place on middle rack. Set table; include sharp steak knives. Continue serving drinks.

4:30 pm   **1**- Start Snack Platter recipe. Serve when ready. Add ginger ale to Tropical Breeze Punch and serve with Snack Platter.

4:45 pm   **2**- Start soup recipe and continue until ready to serve at 6:00 pm.
4- Set out punch glasses for **1** to use.

5:00 pm   **1, 2, 3 & 4**- Eat snacks in the kitchen as they are ready, and drink punch and cocktails while you merrily work on your other food preparations.
3- Place cake in oven on bottom rack at 350° for 30 to 35 minutes.
4- Slice baguette into 1" pieces and wrap in foil. Set aside for salad course.

5:15 pm   **1**- Start Baked Zucchini Recipe and place in shallow baking dish ready for oven. Set aside. Place on top rack of oven at 6:15 pm.

5:30 pm   **2**- Complete final step for soup by adding remaining broth, evaporated milk and cheese. Turn heat back up but do not allow the soup to boil.
3- Check cake with a toothpick for doneness. When done remove from oven and reduce temperature of oven to 325°. Place pork roast

on bottom rack. Move middle rack to top rack position. Let cake cool for 10 minutes and then de-pan the cake. Place upside down cake on platter at room temperature until ready to serve.

5:45 pm.   2- Plate soup with garnish and serve with help from **4** at 6:00 pm.
4- Help **2** serve soup.

6:00 pm   **Eat Soup in Dining Room**
 At 6:15 everyone helps clear soup dishes to the kitchen.

6:15 pm   1- Place baking dish with zucchini in oven on top rack.
2- Retrieve cup of cut mangos from refrigerator and complete assembly, dressing, tossing and plating of salad. Serve salads at 6:30 pm with help from **4**.
3- Start Black Bean recipe. Complete and keep warm until ready to plate.
4- Place foil-wrapped baguette in oven to warm. When warm place baguette in a basket covered with a napkin. Place butter and bread basket on table at 6:25 pm for salad course. Help **2** serve salads.

6:30 pm   **Eat Salad in Dining Room**
 At 6:45 everyone helps clear salad dishes to the kitchen.

7:00 pm   1- Take zucchini from oven, cover and keep warm on top of stove.
4- Remove pork roast from oven. Remove from bag and place in a pan covered with foil. Strain liquids in bag according to instructions, skim fat and reserve liquid. Warm dinner plates.

7:15 pm   1- Plate and serve zucchini in coordination with **3** and **4**.
3- Plate Black Beans and Pork Roast with **4**.
4- Follow directions for slicing roast and covering slices in pan with reserved juices. Plate and serve Pork Roast with help from **3**. Strain remaining juices into a gravy boat and place on table.

7:30 pm   **Eat Entree in Dining Room**
 At 8:00 everyone helps clear dishes to the kitchen.

8:00 pm   2- Remove ice cream from freezer to soften. Assemble dessert plates and reserved toasted pecans chopped by **3** for garnish.
4- Set up coffee cups, teaspoons and tablespoons for dessert service. Brew coffee and tea.

8:15 pm   1- Work with **4** on coffee and tea service.
2- Help **3** plate dessert. Add ice cream and pecans.
3- Final preparation of upside-down cake. Slice and serve according to instructions with help from **2**. Serve when ready.
4- Serve coffee and tea when ready.

8:30 pm   **Eat Dessert and Have Coffee and Tea in Dining Room**
 Relax! Job Well Done!

Tropical Breeze Punch

The punch is perfect for the whole family, but can be made wickedly good for adults by adding your favorite dark rum!

Ingredients:

6 cups fresh orange juice
2 cups fresh or unsweetened canned pineapple juice
½ cup fresh lime juice
½ cup fresh lemon juice
3 TBSP pure vanilla extract
1 cup dark rum (optional)
3 cups ginger ale, chilled

Instructions:

Chill ginger ale and juices.

Combine all the juices in a large pitcher. Add vanilla into the juice.

Stir with a whisk.

Add optional dark rum and stir. (This could be added by the glass when you serve if you want to keep the punch in the pitcher non-alcoholic. Put and ounce of dark rum in a single glass with crushed ice, fill with punch and stir.)

Cover pitcher with plastic wrap, refrigerate and chill until ready to serve.

Serving:

Just before serving, add the chilled ginger ale to the pitcher.

Stir and serve in tall ice-filled glasses. If you can crush the ice, all the better.

Puna Goat Cheese Spread, Pineapple and Summer Sausage Platter

Puna goat cheese comes from the big island of Hawaii. It is a creamy cheese between the texture of cream cheese and feta cheese with a less salty taste. Fortunately for you, if you cannot find genuine Puna in your neighborhood, you can make this spread from half feta and half cream cheese and make believe you are in Hawaii.

Ingredients:

1 lb genuine Puna goat cheese or
       ½ lb plain feta cheese; crumbled
       ½ lb cream cheese; softened
1 stick summer sausage
1 can pineapple chunks; drained (save drained juice)
1 box stone ground wheat crackers
1 TBSP parsley; chopped

Directions:

Drain pineapple chunks and reserve liquid for use in cheese spread. Chop parsley.

Puree the cheese in a food processor until it is a smooth spreadable texture. Add a tablespoon of drained pineapple juice to smooth out the texture for spreading. If the texture remains too stiff to spread add more pineapple juice until it thins properly. Transfer cheese spread into a bowl. Garnish with a tablespoon of chopped parsley. Serve or cover and refrigerate until ready for serving.

Slice sausage on the diagonal into ¼" slices.

Plating:

On a large serving platter arrange sliced summer sausage on one end. Garnish with a few sprigs of parsley. Place bowl of cheese spread in center of platter. Stick a cheese spreading knife into the cheese. Place bowl of pineapple chunks stuck with toothpicks next to cheese spread bowl. Place wheat crackers on the opposite end of the platter from sausage.

Serve at the same time as punch.

Zucchini, Potato and Parmesan Soup

Tropical?………..yes……….Delicious?…………..oh yeah!

Ingredients:

1 TBSP extra-virgin olive oil
1 medium onion; finely chopped
2 celery ribs; finely chopped
3 garlic cloves; smashed and minced
3 medium zucchini; scrubbed but unpeeled, cut into ½" cubes
2 medium Yukon Gold potato; peeled and cut into ½" cubes
3 cups chicken broth
1 sprig of fresh thyme
1 cup evaporated milk
3 TBSP freshly grated Parmesan cheese
2 TBSP freshly grated Parmesan cheese for garnish
2 TBSP fresh thyme; chopped for garnish
salt; to taste
ground black pepper; to taste

Instructions:

Wash, chop and mince vegetables according to instructions, above.

Heat the oil in a large pot over medium heat. Add the onion, celery and garlic. Cover and cook. Stir often, until the onions are translucent, about 5 minutes.

Stir in the zucchini and potato. Add enough broth to barely cover the vegetables. Add the sprig of thyme and bring to a boil over high heat. Reduce the heat to low. Simmer, partially covered, until the potato is fork tender, about 15 minutes.

Ten minutes before serving, stir in any remaining broth, the evaporated milk and 3 tablespoons Parmesan cheese. Heat until very hot, but do not boil (soup will curdle if it boils). Season to taste with salt and pepper.

Plating:

Ladle into soup bowls. Garnish with chopped thyme and extra Parmesan cheese. Serve hot.

Light Summer Salad with Mango

Ingredients:

2 packages spring mix salad (mesclun greens)
1 mango; chopped (approx. 1 cup)
1 bottle raspberry vinaigrette dressing
1 package unflavored croutons
coarse salt (kosher, sea, etc)
ground black pepper
garlic powder
1 baguette
1 stick butter

Instructions:

Wash greens. Spin dry or allow at least 10 minutes for thorough draining and drying.

Set oven to 300°. Slice, wrap baguette in foil and warm while you prepare the salad.

Place greens in large salad bowl for tossing.

Season dry greens with coarse salt and freshly ground black pepper.

Add several dashes of garlic powder.

Toss greens once or twice to distribute seasonings.

Peel and chop mango into ¼" cubes.   Place cubes in salad bowl.

Add enough dressing to lightly coat all greens and mango.

Toss salad once or twice.

Add croutons.

Toss salad twice more and serve.

Remove baguette from oven and slice.

Plating:

Wrap sliced baguette in a cloth napkin and place in a bread basket. Serve warm baguette with butter. Use flat salad plates. Evenly distribute salad among 8 plates and serve.

Tropical Pork Roast

Alive with the flavors of the Caribbean, this pork roast has a tart citrus sauce. Sour oranges, which have thick, bumpy skins, are available at Latin markets; substitute a seedless navel orange, if you wish. Cooking the roast in an oven bag makes it so tender you can practically cut it with a spoon. To allow enough time for marinating and then cooking, I am asking the Host to get started early on the marinating of this roast. All of the ingredients are in the Host Shopping List. Starting the marinating two or three hours (or more) ahead of the cooking party starting time will help the flavor and tenderness of the roast.

Ingredients:

One 5-lb boneless pork butt roast; trim off exterior fat

Marinade Ingredients:

4 oranges (preferably sour or seedless navel); sliced into ½" thick rounds (reserve half for garnish)
2-½ tsp cumin seed; crushed
2-½ tsp dried oregano
6 garlic cloves; smashed under a knife
1 cup fresh orange juice
½ cup fresh lime juice

Instructions:

Marinade:

Place half of the orange slices, cumin, oregano and garlic in a large bowl and crush the orange slices into the spices with a large spoon. Stir in the orange and lime juices. Add the pork and turn to coat on all sides. Cover and refrigerate for 1 hour. If you can prepare this and marinate for several hours, all the better. Turn pork over every ½ hour of marinating.

Roasting:

Pre-heat oven to 350°F then follow Preparation Schedule instructions for the timing of changing temperatures. Transfer the meat and marinade into the plastic oven bag. Seal the bag. Place in a roasting pan and cover tightly. Bake until the pork is fork tender, about 3 hours. When pork is fork tender, open the cooking bag and remove the pork. Place pork in a pan and cover with aluminum foil to keep warm. Pour the liquids from the bag through a strainer into a bowl, pressing hard on the solids. Discard the squeezed out solids. Let liquid stand for 5 minutes. Skim any fat from the surface. Season to taste with salt and pepper. Reserve liquid and keep warm. When ready to serve, slice the pork into 8 thick slices, lay back in the pan and rewet all slices with reserved liquid just before plating. Do not pour the liquid over the pork after it is plated. Strain the remaining pork juices into a gravy boat and place on the table for diners to use at their discretion.

Plating:

Use large bowls. Plate beans and tomatoes in center of bowl. Turn the slice of pork over in the pan to wet both sides and then lay the slice over the beans. Garnish the pork with a slice of orange. Dust orange slice with a pinch of crushed cumin seed. Serve baked zucchini in a bowl on the side.

Black Beans and Roma Tomatoes

Ingredients:
2 TBSP extra-virgin olive oil
½ cup finely chopped onion
½ cup green bell pepper; finely chopped
1 tsp ground cumin
1 tsp dried oregano
2 garlic cloves; smashed and minced
¾ cup chicken broth
3 Roma or plum tomatoes; seeded and chopped into ½" dice
3 15-oz cans Goya® black beans, drained and rinsed
salt
ground black pepper

Instructions:

Chop onion and bell pepper. Smash and mince garlic. Seed and chop tomatoes.

Heat the oil in a medium saucepan over medium heat.

Add the onion and bell pepper and cook, stirring often, until softened, about 5 minutes.

Add the cumin, oregano and garlic and cook for 1 minute.

Add the broth and tomatoes and bring to a simmer. Reduce the heat to low and cook for 5 minutes. Drain and rinse black beans while soup cooks.

Stir in the black beans and cook on low heat 10 minutes more.

Season to taste with salt and pepper.

Keep warm.

Plating:
See plating instructions in Tropical Pork Roast.

Baked Zucchini with Herbs and Tomatoes

Ingredients:

12 firm baby zucchini, or 5 medium zucchini; sliced lengthwise into ¼"-thick sticks
1 large sweet onion; medium chop
2 scallions; white part only, thinly sliced
leaves only from 4 inner stalks celery
8 basil leaves, for bake
¼ cup all-purpose flour
3 whole ripe plum tomatoes; seeded and coarsely chopped
coarse salt (kosher, sea, etc.)
½ cup extra virgin olive oil
ground black pepper
16 basil leaves; for garnish

Instructions:

Preheat oven to 325°.

Slice zucchini and scallions. Chop onion. Seed tomatoes and coarsely chop.

In a colander (allow any excess liquid to strain out), combine zucchini, onion and scallions. Tear celery and basil leaves into small pieces and sprinkle on top. Sprinkle flour over all. Using one hand, press and toss ingredients together until well mixed and coated (it will get a little moist, but not gooey). Add tomatoes, season with salt and toss once more.

Note: The baking dish has to be shallow enough to fit on the top rack of the oven.

Pour half the olive oil into a medium baking dish (round preferred) or ceramic pie plate or. Fill dish with zucchini mixture, then grind about a teaspoon of pepper over the top. Sprinkle remaining oil on top, and place in oven.

Bake uncovered for about 30 to 40 minutes on top rack of oven, or until ingredients are just cooked, but firm.

Remove from oven and allow at least 5 minutes for cooling before plating.

Plating:

Use small bowls. Plate each serving of baked zucchini garnished with a few fresh leaves of basil. Serve on the side of the pork and black bean dish.

Tropical Upside-Down Cake

Upside-down cake is an American classic. This variation uses mangos and pineapple to make it Hawaiian-American.

Ingredients:

½ gallon of vanilla ice cream
½ cup toasted pecans; coarsely chopped for garnish

Cake:
1-½ sticks unsalted butter, at room temperature
2 mangos; pitted, peeled, and cubed (1") (about 1-½ cups)
1-½ cups pineapple chunks; cut to 1" cube pieces
1 cup (packed) light brown sugar
2 TBSP dark rum
1 cup toasted pecans; coarsely chopped (½ cup for bake and ½ cup for garnish)
2 cups all-purpose flour
2 tsp baking powder
1 tsp ground ginger
Pinch of salt
1 cup granulated sugar
2 large eggs, at room temperature
1 tsp pure vanilla extract
¾ cup milk

Instructions: Place rack at bottom position of the oven and pre-heat to 350°. Generously butter a 13 x 9-inch baking pan. Cube cut mangos. Drain and cut pineapple chunks to no larger than 1" on a side. Chop 1 cup of toasted pecans. Separate and reserve half for bake and half for garnish.

Heat 4 tablespoons of the butter in a large skillet over medium heat. Add the mango, pineapple, brown sugar and rum. Cook, stirring often, until the sugar is melted and bubbling. Cool until tepid. While cooked fruit is cooling, sift together the flour, baking powder, ginger and salt and set aside. Beat the remaining 8 tablespoons of butter and the sugar in a large bowl with an electric mixer at high speed until light and fluffy, about 3 minutes. Beat in the eggs, one at a time, then the vanilla. On low speed, add the flour in 3 additions, alternating with 2 additions of the milk, and beat until smooth, scraping down the sides of the bowl often with a rubber spatula.

Arrange the fruit in a single layer in the pan, and pour the syrup over all. Sprinkle with ½ cup of pecans. Spread the batter evenly over the fruit.

Bake until a toothpick inserted in the center of the cake comes out clean, about 30 to 35 minutes. Cool for 10 minutes on a wire rack. Invert and un-mold onto a flat platter or cutting board for slicing. (If any pieces of fruit stay in the pan, just remove them and arrange them in their place on the cake.) Pour any juices in the pan over the cake and allow to rest at room temperature until ready to serve.

Plating: You can serve this cake warm or completely cooled. Slice into 3" by 3" pieces. Plate slightly off-center on a large dessert or salad plate. Add a scoop of vanilla ice cream to the side of the cake. Sprinkle chopped toasted pecans on both the cake and the ice cream. Serve immediately.

Tour of Tuscany

Tour of Tuscany

In Italy, especially Tuscany, it is okay to eat a lot. One of the great disappointments for me when I visited Italy was finding the same kind of eating going on as we did in our house in Massapequa, Long Island, but I could not find native Italians of my girth. This proved true in Rome and Sorrento, too. What gives? Can they digest better than me – only a partial Italian? Well, it was good to know they liked to eat, even if they were thin. In fact, in the wonderful city of Florence you can find Ristorante Pane e Olio (Bread and Oil) where you can not order. They feed you what they have. Five or six courses later, no one ever leaves unhappy. Remember Chianti is the wine of the Tuscan hills. Drink some with this meal for true authenticity.

Pasto is the Italian term for meal. Full meals may range through three to six courses or sometimes more and can take hours to eat. Curiously, though, antipasto – before the meal (appetizer) does not rate a course number, even if the range of appetizers offered in some places would constitute a feast like it did in my house. So, for our five course meal (darn, it would have been six or seven if they let me count the appetizers) tonight here is a primer on the Italian names for the parts of the meal you will eat.

The first course –primo piatto-- generally consists of pasta, risotto, polenta, gnocchi or soup. You can have more than one primo which is primi. We will have two, due primi, pasta and soup! The second or main course--secondo piatto or piatto di mezzo-- may be seafood, meat, poultry, game, omelets or other hearty vegetable dishes. We will have one, un secondo! A straight numbering system for the courses stops working when meals include two or more primi or secondi, say when a fish course precedes a poultry course which precedes a meat course or like our meal with two firsts, due primi. MAMA MIA! With the main course will come a contorno (literally, I surround). This is a side dish or garnish of cooked vegetables, salad, rice, noodles or polenta. Since we will have two, a garnish of vegetables and a side salad and they will surround the main course (they surround), we will have circondono. These do not count as courses at all! Courses may continue with formaggio (cheese), frutta (fresh fruit), dolce (sweet also called dessert), caffè (espresso, of course) and digestivo (grappa, brandy or liqueurs, such as amaro or sambuca). We will have a third course, terzo, of cheese and fruit, but since we had two first courses this is really our fourth course (oh boy!). Confused? Our last course, really the fifth not counting the antipasto, will simply be dolce. I suggest you have a digestivo like sambuca as well to make the meal truly authentic. Remember, you don't have to know any of this, just follow the Preparation Plan and eat. That's enough. It should also be nice to know that if you are, in spirit, truly 100% Italian, you won't care in what order the food comes and you won't gain any weight from eating this meal. Fortuna buona! Enjoy!

Tour of Tuscany

5:00 p.m.   *Cocktails*

        Wine, Beer, Mixed Drinks

    Antipasto

        Affettati Misti (Sliced Mixed Meats)
        Fresh Mozzarella
        Baked Stuffed Polenta Cups
        Italian Bread and Olive Oil

6:00 p.m.   *Pasto (Dinner)*

    Beverages   *Water, Wine, Beer and Soda*

    Primi Piatto, Un   *Linguini Carbonara with Artichokes*

    Primi Piatto, Due   *Red Bell Pepper Soup with Cannellini and Basil*

    Piatto di Mezzo   *Tuscan Roasted Pork Tenderloin*

      Circondano

        Contorno Un – Roasted New Potatoes and Carrots
        Contorno Due – Radicchio Salad

    Terzo Piatto   *Formaggio e Frutta*

    Dolce   *Panna Cotta with Berries*
        Café and Tea
        Liqueur

Tour of Tuscany Shopping Lists

Shopper 1

½ lb Prosciutto, thinly sliced
½ lb Genoa salami, very thinly sliced
1 stick pepperoni
½ lb fresh mozzarella
½ lb block Pecorino cheese
1 lb block of ricotta salata
1 roll of pre-made polenta
2 loaves of Italian bread
1 TBSP anchovy paste
24 black olives (any variety)
1 jar green olives with pimientos
1 large jar of marinated artichoke hearts
6 cups chicken stock

Shopper 2

1 small can of peas; Le Seur preferred
1 16-oz can white cannellini beans
1 cup grated Parmigiano-Reggiano
12 cloves garlic
1 bunch fresh parsley
1 bunch fresh basil
1 medium yellow onion
2 large white onions
12 medium carrots
12 small, new potatoes
5 red bell peppers
6 heads of radicchio
8 oz Torrone candy; wrapped pieces

Shopper 3

Two 1-½ to 2 lb pork tenderloins
5 ripe medium tomatoes
4 sweet apples; Gala or Golden Delicious
4 pears; Anjou or Bartlett
4 lemons
2 cups blueberries
1 cup raspberries

Shopper 4 (Host)

1 lb dry, uncooked linguini
2 eggs
4 slices of bacon
2 cups extra virgin olive oil
salt
sugar
ground black pepper
4 TBSP dried rosemary
4 TBSP fennel seeds
4 TBSP dried parsley
4 TBSP dried oregano
2 TBSP dried basil
2 TBSP dried thyme
½ tsp cayenne powder
¼ tsp crushed red pepper flakes
2 TBSP capers
1 cup white wine
2 cups whole milk
1-½ TBSP unflavored powdered gelatin
4 cups heavy whipping cream
1 TBSP pure vanilla extract
¼ cup honey
1 cup 10X powdered sugar

Preparation Schedule – Tour of Tuscany

Teams
1/
2/
3/
4/Hosts

4:00 pm	**1, 2, & 3**- Arrive at **4**'s kitchen. Put on chef's aprons. Unpack and stack all groceries in a central location. Put mozzarella, ricotta salata, pork tenderloins, berries, eggs, milk and whipping cream in refrigerator. Have a cocktail.
4:15 pm	**1**- Start Panna Cotta recipe. Continue through refrigerating to chill. **2**- Start Polenta Cups recipe. Serve when ready. **3**- Start Mixed Meat Platter recipe. Serve when ready. **4**- Set table and continue serving drinks.
5:00 pm	**1, 2, 3 & 4**- Eat Antipasto items in the kitchen as they are ready, and drink cocktails while you merrily work on your other food preparations. **3**- Start Linguini Carbonara recipe. Continue until ready to serve at 6:00 pm. **4**- Start Pork and Vegetables recipe. Carefully watch oven time for pork and vegetables to avoid overcooking. Continue until ready to serve at 7:30.
5:15 pm	**1**- Start Red Bell Pepper Soup recipe. Continue until ready to serve at 6:30 pm.
5:45 pm	**2**- Help **3** plate and serve pasta. **3**- Plate pasta with help from **2** and serve at 6:00 pm.
6:00 pm.	**Eat Pasta in Dining Room** **At 6:15 everyone helps clear dishes to the kitchen.**
6:15 pm.	**1**- Plate soup with garnish and serve with help from **2** at 6:30 pm. **2**- Slice Italian bread to go with soup and warm in oven. Put Italian bread in a basket when soup is ready to be served. Help **1** serve soup and bread.
6:30 pm	**Eat Soup in Dining Room** **At 6:45 everyone helps clear soup dishes to the kitchen.**

7:00 pm	**2-** Start Radicchio Salad recipe. Hold off tossing and plating for last 5 minutes before entrees are plated. **4-** Warm dinner plates. Continue Pork and Vegetable recipe.
7:15 pm	**1-** Help **2** serve salads. **2-** Time tossing and serving of salad. Serve at same time as entree. **3-** Plate pork and vegetables with **4**. **4-** Slice pork. Deglaze pan. Work with **3** to plate and serve entree.
7:30 pm	**Eat Entrée and Salad in Dining Room** **At 8:00 everyone helps clear dishes to the kitchen.**
8:00 pm	**2-** Wash and platter fruit for Formaggio e Frutta course. Sprinkle Torrone candy on the fruit platter. Set out on table family style. **3-** Slice and platter cheese for Formaggio 3 Frutta course. Set out on table family style. **4-** Set out small plates for cheese and fruit and knives for peeling fruit.
8:15 pm	**Eat Formaggio e Frutta in Dining Room** **At 8:45 everyone helps clear dishes to the kitchen.**
8:30 pm	**4-** Set up coffee cups, teaspoons and tablespoons for dessert service. Brew coffee and tea.
8:45 pm	**1-** Remove Panna Cotta from the refrigerator and complete the final preparation steps in the recipe. Complete and serve with help from **2**. Serve when ready. **2-** Help **1** plate and serve the Panna Cotta. Serve when ready. **3-** Work with **4** on coffee and tea service. **4-** Serve coffee and tea when ready.
9:00 pm	**Eat Dessert and Have Coffee and Tea in Dining Room** **Relax! Job Well Done!**

Cold Sliced Mixed Meat Platter

Always a favorite in my mother's entertaining planning was the tray of folded or rolled cold, sliced meats and cheese. This can be found in Florentine restaurants and all over Tuscany. You will enjoy the ease with which this delightful appetizer comes together.

Ingredients:

½ lb Prosciutto, thinly sliced
½ lb Genoa salami, very thinly sliced (or it won't roll)
1 stick pepperoni
½ lb fresh mozzarella
1 jar green olives with pimientos
1 loaf of Italian bread
½ cup extra virgin olive oil

Instructions:

Drain olives.

Slice mozzarella into 1/8" to ¼" slices. Use a wire cheese cutter if you have it.

Slice about ½ of the loaf of Italian bread into thin slices.

Cut the pepperoni into ¼" slices. Cut on the diagonal so the slices come out in oval rather than round shapes.

Roll the Prosciutto into loose spiral tubes. Roll Genoa salami into tight tubes.

Pour olive oil into a small bowl for dipping.   Sprinkle a small amount of dried oregano, thyme, rosemary or basil in the oil. Your choice or use several dried spiced together in the oil.

Plating:

Place bowl of oil in the center of a large platter. Place sliced bread on one end of the platter. Place mozzarella slices at the other end of the platter. Place the rolled Prosciutto on one side of the platter. Place the rolled Genoa salami on other side of the platter. Sprinkle the meat and cheese part of the platter with pimento stuffed olives.

Serve as finger food, family style. Provide toothpicks, napkins and small plates.

Baked Stuffed Polenta Cups

Cristoforo Colombo, better known to most of us as Christopher Columbus, is most famous in the USA for his "discovery of America" (one wonders who misplaced it), but his true contribution to mankind was setting off what has been called "The Colombian Exchange." This was a 300-year exchange of cultural and biological material between the Europeans and the Indians of the Americas. One of the items "exchanged" was corn going to Europe. There was no corn in Europe before Columbus. The Italians took this odd vegetable and couldn't just boil it and eat it. They had to do more. So they created a wonderful corn cake, polenta, which has only found its way back to the Americas in the last 100 years with the massive emigration of Italians and their recipes to the shores of America. The northern and western regions of Italy were the best climate for growing this relatively new vegetable, so Tuscany became a hot spot for developing ways to use the corn and its polenta. Here is one way!

Ingredients:

1 roll of pre-made polenta; sliced into 16 rounds
6 TBSP extra virgin olive oil
1 small can of peas; Le Seur preferred, drained
4 slices of bacon; chopped to ½" lengths
2 TBSP grated Parmigiano-Reggiano
2 cloves garlic; smashed and minced
4 TBSP chopped parsley; reserve half for garnish
¼ tsp crushed red pepper flakes (optional)
salt

Instructions:

Pre-heat oven to 350°. Chop bacon and parsley. Mince garlic. Cut polenta into 16 rounds.

Using a spoon or melon baller, scoop out the centers of the polenta slices to form small cups with a thin bottom. This can also be done with a sharp tipped knife. Just avoid cutting through the bottoms of the cup. If you do, brush with a small amount of olive oil and "paste" some of the cut-away polenta back in the cup. When the oven is heated, brush the bottoms of the cups with olive oil and place them onto a non-stick cookie sheet. Bake in the pre-heated oven for 15 minutes, or until the cups are golden brown.

While you are baking the polenta cups, warm 2 tablespoons of olive oil in a sauté pan over medium heat. When the oil is warm, add the chopped bacon. Sauté for 2 minutes. Push the bacon aside in pan and add the minced garlic, parsley, peas and a pinch of salt. Sauté for 2 minutes and then stir all of the ingredients in the pan together and continue sautéing for a few more minutes until the bacon crisps. At your option, sprinkle (¼ teaspoon) crushed red pepper flakes and stir well into the cooked ingredients in the pan. Remove from heat.

Plating:

Fill the baked polenta cups with a teaspoon of the cooked mixture. Place all filled cups tightly clustered in the center of a serving platter. Sprinkle all with Parmigiano and some chopped parsley. Get some of the parsley on the edges of the platter. Serve as a finger food.

Linguini Carbonara with Artichokes

The carbonara in the name of this dish refers to the specks of ground black pepper as if they are little pieces of charcoal. This original recipe for carbonara does not include cream. You will find a wonderful creamy finish is achieved when the beaten eggs and cheese are rapidly mixed into the hot, drained pasta. This family recipe from the heart of Tuscany adds a special twist in substituting delicious artichoke for the normally used pancetta (Italian bacon). Be sure to use the very good grated Parmigiano-Reggiano for a robust flavor.

Ingredients:

1 lb dry, uncooked linguini
2 TBSP extra virgin olive oil
1 medium yellow onion; chopped fine
2 cloves garlic; smashed and minced
2 eggs; beaten
½ cup grated Parmigiano-Reggiano
1 large jar (2 small jars) of marinated artichoke hearts; drained and quartered
½ cup chopped parsley
salt; to taste
ground black pepper; to taste

Instructions:

Boil a large pot of water for the linguini. After the water boils, season it with a generous pinch of salt and toss in the dry linguini. When the pasta softens and sinks below the surface, give it a quick turn to stir and separate the strands. Do not add oil to the water, since this would interfere with the ability of the cooked pasta to absorb the flavoring of the sauce. Cook the pasta about 8 to 10 minutes, until it is al dente. Taste a strand. It should be softened all the way through but still firm in the center. Don't overcook the pasta. Drain it well, but don't rinse it. You want it hot and the starch on the strands to thicken the sauce.

When you put the water pot on to boil, quarter the artichoke hearts, chop the onion and mince the garlic. Heat the olive oil in a large skillet over medium heat. Add the garlic and onion and sauté for about 5 minutes or until the pieces become translucent and the air is fragrant. Add the artichoke pieces and lightly season with salt and pepper (lightly! - you will be able to add more salt and pepper to taste later on). Stir well, cover the pan and reduce the heat to low. Simmer for up to 15 minutes (actually, only until the time the linguini is cooked to al dente and drained).

While the linguini is cooking and the artichokes are simmering, beat the 2 eggs with the Parmigiano cheese. Add a pinch of salt and continue to beat until the eggs and cheese are well combined. Reserve. After draining the linguini well, immediately add it to the skillet on top of the artichokes and onion. Turn the heat to very low. Pour the egg-cheese mixture all over the linguini and immediately toss the linguini. The heat of the linguini cooks the eggs and makes the dish creamy. Toss with the artichokes and onion. Turn off the heat.

Plating:

Evenly divide the linguini and sauce among 8 pasta bowls. Toss on another spoonful of grated cheese and a wild sprinkle of chopped parley. Serve immediately.

Red Bell Pepper Soup with Cannellini and Basil

Another family recipe, this time from Pistoia, near Florence.

Ingredients:

5 red bell peppers
1 large white onion
1 16-oz can white cannellini beans; drained
5 ripe medium tomatoes; chopped and seeded
6 cups chicken stock
5 TBSP chopped fresh basil
Salt
5 TBSP extra virgin olive oil

1 loaf Italian bread, sliced and warmed in the oven

Instructions:

Slice the onion and chop the pepper. Seed and chop the tomatoes.

Heat the olive oil in a large sauce pan on medium high heat. Sauté the sliced onion for 5 minutes and then add the chopped pepper. Sauté for 5 more minutes.

Add the chopped tomatoes, the drained cannellini beans and a pinch of salt. Stir gently, sauté uncovered for 2 minutes, cover the sauce pan and continue cooking for 3 more minutes.

Add chicken stock and blend well by stirring. Bring to a boil and then reduce heat to medium low. Simmer for 15 minutes without the lid.

Slice the loaf of Italian bread and warm it in the oven just before serving the soup.

Chop and add the basil just before plating soup. Stir the basil into the soup and plate.

Plating:

Serve hot in large soup bowls with some extra virgin olive oil drizzled over the top, just a light sprinkling of grated Parmigiano, and warm Italian bread on the side. Place the warmed, sliced loaf of bread in a basket covered with a cloth to keep it warm.

Tuscan Roasted Pork Tenderloin, Carrots and Potatoes

Ingredients:
Two 1-½ to 2 lb pork tenderloins
8 cloves garlic; cut into slivers
4 TBSP dried rosemary
4 TBSP fennel seeds; ground in mortar and pestle (or in a bowl with a spoon)
4 TBSP dried parsley
4 TBSP dried oregano
2 TBSP dried basil
2 TBSP dried thyme
½ tsp cayenne powder
4 tsp dried chopped onion
4 tsp salt
2 lemons; cut into 8 wedges
1 cup white wine
extra virgin olive oil
12 medium carrots; peeled, sliced in half lengthwise and cut in 2-½" long pieces
12 small, new potatoes; wash, remove eyes, cut in half (leave skins on)

Instructions:
Wash the tenderloins and pat dry thoroughly. Sliver garlic. With a sharp pointed knife, cut slits in the meat at ½" intervals and force the garlic slivers into the slits. Rub the tenderloins thoroughly with olive oil. Mix the dried herbs in a small bowl (rosemary, crushed fennel seeds, parsley, oregano, basil, thyme, cayenne, dried chopped onion and salt). Rub the dry herb mixture on the tenderloins, patting and pressing the herbs into the meat. Allow the rubbed tenderloins to rest at room temperature for 30 minutes. Cut carrots and potatoes while tenderloins rest. Pre-heat oven to 300°.

On the stovetop over medium heat, heat 2 tablespoons of olive oil in a heavy ovenproof pan. Brown the tenderloins on all sides. Then turn off the heat. Squeeze the lemon wedges into the hot pan and add ½ cup wine. Allow the pan to deglaze slightly and scrape the bottom a bit with a wooden spoon to bring up the bits of meat and spices from the browning. Baste the tenderloins. Place the squeezed lemon wedges, cut potatoes and cut carrots in the pan. Partially cover the pan with a lid or piece of loose aluminum foil and place in oven at 300°. Roast until the meat reaches 140° internal temperature (about 25 minutes, but use a meat thermometer if you have one). Warm an oven-proof platter 5 minutes before tenderloins are done. Move the meat out of the oven to the warm platter, cover tightly with foil and toss on a dishtowel for insulation. Return the pan and vegetables to the oven, again partially covered, raise heat to 375° and roast vegetables 20 minutes (until fork tender). When done, remove vegetables. Skim off any fat in the roasting pan. Deglaze the hot pan with a ½ cup of white wine; scrape the bits off the bottom of the pan with a wooden spoon. At the same time as deglazing occurs, slice the tenderloins into 16 total pieces to plate.

Plating:
Use a large dinner plate. Place 2 slices of tenderloin, slightly overlapping, in the center of each plate and sprinkle the carrots and potatoes onto the meat as a garnish (no lemons). A few vegetables may fall to the edges of the plate (that's okay). Spoon the liquid and bits from the deglazed pan over the meat and vegetables. Serve with the salad on a side plate.

Radicchio Salad with Pecorino and Olives

There are over a dozen different varieties of Pecorino, sheep's milk cheese, produced in the southern and central parts of Italy. While there is a Tuscan variety, Pecorino Toscano, it is likely when you go shopping you will only be able to find the most popular variety, Pecorino Romano which oddly enough comes from Sardinia, not Rome. Regardless, enjoy this simple salad with the Pecorino cheese as a magnificent Contorno (side dish).

Ingredients:

6 heads of radicchio; sliced
½ cup extra virgin olive oil
1 lemon; juiced
1 TBSP anchovy paste
24 black olives (any variety); pitted and cracked
2 TBSP capers; chopped coarsely
½ lb block of Pecorino cheese; sliced into 16 long pieces
salt; to taste
ground black pepper; to taste

Instructions:

Wash and dry the radicchio. Trim off any brown from the base of the stem and discard. Slice the radicchio into ½" thick slices. Slice through the stems, too, leaving them as part of the slice. Reserve.

Slice the Pecorino cheese into 16 pieces, as long as you can make them. Reserve.

Chop the capers. Crack and pit the black olives. Reserve.

Select a large salad bowl, in which you will be able to generously toss the salad. Before adding the radicchio, mix the dressing in the bottom of the bowl. Add in the anchovy paste and lemon juice and mix until well combined. Whisk in the olive oil and a pinch of salt and ground pepper. Whisk well. Add the capers and olives. Keep the sliced Pecorino cheese on the side to use as a garnish when you plate. Toss everything in the bowl coating the radicchio well with all of the ingredients. It is okay if some of the radicchio slices do not fall apart during the tossing.

Plating:

Use flat salad plates. Evenly distribute the tossed salad on the 8 plates. Evenly distribute the sliced Pecorino cheese on the salads. Serve the salad on the side with the main course.

Formaggio e Frutta (Cheese and Fruit Course)

For fun, I thought I would add a touch of Sicily to this otherwise Tuscan-exclusive meal. Ricotta Salata, despite its name, is not ricotta at all. It is a dense but slightly spongy sheep's milk cheese from Sicily with a slightly salty, milky flavor. A small piece of this with some sweet fruit will provide a good transition from the savory items in the main meal and our deliciously sweet dessert. I am also suggesting that you place a few pieces of the wonderful almond-nougat candy from Italy, Torrone, on the fruit plate. Buy the candy. It is a lot easier than making it. Take a little extra time to sit and talk during this course.

Ingredients:

1 lb block of ricotta salata
4 sweet apples; Gala or Golden Delicious
4 pears; Anjou or Bartlett
8 oz Torrone; individually wrapped pieces

Instructions:

Wash fruit and dry.

Slice cheese from block into long flat pieces about ½" thick by 1" wide by 2" to 3" long.

Plating:

Stack pieces of cheese on a flat plate like a pile of pick-up sticks. No garnish!

Stack fruit high on a flat serving platter. Sprinkle the Torrone candy pieces onto and around the fruit. Provide small plates and knives for peeling fruit.

Place cheese plate, fruit platter, plates and knives on table family style.

Panna Cotta and Berries

Panna cotta has been enjoyed in Italy in one form or another for more than a thousand years. Prepared this way it is a smooth, creamy delight. The zest will add a slight tang for your tongue in the backdrop of the sweetness. The berries provide fun colors and fresh, cool tastes. It is reported that in the early years of this dessert fish bones were used to provide the gelatin that set up the finished dessert. Thankfully we can skip that step. Using unflavored gelatin also lets us skip using the oven and a bain marie to set up.

Ingredients:

2 cups whole milk

1-½ TBSP unflavored powdered gelatin
4 cups heavy whipping cream
1 TBSP pure vanilla extract
¼ cup honey
1 TBSP granulated sugar
zest of ½ lemon
pinch salt

2 cups blueberries
1 cup raspberries
10X powdered sugar

Instructions:

Remove any stems in the berries. Wash, drain and chill berries.

Place the milk in a small bowl. Add gelatin and stir to combine. Set aside for 5 minutes to soften the gelatin.

Stir milk and gelatin a second time. Pour the milk-gelatin mixture into a saucepan. Place the pan over medium heat. Stir until the gelatin dissolves but the milk does not boil, about 5 minutes.

When you zest the skin of the ½ lemon into the saucepan in the next step avoid zesting down to the white pith of the lemon. It is bitter.

Add the cream, vanilla extract, honey, sugar, lemon zest and pinch of salt. Stir until the sugar dissolves, 5 to 7 minutes. Remove from the heat and let cool for 5 minutes.

Stir the finished panna cotta and pour into 8 of your largest stemmed wine glasses so that they are ½ to ¾ full. Cool at room temperature, slightly. Refrigerate until set, at least 2 hours.

Plating:

Spoon the berries on top of the set-up panna cotta. Dust with a light coating of 10X powdered sugar. When you serve this, place a flat dessert or salad plate on the table beneath the wine glass at each setting.

A Calabrian Festival of Food

A Calabrian Festival of Food

No one had a simple name in the Canarsie neighborhood and culture that surrounded my father's butcher shop in Brooklyn. One of the characters that worked in the store for a couple of years was Freddie the Actor. I didn't know him by any other name. All I remember is that he was a handsome guy in his late twenties or early thirties and he was Calabrese. The butchers in the store were all Italian except for my Greek dad, but if you know about Italians, you can never just say you're Italian. You must be identified by your region of origin. Well the butchers in the store were Calabrian, Sicilian and Neapolitan. Naturally in the store and around the neighborhood these were pronounced the Italian way – Calabrese – Siciliano – Napolitano. While the crew loved one another and would have fought to the death on the street to defend each other if there was ever trouble, this did not stop the daily sniping that went back and forth from butcher block to butcher block inside the store. So my entire knowledge about Freddie and the Calabrese was that they were thick-heads – stubborn. Freddie was constantly accosted with this label. He gave as good as he got, but he was permanently labeled "thick-head", and he kinda was....

Now move forward in time 40 years. Diane and I are cruising with our church group through the Straight of Messina in the early morning. That's the spot in the Mediterranean between the toe in the Italian boot and Sicily. I walk out on deck immediately following morning mass that was conducted by our priest and our deacon from home who were both on the trip with the group. I look over the port side and there was Calabria unfolding before me and for the first time in 40 years I understood. "Understood what?" you might say. I understood why the Calabrese were the most stubborn of the Italian people. The landscape seemed to rise almost vertically from the sea into high mountains. You had to be stubborn if you were going to live in a place like that! So I turn to my companions, tell the story of Freddie the Actor, and how the Calabrese got the rap of being the most thick-headed and stubborn people of Italy. Joey, our deacon, was standing there, looking at me with a bit of a blank stare and he says, "I'm Calabrese." Naturally, I say, "Oh, not you, Joey!" Meanwhile his wife, Marie, is standing behind him, tapping her finger on her temple and mouthing the words, "He is thick!" So it must be true. Freddie the Actor and Joey the Deacon were separated by 40 years, but peas in a pod. The Calabrese are the most stubborn and hearty people of Italy, and they pass the traits to their offspring.

Their food is hearty, too. Simple, but hearty. You will love it. It seems to unite and balance the cuisines of the nearby Italian regions of Campania, Basilicata and Apulia. The land produces pigs, sheep and beef. The eggplant is the king of vegetables; the

121

sunny warm climate yields all sorts of citrus, olives and herbs; and the abundant sea surrounding on three coasts provides seafood of all types.

This meal will be spread over a bit more time because there are so many good tastes to experience from Calabria. I am suggesting smaller sized portions so you can taste everything. We will eat the sausage, cheese, olives, citrus, lamb, fish, herbs, eggplant, nuts and simple sweets. We will even sample the famous Caviale dei Poveri or Poor Man's Caviar of the region, although some of you may have to plug up your nose to have this strong smelling and tasting treat. There will be soup. There will be salad. There will be pasta. Before our double dessert, we will have two main courses! So settle in for a good old fashion big Italian family meal.

Enjoy!

A Calabrian Festival of Food

5:00 p.m.	*Cocktails*	
		Wine, Beer, Mixed Drinks
	Antipasto	
		Baked Bread Dough Stuffed with Pig Meat *with an Olive Oil and Dry Herb Dip*
		Antipasto Platter *Caviale dei Poveri (Poor Man's Caviar)* *Soppressata* *Grilled Caciocavallo Cheese and Fresh Tomatoes* *Buttery Flavored Crackers*

6:00 p.m.	*Pasto (Dinner)*	
	Beverages	*Water, Wine, Beer and Soda*
	Primo, Un	*Fusilli Pasta and Mushrooms in Citrus Sauce*
	Primo, Due	*Chicory and Poached Egg Soup*
	Insalata	*Fennel Salad*
	Secondi, Un	*Grilled Swordfish with Lemon and Oregano*
		Accompanied by
		Eggplant with Almonds and Walnuts
	Secondi, Due	*Lamb Chop Arancia*
		Accompanied by
		Potatoes and Olives
	Dessert	*Half-Moon with Jam and Almonds* *Lemon Crème Crostata* *Café and Tea* *Liqueur*

A Calabrian Festival of Food Shopping Lists

Shopper 1

8 lamb leg sirloin chops; ¾" thick and about 6 to 8 oz each, bone-in
¼ lb bacon
1 cup of orange juice
1 orange for zest
2 limes
8 lemons
1 pkg Pepperidge Farm® Puff Pastry Sheets
1 cup fig preserves (substitute: strawberry or grape jam)
1 quart extra virgin olive oil

Shopper 2

¾ cup Italian black olives
½ cup large green olives stuffed with pimentos
½ cup grated Parmesan
1 lb fusilli pasta
¼ cup capers
¼ cup Anchovy fillets
1 package buttery flavored crackers
8 oz of Soppressata; sliced thinly
1 lb block of caciocavallo cheese; about 1" thick (substitute: 1 lb block of imported provolone)
1 quart red wine vinegar
2 quarts vegetable stock
¾ lb fresh or frozen bread dough (substitute: 1 tube Refrigerated Pillsbury® Biscuits 8 or 10 oz)

Shopper 3

12 oz fresh mushrooms; any variety
3 bunches fresh Italian parsley
1 bunch fresh basil
1 large head of chicory
4 large starchy baking potatoes
4 bulbs fennel
26 cloves of garlic
2 large white onions
1-½ lbs ripe tomatoes
4 large eggplants
1 bag all-purpose flour
1 bag sugar
1 box 10X powdered sugar
8 oz sliced almonds
¼ lb walnut pieces

Shopper 4 (Host)

8 4-ounce swordfish fillets; ½" thick
4 links (¾ lb) Italian sweet sausage
1 loaf of day-old (stale) Italian bread
13 eggs
Kosher or Sea Salt
6 TBSP dried oregano
1 tsp dried basil
1 hot chili pepper (substitute: crushed red pepper)
1 tsp paprika
1 cup golden raisins
2 teaspoons dried mint
2 TBSP honey
½ tsp cinnamon
1 TBSP unsweetened cocoa powder (substitute 3 TBSP sweetened coca mix)
1 stick unsalted butter
1 stick butter
2 tsp vanilla extract
3 TBSP cornstarch
Table Salt
ground black pepper
1 ounce Strega® Liqueur (substitute Crème de Menthe or Sambucca)
½ cup white wine

Preparation Schedule – A Calabrian Festival of Food

Teams
1/
2/
3/
4/Hosts

4:00 pm	**1, 2, & 3**- Arrive at **4**'s kitchen. Put on chef's aprons. Unpack and stack all groceries in a central location. Put lamb, fish, Italian sausage and eggs in refrigerator. Leave puff pastry, butter, cheeses, Soppressata, orange juice, bread/biscuit dough, and Italian bread at room temperature. Have a cocktail.
4:15 pm	**1**- Start Poor Man's Caviar recipe. Serve with Antipasto Platter. **2**- Start Baked Stuffed Bread dough recipe. Serve when ready. **3**- Start Grilled Cheese and Antipasto recipes. Serve when ready. **4**- Set table and continue serving drinks.
4:30 pm	**1**- Start Chicory Soup recipe. Serve at 6:30 pm. **4**- Prepare swordfish marinade and place marinating swordfish in refrigerator by 5 pm.
5:00 pm	**1, 2, 3 & 4**- Eat Baked Stuffed Dough and Antipasto Platter in the kitchen as they are ready, and drink cocktails while you merrily work on your other food preparations. **2**- Pre-heat oven to 350°. Start Lamb recipe. Place in oven by 5:30 pm. **3**- Peel and cube eggplant. Salt and place in colander by 5:30 pm. for 1 hour of draining.
5:15 pm	**4**- Start Fusilli and Mushroom recipe. Serve at 6 pm.
5:30 pm	**2**- Place lamb in oven. **3**- Start and complete Half-Moon recipe through placing on baking sheet. Set sheet aside at room temperature. Place in oven at 8:00 pm.
5:45 pm	**2**- Help **4** plate pasta. Serve at 6 pm. **4**- Plate pasta with help from **2**. Serve at 6 pm.
6:00 pm.	**Eat Pasta in Dining Room** **At 6:15 everyone helps clear dishes to the kitchen.**
6:15 pm.	**1**- Plate soup with garnish and serve at 6:30 pm. **2**- Wash, trim and slice fennel for salads. Cover and refrigerate. Check liquid level on lamb in oven at 6:25 pm. Supplement according to recipe.
6:30 pm	**Eat Soup in Dining Room** **At 6:45 everyone helps clear soup dishes to the kitchen.**

6:45 pm	**1-** Start Lemon Crème Crostata recipe. Put in oven at 8:00 pm. **2-** Dress, toss and plate salad. Serve at 7:00 pm. **3-** Complete cooking and dressing of Eggplant. Serve at 7:30 pm. **4-** Warm dinner plates. Make preparations for completing Swordfish recipe. Don't cook it yet, just get set up.
7:00 pm	**Eat Salad in Dining Room** **At 7:15 everyone helps clear salad dishes to the kitchen.**
7:15 pm	**2-** Start Potatoes and Olives recipe. Serve at 8:30 pm. **3-** Plate and serve Eggplant and Swordfish Entrée with **4**. **4-** Sauté swordfish. Help **3** plate Eggplant and Swordfish Entrée.
7:30 pm	**Eat Fish Entrée in Dining Room** **At 8:00 everyone helps clear dishes to the kitchen.**
8:00 pm	**1-** Put Crostata in 375° oven on lower rack at 8:00 pm. Check doneness of crostata at 8:30 pm. **2-** Remove lamb from oven and rest on stove. Raise oven to 375°. **3-** Put Half-Moons in 375° oven on middle rack at 8:00 pm. Check doneness of Half-Moons at 8:30 pm.
8:15 pm	**1-** Check doneness of both desserts in oven. Remove from oven when done. **2-** Plate Meat Entrée, Potatoes and Olives with **4**. Serve at 8:30 pm. **3-** Check doneness of both desserts in oven. Remove from oven when done. **4-** Help **2** plate and serve Meat Entrée, Potatoes and Olives.
8:30 pm	**Eat Meat Entree in Dining Room** **At 9:00 everyone helps clear dishes to the kitchen.**
9:00 pm	**1-** Final preparation of desserts. Plate and serve with help from **3**. Serve when ready. **2-** Work with **4** on coffee and tea service. **3-** Final preparation of desserts. Plate and serve with help from **1**. Serve when ready. **4-** Set up coffee cups, teaspoons and tablespoons for dessert service. Brew coffee and tea.
9:15 pm	**2-** Work with **4** on coffee and tea service. **4-** Serve coffee and tea when ready.
9:30 pm	**Eat Dessert and Have Coffee and Tea in Dining Room** **Relax! Job Well Done!**

Baked Bread Dough Stuffed with Pig Meat

For the sake of time, we are going to cheat on this item. You may not be able to find pig's feet, snout, skin and lard. So I suggest using Italian sweet sausage as a flavorful and simple alternative. If you run into trouble finding ¾ of a pound of fresh (or frozen) raw bread dough, pick up a tube of Pillsbury® Biscuit Dough. The sweetness of the biscuit dough is probably better suited to mix with the sausage meat, anyway.

Ingredients:

1 tube Refrigerated Pillsbury® Biscuits (8 or 10 ounce) (**Alt:** ¾ lb bread dough)

4 links (¾ lb) Italian sweet sausage

For dipping:
½ cup extra virgin olive oil
½ tsp dried oregano
½ tsp dried basil
ground black pepper

Instructions: Pre-heat oven to 375°.

I am going to presume you followed my recommendation to get Italian sweet sausage in place of pig snout and feet. Remove sausage meat from casing (skin). Heat a skillet over medium heat. Add one tablespoon of olive oil to pan. Place sausage meat in pan. Fry and stir continuously with a wooden spoon to avoid having meat stick to the pan. Remove from heat before meat browns. Tilt pan and drain off excess liquid. Leave cooked meat in tilted pan allowing more liquid to drain off.

Dust the surface of the kitchen counter, large cutting board or table top with flour. Open package of prepared biscuit dough. Separate biscuits and place on floured surface. Cut biscuits in half. Spread, stretch and flatten one cut piece of dough to about 2"x3". Use a teaspoon to place a dollop of cooked sausage meat onto one end of the flattened dough. Roll the dough up and over the meat and continue rolling once or twice more wrapping the meat completely inside. Pinch any openings closed. Place stuffed dough ball onto an ungreased non-stick cookie sheet. Repeat. Leave an inch of separation between the dough balls on cookie sheet. They will puff as they bake.

Place the cookie sheet of dough balls in the pre-heated oven on the middle rack. Bake for 10 minutes and check them for doneness. They should be slightly puffed up and golden brown on the outside. These go from golden brown to black quickly, so get them out of the oven as soon as they brown.

While the dough balls bake, place the ½ teaspoon of dried oregano, ½ teaspoon of dried basil, pinch of salt and pinch of ground black pepper into a small dipping bowl. Use a spoon to slightly grind the four dry ingredients together. Add ½ cup of olive oil to the dipping bowl. Stir ingredients together.

Plating:

Use a large flat platter. Place all baked stuffed bread dough on the platter. Push slightly to clear one side. Place dipping bowl on platter in cleared out area. Serve family style. Provide toothpicks.

Caviale dei Poveri (Poor Man's Caviar)

This is eaten all over Italy. There are as many recipes as there are mouths. This one is truer to the Calabrian area, but there are other variations. It has a strong flavor due to the anchovies. If you are a timid eater, spread it on a cracker, hold your nose and bite down. You might find a new way to enjoy anchovy other than Caesar salad.

Ingredients:

¾ cup Italian black olives; crushed and pitted
¼ cup capers; drained
¼ cup Anchovy fillets
¼ cup extra virgin olive oil
4 TBSP lemon juice; fresh squeezed
1 tsp paprika

1 package buttery flavored crackers

Instructions:

Crush olives and remove pits. Be careful to get all of the pits and discard them.

Rough chop the capers and anchovies.

In food processor or blender, mix all ingredients (except crackers) together until you have a smooth spread, about 10 seconds.

Plating:

Transfer the spread into a medium bowl. Stick a cheese spreading knife into the spread. Serve with buttery flavored crackers with the spread. Place both on large platter with Soppressata and grilled cheese. Serve family style with platter of stuffed dough balls.

Soppressata

This Calabrian salami is the best known and widely available. It is pressed before curing, so it holds up as thin slices. Natural flavors such as black pepper, red pepper, cumin and chili peppers are added to meat which is then aged for up to 100 days. Buy this thinly sliced. Lay the slices out on a platter with the Poor Man's Caviar, Grilled Caciocavallo and buttery flavored crackers.

Ingredients:

8 oz of Soppressata; sliced thinly

Instructions:

If they only have sticks of the sausage at your store, take it to the cold cut counter and ask them to slice it thin for you. I must have done that 1000 times for customers when I worked the cold cut counter in my father's store. If you have to buy a chunk of this, try to slice the 8 ounces into more than 16 slices. The thinner you can make this the better it tastes as you lay it on your tongue.

Plating:

Lay out the slices on one end of the large platter that you will be using for the Soppressata, Grilled Caciocavallo and Poor Man's Caviar.

Grilled Caciocavallo Cheese

The Italian name of this cheese, caciocavallo, means "Cheese on horseback." Folklore says that it was originally made from mare's milk, but the only hard evidence is that cow's milk has been used dating way back. The name really comes from the fact that the curd is left to dry by straddling it upon a horizontal stick like the saddle over a horse's back. This leaves the cheese with a tear-drop shape. The flavor is quite similar to aged provolone. While the rind of caciocavallo is hard, it is edible. Try grating it and using as a garnish in other meals. If you have too much difficulty in locating the caciocavallo, feel free to use aged provolone.

Ingredients:

1 lb block of caciocavallo cheese; about 1" thick
2 ripe tomatoes

Instructions:

Cut each tomato into 8 wedge pieces. Place in a medium serving bowl, cover with plastic wrap and refrigerate until cheese is ready to be served.

Trim the cheese rind and save for grating and other uses.

Cut ½" slices off the trimmed block of cheese. The slices will be ½"x1" by whatever length the original block of cheese was. Cut the slices into ½"x1"x1" squares.

Heat a dry flat non-stick surface griddle on the stove over medium heat. Place the square slices of caciocavallo cheese on the dry hot griddle. Leave until a caramelized crust forms on the bottom of the cheese. Flip the cheese over with a non-stick spatula and leave until a crust forms on the second side. You may need a fork to push the cheese onto the spatula in order to flip it.

There is so much naturally occurring oil in either the caciocavallo or provolone that when you place the cheese on the dry hot pan, oil will immediately start to come out of the cheese. The cheese will also melt and lose its shape a bit while it is browning. Use your spatula and fork to push it back into shape. It will take several minutes for the cheese to brown. Don't rush flipping it over, but if you do it is okay to flip it back after the second side browns. When it is done on both sides the cheese will have lost its shape completely, almost forming flat discs. Place the grilled cheese on a paper towel to absorb the excess oils. Then plate.

Serve the pieces of cheese warm and brown.

Plating:

Place grilled cheese on the opposite end of the large platter from the Soppressata. Place the bowl of Poor Man's Caviar with the cheese spreading knife in the center of the platter. Surround the bowl with crackers. Serve this platter with the platter of Baked Stuffed Bread Dough and the bowl of chilled tomato wedges on the side. Provide small plates, forks and napkins.

Fusilli and Mushrooms in Citrus Sauce

Enjoy a different combination of flavors on your pasta this time. Cheese is not recommended. If you must, just add a small amount, but hey, taste it without the cheese, first.

Ingredients:

½ cup extra virgin olive oil
12 oz fresh mushrooms; any variety
1 lb fusilli pasta
1 bunch Italian parsley; chopped (half for sauce; half for garnish)
salt; to taste
ground black pepper; to taste
2 limes
zest of 1 lemon

Instructions:

Wash mushrooms and drain well. Slice mushrooms. Reserve.

Put a large pot of water on to boil for pasta. When water boils add a generous pinch of salt and fusilli pasta. When the pasta is submerged, stir it with a large spoon to prevent it from sticking to the bottom of the pot or to itself. Do not add any oil to the boiling pasta water!

Start preparing the sauce as soon as the water for the pasta goes on the stove. Heat a saucepan over medium-high heat. Add 2 tablespoons of oil from the ½ cup. When oil is hot fry sliced mushrooms. When they start to break down add a generous pinch of salt, pepper and half of the chopped parsley.

Remove saucepan from heat and add juice of one lime.

When the pasta is cooked al dente (slightly firm), transfer 1 full serving spoon of the starchy pasta water into the mushroom sauce and stir. Drain (do not rinse) the pasta and pour it into the saucepan with the mushroom sauce. Toss slightly to distribute the mushroom sauce. Add the rest of the ½ cup of oil, spreading it all over pasta. Add some fresh ground pepper. Squeeze on the juice from the second lime. Toss all ingredients together 2 or 3 more times to distribute flavors.

Plating:

Use pasta bowls. Evenly distribute the pasta and mushrooms among the eight plates. Zest some lemon over the pasta. Sprinkle the edges of each plate with chopped parsley. Serve immediately.

Chicory Soup with Stale Bread and Poached Egg

Trust me on the stale bread. Old Italians have been eating it since the beginning of time, or at least since the beginning of bread. I finally have figured out they're not nuts.

Ingredients:

1 large head of chicory; chopped
2 quarts vegetable stock
1 loaf of day or two day-old (stale) Italian bread

3 TBSP extra virgin olive oil
4 cloves of garlic; smashed and minced
2 large white onions
salt; to taste
1tsp dried mint
1lb ripe tomatoes
1 hot pepper(chili) (substitute ¼ tsp crushed red pepper)

8 poached eggs; see poaching directions, below
    4 cups water for poaching
    3 TBSP vinegar
    4 cups slightly warm salted water (¼ tsp salt) to stop cooking

extra virgin olive oil for garnish
½ cup grated Parmesan for garnish

Instructions:

Slice stale Italian bread into 1" thick slices. Spread out on a platter. Do not stack. Leave out on counter for at least 30 minutes to get even staler.

Put a large pot of salted water on to boil.

Smash and mince garlic. Cut onion into thin slices. Seed and dice tomatoes. Reserve.

Wash head of chicory by soaking in water and then rinsing well. Shake excess water from head. Chop the chicory into soupspoon size pieces. Plunge into the pot of boiling salted water for 2 minutes and then strain away all water. This step removes and bitterness from the chicory and washes it down the sink with the strained out water. Reserve the wilted chopped leaves.

Bring 2 quarts of vegetable stock to a boil in a very large pot and reduce heat to low. Put the wilted chicory into the vegetable stock to simmer at the same time you are adding the mint and chili to the tomatoes, onions and garlic in the next step.

Start this step when you put the vegetable stock on the stove to boil. In a sauté pan add 3 tablespoons of olive oil. Heat oil over medium-high heat. When oil is hot add sliced onion and sauté for 5 minutes until onion becomes transparent and fragrant (do not brown). Push onion away from center of pan and add minced garlic. Sauté for another minute (do not brown). Add seeded, diced tomatoes and stir everything in the pan together. Reduce heat to medium and cook down for 5 minutes. Add mint and optional sliced chili (or crushed red pepper). Stir together and simmer for another minute. Turn off heat and pour contents of pan into simmering pot of vegetable stock and chicory. Stir together, and continue to simmer.

Poaching Eggs. It's imperative that the eggs be very fresh and cold! Put a bowl of warm, not hot, water (4 cups) on the counter next to the stove to hold the eggs after they are poached. Add ¼ teaspoon of salt to this bowl of water. Place a medium saucepan with the 4 cups of water and vinegar on the stove and boil. (No salt in this saucepan). When the water begins to boil, turn the burner to low and keep water at "almost boiling" point. If it is at a rolling boil, the egg white will not surround the yolk in the proper shape. Select the first egg, crack it and slide it into a large metal serving spoon (or ladle). Carefully and slowly pour the egg into the pan without dipping the spoon. Repeat until all 8 eggs are in the water. Each egg should be in the simmering water for almost 3 minutes. Take each egg out of the water as it approaches the 3 minute point, and submerge it in the bowl of warm salted water on the counter. This will quickly halt the cooking process. The eggs should be somewhat round and smooth. Don't worry about the shape, too much, or whether or not they are cooked white over the top of the egg. Funny shapes are good for a laugh when you sit down to eat the soup.

Plating

Use large soup bowls. When ready put one piece of stale bread in the center of the bowl. Pour some of the cooking broth on it directly to assure it is soaking. Place one poached egg on top of bread. Top off the bowl with more broth and the solids from the broth. Cover each plate with a dish. Let the soup rest in the covered plates for 5 minutes to allow the bread to absorb the broth. Just before serving, remove half of the unabsorbed broth from each bowl. Garnish the egg in each bowl with a swirl of extra virgin olive oil and a dash of grated Parmesan cheese.

If you decide to leave out the hot chili, provide crushed red pepper on the table for individual choice.

Fennel Salad

This licorice flavored salad is meant more as an intermezzo rather than a full course, just to clear the palate before the fish.

Ingredients:

4 bulbs fennel; very thinly sliced
extra virgin olive oil
red wine vinegar
salt; to taste
ground black pepper; to taste

8 stalks of fresh Italian parsley for garnish

Instructions:

Clean and wash fennel under running water.

Cut away most of the stalk, especially dry parts. Pick off and discard any sprouts. You mostly want the crunchy moist bulbs. Trim off dry bottom of bulbs.

Slice every bulb (and moist parts of stalks) thinly and place in a large bowl. Dress all with olive oil. Give a slight toss to the fennel. Dress with a small amount of red wine vinegar. Toss fennel slightly. Add and pinch of salt and ground black

Toss well and taste. Adjust oil or vinegar to taste. Plate.

Plating:

Use small flat salad plates. Divide the tossed and dressed fennel among the 8 salad plates. Garnish each with one stalk of Italian parsley on top of the fennel. Serve.

Grilled Swordfish with Lemon and Oregano

Ingredients:

8 4-ounce swordfish fillets; ½" thick

3 TBSP olive oil

1 cup chopped fresh Italian parsley for garnish

½ cup white wine for deglazing pan (and stretching marinade)

Marinade Ingredients:
¾ cup lemon juice (about 4 medium lemons)
8 cloves garlic; smashed and minced
3 TBSP dried oregano
1-½ TBSP salt
½ cup olive oil
2 cups chopped fresh Italian parsley

Instructions:

Chop 3 cups of parsley. Reserve 1 cup for garnish. Smash and mince garlic. Squeeze 4 lemons to collect ¾ cup of juice for marinade.

Place fish in one layer in a shallow casserole.

In a small bowl, combine marinade ingredients, lemon juice, garlic, oregano, salt, olive oil and parsley; pour over fish. Cover and marinate for 1-½ hours in refrigerator.

When you are about 15 minutes from the desired time to serve the fish, preheat 3 TBSP olive oil in a pan over medium-high heat. Sauté marinated fish for 2 minutes per side, turning once. When you transfer the fish to the pan to sauté, transfer a bit of marinade to the pan, as well. Some of the marinade will remain in the casserole dish. Reserve it. Add another tablespoon of olive oil as you cook successive batches of fish if the pan looks like it is drying out. If you have to do multiple batches of fish, after cooking each batch, pile the cooked fish on a platter over the stove to retain heat while awaiting plating. Cover the cooked fish with a piece of aluminum foil.

When all of the fish is sautéed, put any remaining marinade in the sauté pan and heat. It will brown slightly. Add ½ cup of white wine to stretch the marinade.

Plate fish and serve immediately.

Plating:

Use flat dinner plate. Place eggplant with almonds and walnuts in center of dish. Place swordfish fillet on top of and in the center of the eggplant. Spoon 2 tablespoons of the heated marinade over the fish. Garnish edges of plate with more chopped parsley. Serve immediately. Use steak knives.

Eggplant with Almonds and Walnuts

Ingredients:

4 large eggplants; peeled and cubed
1 TBSP salt; kosher or sea, for leaching water/bitterness from eggplant
½ cup olive oil for frying eggplant

6 cloves garlic; smashed and minced
1 oz sliced almonds (use 7 oz from 8 oz bag for Half-Moon recipe)
¼ lb dried walnuts; coarsely chopped (or buy walnut pieces)
½ cup golden raisins
16 basil leaves
8 mint leaves or ½ teaspoon dried mint

1 cup red wine vinegar
2 TBSP honey

Instructions:

To reduce the bitterness of the eggplant, clean, peel and cube eggplants, place the pieces in a colander and sprinkle with salt. Cover the cubes with a flat dish to weigh the eggplant down and hasten draining. Leave covered for 1 hour at room temperature. After the hour is up, rinse the eggplant and then squeeze out the excess water from eggplant.

Mince the garlic and chop the nuts. Reserve.

When eggplant has been rinsed and squeezed, place oil in saucepan and heat over medium heat. When oil is hot, fry a batch of eggplant until lightly browned. Use a slotted spoon or spoon with holes to strain the cooked eggplant out of the oil. Place the cooked eggplant on several layers of paper towels on a plate or on a brown bag on a plate to drain the excess oil. This should take 3 or 4 batches to complete.

In a casserole dish add browned and drained eggplant, garlic, raisins, walnuts, almonds, basil and mint leaves. Mix and cover. Do this as you fry and drain each batch of eggplant. Recover the casserole each time to retain heat.

After all eggplant batches have been placed in the casserole, combine the vinegar and honey in a small saucepan and heat gently until honey melts. Just before the solution boils it will froth on the bottom of the pan. Before it boils, turn off the heat, remove and whisk honey and vinegar completely together. Pour onto eggplant mixture. Toss mixture once or twice to distribute heated liquid. Cover and leave to rest at room temperature until ready to plate with swordfish.

Plating:

See plating instructions for swordfish.

Lamb Chop Arancia (Orange Flavor)

Lamb leg sirloin chops are cut from the sirloin section of the leg and contain backbone and part of the hip bone, which vary in shape. Muscles include the top sirloin, tenderloin, and flank. There is fat on the outside, but the fell (a thin, paperlike covering of tissue) is removed. We will pan sear and then braise our chops in the oven in a wonderful combination of herbs, spices and citrus flavors. If you are stuck buying heavier chops, buy half as many and cut them in half before cooking.

Ingredients:

8 lamb leg sirloin chops; ¾" thick and about 6 to 8 oz each, bone-in
¼ lb bacon
4 cloves of garlic; smashed and minced
2 TBSP dried oregano
1 cup of orange juice
1 orange for zest
olive oil
salt
ground black pepper

Instructions:

Trim off excess fat around the outside of the lamb chops. Mince garlic. Finely dice bacon.

In a bowl mix bacon, garlic, oregano, a pinch of salt and fresh ground pepper. Mix well.

Lay out the 8 chops on a flat plate or tray. Sprinkle half of the mixture of herbs and spices over the chops. Press the mixture into the chops and then flip them over and use the other half of the mixture on the second side of the chops. Press the mixture into the chops.

Wipe a light coat of olive oil on the inside of a large baking pan capable of holding all of the chops in a single layer on the bottom of the pan.

Heat a dry sauté pan over medium-high heat. Sear the chops two at a time in the sauté pan for 2 minutes per side on both sides and transfer them into the large oiled baking pan, so all chops are in a single layer.

When all chops are seared, deglaze the sauté pan with 1 cup of the orange juice. Immediately after adding the orange juice, use a spatula to scrape all of the spices and meat bits off the bottom of the sauté pan. Add 2 tablespoons of olive oil to the juice in the pan. Stir well and heat until near boiling. Remove from heat and pour the deglazing juice over the chops in the baking pan. Top off the chops with additional orange juice, if necessary, so the top surface of the chops is just peeking out above the surface of the juice. Cover the baking pan with a lid or aluminum foil. Place in preheated 350° oven on the middle rack for 2 hours or more. Check the liquid level in the pan after an hour. If the level is down, add more orange juice to bring the level back up to where the top surface of the chops is just peeking out above the surface of the juice.

Plating:

See plating instructions for Potatoes and Olives. Leave braising pan juices in the pan when you plate the chop. We are transferring the orange flavor cooked into the chop, not the juice.

Potatoes and Olives

Ingredients:

4 large starchy baking potatoes; peeled and each cut into 10 to 12 pieces
½ cup of large pitted green olives stuffed with pimentos; cut in half
4 cloves garlic; smashed and minced
1 bunch fresh Italian parsley; chopped for cooking and garnish
salt
ground black pepper
½ cup olive oil

Instructions:

Wash, peel and cut potatoes into pieces sized to provide approximately 10 to 12 pieces out of each potato. As you peel and cut, place the cut pieces of potato into a pot of cool water, so all cut pieces are submerged. You will use a cup of this starchy water later to cook the potatoes.

Smash and mince garlic. Chop parsley. Cut olives in half. Reserve.

Place 2 tablespoons of olive oil in saucepan over medium-high heat. Add minced garlic and sauté for 1 minute until garlic gets fragrant. Add cut olives to pan, heat and mix well for 1 minute. Push olives and garlic to edges of the pan. Place cut potatoes in saucepan (save the starchy water in the pot where you stored the cut potatoes). Sauté the cut potatoes for 2 minutes to brown some of the potato edges a bit. Add 1 cup of starchy water, ½ cup of olive oil and 2 tablespoons of parsley. Season with a pinch of salt, fresh ground pepper. Reduce the heat to low, cover the pan and cook for 25 minutes or until potatoes are fork tender.

If liquid is runny after the potatoes are tender, remove the cover and allow the liquid to reduce and thicken.

Turn off heat, put cover back on pan and leave pan on stovetop until ready to plate with lamb chop.

Plating:

Use a large bowl. Plate 4 to 6 pieces of potato (depending upon appetite) in the center of the bowl. Add a few pieces of olives and pimentos in each bowl. If there is enough liquid, spoon a bit of the starchy sauce over the potatoes and olives. Place one lamb chop partially over the potatoes. Do not add any extra juices from the braising pan after plating the chop. Garnish the edges of the plate with a sprinkle of chopped parsley. Grate a small amount of orange zest over the chop. Serve. Use sharp steak knives.

Half Moon Filled with Jam and Almonds

Frozen puff pastry for a true Calabrian dessert? The alternative is getting the proportions and handling wrong for making a delicious pastry crust. Since we are mostly amateurs in the kitchen, pre-made puff pastry is a great way to go. You will be happy to know that the ingredients in the store bought stuff are the same as doing it yourself – flour, grease and sugar. Now if you are a pastry crust a purist, you would be using pork lard, cold for flaky and warm for tender crust. You would work the dough just right to not overwork the glutens and would get great pie crust. To go the puff pastry extra mile, your grease would be cold butter for taste and the liquids in the butter. When you have worked the dough perfectly, you would then fold and roll out the dough numerous times to get the so-called hundreds of layers that will puff up when the butter steams up the crust. Most experts agree, buy the frozen puff pastry. You will save a lot of effort with no compromise of results. The filling matters here.

Ingredients:
1 package Pepperidge Farm® Puff Pastry Sheets
sugar for dusting inside of pastry
all-purpose flour for dusting the outside of the pastry
10X powdered sugar

Filling Ingredients:
1 cup fig preserves (substitute: strawberry or grape jam)
7 oz sliced almonds (use 1 oz from 8 oz bag for Eggplant with Almond recipe)
2 oz golden raisins
½ tsp cinnamon
1 TBSP unsweetened cocoa powder (substitute 3 TBSP sweetened coca mix)
2 TBSP sugar (if you have sweetened coca mix leave out the sugar)
1 oz Strega® Liqueur (substitute Crème de Menthe or Sambucca)

Instructions: In a medium bowl add preserves (jam), sliced almonds, cinnamon, golden raisins, cocoa powder, sugar (if needed) and a shot glass of the liqueur and mix all ingredients well. Reserve at room temperature. Pre-heat oven to 375°.

Allow at least 30 minutes of thawing time before you work with the pastry. Take it out of the box and wrap it in a cloth kitchen towel to soak up the moisture that may form as it thaws. When you start to unfold it, if it is still stiff stop unfolding it until it is completely thawed. Unfold it on a lightly floured surface. When it is unfolded, crimp the seams together. Using a floured rolling pin and light pressure, roll out the pastry to a 12"x12" sheet. Lightly dust the top surface with sugar. Using a sharp knife, cut four 6" discs out of the dough. Don't worry about having perfect circles, just sort of round. In the center of each disc add two tablespoons of the filling. Wet the top edges of the discs and fold in half over the filling so they resemble half moons. Seal borders well so filling does not escape during cooking. Repeat with a second sheet to make another four half-moons. Lightly flour the outside of each half-moon and place on it on a non-stick cookie tray. Use a double bottom cookie tray. It will help to avoid over-browning the bottom. Cover the two sharp ends of the half-moon with small patches of aluminum foil to avoid over-browning in that spot. Bake for 25 minutes or until entire outside of a light golden brown. Set out on counter and allow to cool.

Plating: Use a large flat dessert or salad dish. Place Half-Moon with round edge to the outside of the plate. Add a slice of Lemon Crème Crostata to the plate. Dust all with 10x powdered sugar. Serve.

Lemon Crème Crostata

My cousin Larry makes fruit-filled crostata. We are always happy to see him show up at family gathering. He's a bit mysterious. I don't know much about him, but the crostata is fantastic. This version has a rich lemon cream filling in keeping with Calabria's plentiful citrus. The dough method is a bit easier, so we will make this one from scratch ingredients, and you will have a fully homemade dessert. Good luck.

Dough Ingredients:
5 cups all-purpose flour
3 eggs
1-¼ cups sugar
1 stick unsalted butter; melted
1 tsp vanilla extract

Filling Ingredients:
3 large lemons
¾ cup flour
3 TBSP cornstarch
2 cups warm water
1 cup sugar
2 TBSP butter; melted
1 tsp vanilla extract
2 eggs

Dough Instructions: Melt unsalted butter. Place flour on board and make a well in the center. Place eggs, sugar, melted butter and vanilla. Incorporate all ingredients until soft dough is formed. If dough is too stiff or dry, add a tablespoon of cold water and knead. Add more cold water tablespoon by tablespoon until it softens. If no water is needed, that is okay. Knead and then leave to rest while you prepare the filling.

Filling Instructions: Melt butter. Grate the zest from lemon skin and juice the lemons into a cup. Using and electric mixer, add flour and cornstarch, slowly add 2 cups of warm water making sure no lumps form. Add sugar, vanilla and melted butter. Continue mixing. Beat 2 eggs, separately, and add gradually. Finally, add the zest and juice from the 3 lemons, and mix well. Pour into a cold saucepan and cook over low heat. Keep stirring with a wooden spoon and when the mixture thickens and coats the spoon it is ready. Remove from heat and cover. Allow to stand at room temperature while you prepare dough in pan.

Assembly and Baking: Pre-heat oven to 375°. Use a tart or pie pan (9" or 10"). Knead the dough again. Flour a surface to roll out the dough. Flour the rolling pin. Roll out the dough into a 12" circle. Place it in the tart pan and carefully form it up the sides of the pan (no breaks in the dough). Allow 1" to hang outside of the pan. Cut off the excess dough and save. Fold the 1" back under itself to form a double crust at the top of the pan that protrudes ¼ to ½" straight up from top of pan. Pinch the double crust to decoratively flute the dough. Place the cooled lemon mixture into the crust in the tart pan and level the filling in the crust. The extra dough you cut off can be rolled out again, cut into strips and used for decoration on the top of the crostata. Make any pattern you would like. When the oven is pre-heated to 375°, place on the lower rack and bake 30 to 40 minutes, until the crust is golden brown.

Plating: See plating instructions in Half-Moon dessert.

Appetizers All Night Long

Appetizers All Night Long

"What the heck is pear chutney?" she said, and with that I learned sometimes when you send a shopping list to a friend, you will not always get a great response. Kathy was excited about coming to the Appetizers All Night Long dinner party. She and Matt had never been involved in an evening like this before. They had given and been to many dinner parties, but an evening of working together with friends and sharing an unusual bill of fare struck her as just the entertainment she and Matt needed. When she said yes to the evening, I immediately e-mailed her the complete menu, shopping list and preparation schedule along with the recipes. She wanted to see it all! I send out a lot of e-mails and communications, and I sometimes lose track of what I have sent and when. The next day I received one those infamous computer messages saying that there was a failure to deliver a message to Kathy. Was this the shopping list? Was it something else? A call was in order. I had to be sure she had gotten the menu, especially the shopping list. Without one-quarter of the food where would we be on Saturday night preparing the dinner?

I reached Kathy at work and was immediately met with the resounding pear chutney question. At least I knew she had the shopping list. I shot back, *"It is chutney made out of pears!"* She had already figured that out. Her real dilemma was where she was going to find pear chutney. Between us we had some ideas, and I certainly did not want her to make the pear chutney from scratch at home before coming to the dinner. That is not the idea of these dinners. Everyone is supposed to come to the dinner with purchased ingredients and prepare the meal right then and there. No advance work. This is not a pot-luck dinner! Our solution was simple. We both knew of some specialty foods stores in our area, and I calmed her with, *"Look a little bit in some of those stores, and if you can't find pear chutney, get mango sauce or pear sauce or whatever fruit preserve you can find and that will do fine!"* It is not important that these recipes be followed to the letter. If you find that you are short on one ingredient, especially when you start the dinner prep at the start of the evening, don't panic. Stop. Think. Talk it over, and with the eight brains you have handy, I am confident that you will come up with a fabulous substitute. You may even decide to forgive yourself and leave the ingredient out. Any one of these solutions is okay. Revel in your own inventions. That night we had authentic pear chutney on the baked brie thanks to Kathy's eagle eyes and shopping ability, and it was delicious beyond telling. You'll find out.

Tonight's meal will meander through a whole forest of flavors. Wave after wave after wave of food and all will be appetizers. Taste everything. Portion control and pacing is important. Leave room for dessert. This is a big night for your oven. Enjoy!

Appetizers All Night Long

5:00 p.m.   Cocktails/Beverages throughout the Evening
                     Wine, Beer, Mixed Drinks

              Appetizing Snacks
                     Stuffed Celery and Black Olives
                     Smoked Almonds

                     Baked Brie with Pear Chutney
                     Wheat Crackers

6:30 p.m.   Appetizing Starter
                     Potato Crisps and Wild Mushroom Napoleons

7:00 p.m.   Appetizing Soup
                     Soupe au Pistou with
                     Blue Cheese Gougeres

7:30 p.m.   Appetizer Later On
                     Shrimp Toasts

8:30 p.m.   Appetizer Even Later
                     Beef Short Ribs with Cheddar Polenta

9:15 p.m.   Appetizing Dessert
                     Warm Granny Smith Fruit Tart
                     with Whipped Cream and Nutmeg
                     Café and Tea
                     Liqueur

Appetizers All Night Long Shopping Lists

Shopper 1

1 package Pepperidge Farm® Puff Pastry Sheets
8 Pepperidge Farm® Puff Pastry Shells (preferred), or a second package Pepperidge Farm® Puff Pastry Sheets
1 loaf homemade-style white bread
8 oz pitted black olives; any variety
1 can smoked almonds
1 box wheat crackers
One 5" round of French Brie Cheese
1 cup Pear Chutney
1 jar apricot jam
3 lbs beef short ribs; bones-in, cut into eight 6-ounce portions
1 doz large eggs
1 can albacore tuna

Shopper 2

½ lb unsalted butter
1 stick butter
¼ lb blue cheese
1 quart whole milk
1 pint heavy cream
1 can Reddi Wip® whipped cream
4 oz cream cheese
6 oz grated Parmesan cheese
½ cup grated cheddar cheese
1 bottle Cajun spice; Emeril's Essence®
1 bottle Crystal® Hot Sauce or Tabasco®
1 cup chicken stock
2 quarts vegetable stock
1 lb peeled cooked shrimp; frozen
4 Granny Smith apples
2 lemons

Shopper 3

6 shallots
2 fresh black or white truffles (optional)
4 medium zucchini
4 carrots
2 large baking potatoes (about 1 lb)
1 medium yellow onion
1 head garlic
4 medium white onions
14 stalks celery (about 2 bunches)
2 large ripe tomatoes
1 bunch fresh chives
1 bunch fresh thyme
1 bunch fresh parsley
1 bunch green onions/scallions
1 bunch fresh cilantro
12 oz wild mushrooms such as chanterelle, shiitake or morel
1 jalapeno pepper

Shopper 4 (Host)

1 TBSP mayonnaise
1 tsp mustard, any variety
2 tsp dried dill weed
1 bay leaf
nutmeg
paprika
2 TBSP ancho chile powder
1 TBSP soy sauce
6 TBSP Worcestershire sauce
6 TBSP light brown sugar
¼ cup kosher salt
salt
ground black pepper
granulated sugar
1 cup all-purpose flour
1 cup polenta (corn meal)
1 quart extra virgin olive oil
1 quart canola oil
1 pint sesame oil
2 TBSP white or black truffle oil
parchment paper for baking

Preparation Schedule – Appetizers All Night Long

Teams
1/
2/
3/
4/Hosts

4:00 pm	**1, 2, & 3-** Arrive at **4**'s kitchen. Put on chef's aprons. Unpack and stack all groceries. Put meat, milk, cream, cream cheese, whipped cream in refrigerator. Leave all other cheeses, butter, eggs and puff pastry (see note in Baked Brie recipe) at room temperature. Put frozen shrimp in cool water to thaw. Have a cocktail.
4:15 pm	**1-** Start Beef Short Rib recipe and place ribs in oven by 5:45 pm. **2-** Start Celery Platter recipe. Serve family style when ready. **3-** Start Baked Brie recipe. Put in oven on middle rack by 4:40 pm **4-** Pre-heat oven to 400°. Set table and continue serving drinks.
4:30 pm	**4-** Prep vegetables for soup and napoleon recipes. Reserve soup vegetables for **3** to complete the soup recipe. Prepare thin potato slices to be crisps for Napoleons to go in oven at 5:15 pm.
5:00 pm	**1, 2, 3 & 4-** Eat Celery Platter family style in the kitchen and drink cocktails while you merrily work on your other food preparations. **3-** Check on Baked Brie. Turn oven down to 325°, if first 20 minutes have elapsed. Continue baking brie for an additional 20 minutes.
5:15 pm	**3-** Turn oven up to 375°. Remove Baked Brie from oven as soon as it is golden brown. Put on platter. Cool for 5 minutes. Top with chutney and serve family style in kitchen. **4-** Bake potato slices in 375° oven on top rack. Rotate baking pans at 5:30 pm. Bake on top rack. Continue with recipe directions.
5:30 pm	**1, 2, 3 & 4-** Eat Baked Brie family style in the kitchen and drink cocktails while you merrily work on your other food preparations. **2-** Begin Blue Cheese Gougeres recipe
5:45 pm	**1-** Place short ribs in oven on bottom rack to braise for 2-½ hours. Allow oven temperature to change for Gougeres requirements. **2-** Raise oven to 400° and place Gougeres on top rack for 10 minutes, then turn oven down to 350° and continue baking. **3-** Begin Pistou Soup cooking. Vegetables were cut and prepared by **4**. Complete soup and simmer on low heat. Complete prep of pistou garnish and reserve at room temperature until ready to plate soup. **4-** Get crisps from oven and cool on rack or plates. Continue recipe.
6:00 pm	**1-** Start Shrimp Toast recipe. Complete through placing bread with spread in refrigerator to chill. Fry later, just before plating.

2- After Blue Cheese Gougeres have baked for 10 minutes at 400°, turn oven down to 350° and continue baking for 25 more minutes.

6:15 pm	**2-** Remove Blue Cheese Gougeres from oven at 6:25 pm, just before sitting down for Potato Crisps Napoleons. Cool on stovetop. **4-** Plate Potato Crisps Napoleons and serve at 6:30 pm.
6:30 pm	**Eat Potato Crisps Napoleons in Dining Room** **At 6:30 everyone helps clear dishes to the kitchen.**
6:45 pm	**2-** Place Blue Cheese Gougeres in a serving bowl and serve family style in Dining Room with soup at 7:00 pm. Help **3** serve soup. **3-** Complete plating and serving of soup with help from **4**.
7:00 pm	**Eat Soup and Gougeres in Dining Room** **At 7:15 everyone helps clear dishes to the kitchen.**
7:15 pm	**1-** Set up frying pan and pre-heat oil to 360° for Shrimp Toasts. Prepare dipping sauce for toasts. Fry toasts when oil is hot. **4-** Start Cheddar Polenta recipe. Serve with Short Ribs at 8:30 pm.
7:45 pm	**1-** Continue frying the Shrimp Toasts. Drain excess oil on paper towels. Plate Shrimp Toasts according to directions on recipe and serve with dipping sauce at 8:00 pm with help from **2**. **2-** Help **1** plate and serve Shrimp Toasts. **3-** Start Granny Smith Fruit Tart recipe. Complete up to point of having the tarts ready to bake. Wait until 8:30 pm to bake these.
8:00 pm	**Eat Shrimp Toasts in Dining Room** **At 8:15 everyone helps clear dishes to the kitchen.**
8:15 pm	**1-** Turn oven up to 400° for fruit tarts. Remove Beef Short Ribs from oven. Plate and serve with Polenta with help from **2**. **3-** Put Fruit Tarts into 400° oven on middle rack at 8:30 pm just before sitting down to eat Beef Short Ribs. Keep an eye on these. **4-** Complete Polenta recipe and help **1** plate Polenta and Ribs.
8:30 pm	**Eat Beef Short Ribs and Polenta in Dining Room** **At 9:00 everyone helps clear dishes to the kitchen.**
8:45 pm	**3-** Take a peek at the fruit tarts in the oven. Brown, don't burn.
9:00 pm	**1-** Work with **4** on coffee and tea service. **2-** Help **3** plate and serve the dessert. Serve when ready. **3-** Complete dessert recipe, plate and serve with help from **2**. **4-** Set up coffee cups, teaspoons and tablespoons for dessert service. Brew coffee and tea. Serve coffee and tea when ready.
9:15 pm	**Eat Dessert and Have Coffee and Tea in Dining Room** **Relax! Job Well Done!**

Stuffed Celery, Black Olives and Smoked Almonds

This platter was always on the bar along with many other goodies at all of our family get-togethers. Working as my mother's assistant (like I had a choice), I made approximately four million canapés and an equal amount of stuffed celery. These are tasty and light appetizers to start off your evening.

Ingredients:

8 stalks of celery
3 hard-boiled eggs
1 can albacore tuna
3 TBSP mayonnaise; 1 for eggs and 2 for tuna
1 tsp mustard; any variety
2 tsp dried dill weed
½ tsp Crystal® Hot Sauce or Tabasco® Sauce
Salt
pepper
3 TBSP fresh parsley; chopped

½ lb pitted black olives; any variety
1 can smoked almonds
wheat crackers; as needed
paprika; as needed

Instructions:

Hard boil 3 eggs.

While eggs boil, wash celery stalks, trim and cut in half to get 16 shorter stalks. Chop parsley.

Egg Salad: Peel and chop eggs. Combine with one tablespoon of mayonnaise, 1 teaspoon of mustard, several dashes of Hot Sauce, salt and pepper to taste. Generously stuff the small halves of 8 stalks with egg salad. If you have some egg salad left over make a few canapés using the wheat crackers from the brie recipe. Dust the egg salad stuffed celery stalks and canapés with paprika.

Tuna Salad: Combine tuna with 2 tablespoons of mayonnaise and dried dill weed. Generously stuff the large halves of 8 stalks of celery with tuna salad. If you have some tuna salad left over make a few canapés using the wheat crackers from the brie recipe. Dust the tuna salad stuffed celery and canapés with more dill weed.

Plating:

Use a flat serving platter. Place a small bowl at one end of the platter and fill it with the smoked almonds. Alternate egg salad stalks and tuna salad stalks in a fan design on the rest of the platter. Drop black olives among the stalks. If you made a few canapés with the wheat crackers, nestle them into the center of the platter. Garnish the platter with a wild sprinkle of chopped fresh parsley. Serve family style.

Baked Brie with Pear Chutney

This recipe calls for cutting decorations for the top of the pastry wrapped brie and decorating before you put it in the oven to bake. The interesting thing is no matter what you try to make, it won't matter. Any shape on top of the pastry looks good after it is baked. So don't be too fussy. While flat decorations will bake better, your rosettes or bunny ears will be a browned blob that looks and tastes great. Just be sure to brush the top and the decorations well with the beaten egg.

Ingredients:

1 package Pepperidge Farm® Puff Pastry Sheets
One 5" round of French Brie
1 egg; slightly beaten
1 cup Pear Chutney
salt
fresh ground black pepper

1 box wheat crackers; any variety

parchment paper for baking

Instructions: Preheat the oven to 400°.

Allow at least 30 minutes of thawing time before you work with the puff pastry. Take it out of the box and wrap it in a cloth kitchen towel to soak up the moisture that may form as it thaws. When you start to unfold it, if it is still stiff stop unfolding it until it is completely thawed. Unfold it on a lightly floured surface. When it is unfolded, crimp the seams together. Using a floured rolling pin and light pressure, roll out the pastry to a 12"x12" sheet. Cut the corners so you have a 12" round of pastry. Save the scrap corners for decorations.

Lay the Brie in the center of the puff pastry circle. Fold the excess pastry around the Brie wheel, completely enclosing it. Turn it over, smooth side up and place it on a parchment lined sheet tray.

Use the Puff pastry scraps to cut decorations for the top of the pastry. Cut out decorations using a paring knife or small cookie cutters. Let your imagination run wild as you cut and decorate. Place your decorations flat on the top of the pastry.

Brush top and sides of pastry well with egg. Brush the decorations well, too, especially if they protrude up or out.

Bake at 400° for 20 minutes or until the outside is golden, then reduce the oven temperature to 325° degrees and cook for 20 minutes longer.

Plating:

Place the finished Baked Brie on a flat, pretty serving platter about twice the diameter of the brie and allow it to sit for 5 minutes. Then top with Pear Chutney. Add a long sharp knife to the platter to cut the Baked Brie. Put wheat crackers in a bowl on the side. Serve family style.

Potato Crisps and Wild Mushroom Napoleons

The first time we staged this dinner, my friend Kenny went all over town looking for WHITE truffle oil. He showed up with a 3 ounce bottle that cost him as much as his first college degree. You will find black truffle oil works great for this mushroom filling and is less than half the cost. Extra virgin olive oil is even good for this dish!

Ingredients - Potato Crisps:
¼ cup olive oil
2 large baking potatoes (about 1 lb); peeled and cut on a mandolin into 1/8-inch slices
1 tsp of Cajun spice; Emeril's Essence®
½ tsp salt

Ingredients - Mushroom Filling:
3 TBSP unsalted butter
½ cup shallots; sliced
1 tsp salt
½ tsp freshly ground black pepper
1 cup chicken stock
1 cup heavy cream
2 tsp fresh chopped thyme
12 oz wild mushrooms such as chanterelle, shiitake, morel; cleaned, stems removed, and thinly sliced
2 TBSP white truffle oil (or black truffle oil or extra virgin olive oil)
¾ cup grated Parmesan cheese (about 3 oz)
24 slices fresh black or white truffle; (optional garnish)
32 chives, long, not chopped, for garnish

Instructions: Slice shallots. Chop thyme. Clean and slice mushrooms. Peel and slice raw potatoes. If you have a mandolin to slice the potatoes very thin, great.

Potato Crisps: Preheat oven to 350°. Brush 2 baking sheets with oil. Arrange potato slices in one layer. Brush the tops of the slices with oil. Stack one sheet on the other, and top with a third baking sheet to stop curling. If you don't have this many baking sheets, just use what you have. If they curl, they curl. Bake on upper rack of oven for 20 minutes. Then rotate sheets so the middle sheet is on the bottom and vice versa. Replace the empty sheet on the top. Bake on upper rack until slices are golden brown (about 15 minutes). Transfer with a spatula to cooling racks. Sprinkle with the Cajun Spice and salt, and set aside.

Mushroom Filling: After potato crisps are cooling on rack, in a large, heavy skillet, melt the butter over medium-high heat. Add the shallots and cook, stirring, for 1 minute. Add the mushrooms, salt and pepper, and cook, stirring, until soft and most of the mushroom liquid is evaporated, about 8 minutes. Add the stock, cream, and thyme, and simmer until the liquid has reduced by 50 percent in volume, about 5 minutes. Remove from the heat and stir in the truffle oil (or Extra Virgin Olive Oil).

Plating: Place 2 potato crisps on each of 8 serving plates. Spoon a generous tablespoon of mushroom filling on top, topped with a very light sprinkling of grated Parmesan cheese. Continue layering the napoleon so that you have 3 layers of potato crisps and 3 layers of mushrooms in all, ending with mushrooms on top. Garnish the top of each napoleon with a generous sprinkle of grated cheese (and 3 slices of truffle, optional). Arrange 4 chives on each plate randomly around the outer edge of the plate and serve.

Blue Cheese Gougeres

Ingredients:

1 cup whole milk
4 TBSP unsalted butter
¼ tsp salt
1/8 tsp freshly ground black pepper
1/8 tsp of Cajun spice; Emeril's Essence®
1 cup all-purpose flour
4 large eggs, at room temperature
¼ lb blue cheese, or other creamy blue cheese

Instructions:

Preheat the oven to 400°. Line a baking sheet with parchment paper.

In a large saucepan, combine the milk, butter, salt, black pepper, and Cajun spice over medium-high heat. Bring to a boil, and then remove from the heat. Add the flour, and stir constantly with a large wooden spoon to incorporate, about 1 minute. Return to medium-high heat and cook, stirring constantly, for another 1 minute. Remove from the heat and add the eggs one at a time, beating in well after the addition of each. Add the cheese and beat until mixed well and a slightly soft dough forms.

Drop the dough by the spoonful on the parchment paper on the baking sheet. Bake for 10 minutes, then reduce the temperature to 350°, and bake until golden brown, about 20 to 25 minutes.

Remove from the oven and serve immediately, or at room temperature.

Plating:

Use a serving bowl to cluster the Gougeres together and keep warm. Dust all with a light sprinkle of Cajun spice. Serve family style along with soup. Pass around the table. Provide bread plates at each place setting to put Gougeres on.

Soupe au Pistou

Ingredients:

4 TBSP butter
2 cups zucchini; julienne ¼" by 2" long
4 carrots; julienne ¼" by 2" long
4 onions; very thinly sliced
6 stalks celery; julienne ¼" by 2" long
2 tomato; peeled, seeded and finely chopped
2 quarts vegetable stock
Salt
freshly ground black pepper

Pistou Garnish:
6 garlic cloves
2 cups fresh basil leaves; packed
8 extra basil leaves; for garnish
½ cup Parmesan cheese; grated
10 TBSP extra virgin olive oil

Instructions:

Julienne zucchini, carrots and celery. Slice onions. Peel, seed and chop tomatoes.

In a large pan, melt the butter. Add the vegetables, and season them well with salt and pepper. Cover the pan and cook on low heat, stirring 3 or 4 times, for 20 minutes. Add vegetable stock, bring to a boil and simmer for about 10 minutes. Season with salt and pepper to taste. Cover pan and continue simmering on very low heat until ready to serve.

To make pistou: While soup cooks blend the garlic, basil and Parmesan cheese in a food processor. Drizzle in the olive oil while machine is still running.

Plating:

Use large soup bowls. Ladle up from the bottom of the pot to get good chunky stuff in every bowl. Garnish each bowl with a dollop of the pistou in the center of the soup. Do not stir in. Place one basil leaf on top of each dollop of pistou and a pinch more of Parmesan cheese on the basil leaf. Serve with Blue Cheese Gougeres on the side.

Shrimp Toasts

You will probably have leftovers of these shrimp toasts and you will be glad for it. Reheat leftovers in a 350° oven for 6 minutes. Don't use a microwave oven to reheat. My buddy Matt was glad that there was enough for leftovers. He decided to have his right then and there. It was his favorite item of the night just nosing out the baked brie.

Ingredients:

1 lb peeled cooked shrimp; frozen are fine
¼ cup green onions/scallions; minced fine
2 TBSP fresh cilantro; minced
1 tsp garlic; smashed and minced
1 tsp jalapeno pepper; minced
1 egg white
1 tsp salt
½ cup heavy cream
4 oz cream cheese; cut into pieces (keep the chunks chilled until use)
16 slices homemade-style white bread; crusts removed
canola oil; for frying

Dipping Sauce:
¼ cup of sesame oil
1/8 cup Crystal® Hot Sauce or Tabasco®
3 TBSP chopped chives; for garnish

Instructions: Mince green onions, cilantro, garlic and jalapeno pepper. Chop chives. Reserve all. Separate egg and reserve egg white.

Cut the ¼ pound of cream cheese into several chunks and refrigerate.

In the bowl of a food processor, combine the shrimp, minced green onions, minced cilantro, garlic, jalapeno, egg white and salt. Process until smooth. Add the cream cheese, chunk by chunk, and pulse to incorporate. Add the heavy cream and pulse just until incorporated, being careful not to over-process.

Spread approximately 2 heaping tablespoons of the shrimp mixture onto each slice of bread, spreading to the edges and smoothing the top. Do not fold the slices. Place flat on a dish with plastic wrap between the layers of slices. Cover the final layer of slices with plastic wrap. Refrigerate the slices until you are ready to fry and serve.

In a large heavy pot, heat 3" of vegetable oil to 360 degrees F. Add the shrimp toasts in batches and fry until golden, fry coated side down for 1 minute first then flip to bread side and fry about 1-½ minutes (until browned). Drain bread side down on paper towels on a plate, cut each slice in half diagonally, plate and serve immediately.

Dipping Sauce for Table: Combine in a small bowl, ¼ cup of sesame oil and 1/8 cup hot sauce.

Plating: Use a flat salad or dessert dish. Place 2 or 3 toast triangles on each plate slightly overlapping with each other. Garnish each plate with a sprinkle of chopped chives.

Beef Short Ribs

Wow, we were getting full by time we reached this last appetizer. If you experience the same thing you can make the portions even more modest than the 6 ounces I propose. Cut some of them in half or thirds if need be and have leftovers. Just make sure that everyone tastes everything. The cheddar polenta that is served with the ribs is fantastic.

Ingredients:

3 lbs beef short ribs; bones-in, cut into eight 6-ounce portions
2 TBSP ancho chile powder
2 TBSP olive oil
1 TBSP soy sauce
1 medium yellow onion; sliced thin
4 cloves garlic; smashed and minced
6 TBSP Worcestershire sauce
6 TBSP light brown sugar
¼ cup kosher salt
2 quarts water; as needed to top off braising pan

Instructions:

Season both sides of the ribs with the ancho chile powder. Wrap tightly in plastic wrap and let sit at room temperature to dry marinate for 1 hour before searing.

During the hour of dry marinating the seasoned ribs, smash the garlic cloves and mince. Set up a roasting pan over 2 burners on the stove with the heat off.

Preheat the oven to 350°. (Note: Allow oven temperatures to vary based on needs of the other items being baked at the same time.)

When the hour of dry marinating for the ribs has elapsed, put the heat under the roasting pan on medium-high. Add the olive oil, heat it and then sear ribs on all sides. Turn the heat off. Add the soy sauce, onion, garlic, Worcestershire sauce, brown sugar and kosher salt. Use as much water as you need to add to the roasting pan to top off. The ribs should be just peeking above the level of the water. Turn the heat back on under the roasting pan and bring to a simmer over medium-high heat. Turn the heat off. Put on hot mitts and tightly cover the pan with aluminum foil or if you have a matching cover just cover the pan. Transfer the pan to the lowest rack in the oven. cook until the ribs are tender and fall from the bones, about 2-½ hours.

The cooked ribs can be served immediately or can sit in the hot liquids until you are ready to plate and serve them.

Plating:
Use a large bowl. Place a medium serving spoon amount of the cheddar polenta in the center of the bowl. Place the serving of ribs over the polenta. Spoon one or two tablespoons of the cooking liquid over the top. Serve.

Cheddar Polenta

Ingredients:

1-½ cups water
2 cups milk
2 tsp garlic; smashed and minced
1 bay leaf
1 tsp fresh thyme leaves; chopped
1-½ tsp salt
½ tsp freshly ground black pepper
1 cup polenta (corn meal)
4 TBSP unsalted butter
½ cup grated cheddar cheese
2 TBSP grated Parmesan

Instructions:

Mince garlic. Chop thyme. Grate cheeses. Reserve.

In a large, heavy saucepan, combine 1-½ cups of water with 2 cups milk, minced garlic, bay leaf, chopped thyme, salt and pepper. Bring to a boil and slowly add the polenta, whisking constantly. Reduce the heat to low and simmer, stirring often with a large wooden spoon, until the polenta thickens, about 25 minutes.

Add the butter and stir until melted. Then add the grated cheddar and grated Parmesan. Stir well. Adjust seasoning, to taste, and serve hot.

Plating:

See plating instruction in Beef Short Rib recipe.

Granny Smith Fruit Tart with Whipped Cream and Nutmeg

When we made this the Granny Smith Apple Fruit Tarts were supposed to be puffy but the dear friend who was our Pastry Chef for the night had so much fun with the rolling pin, she rolled the pastry sheets as flat as pita bread. That was the end of the puff. Instead of puffing up, they were like a double-pane glass tabletop with apples laminated in between layers. We all had a good laugh, but they still tasted great. How could we miss with the baked apples and cream on top? Buy Pepperidge Farm® Puff Pastry Shells and stuff 'em. Next choice would be Pepperidge Farm® Puff Pastry Sheets with very, very light rolling pin action.

Ingredients:
8 Pepperidge Farm® Puff Pastry Shells (preferred), or
4 Pepperidge Farm® Puff Pastry Sheets
granulated sugar; for dusting pastry
4 Granny Smith apples; peeled, cored, and quartered
4 TBSP lemon juice
1 jar apricot jam
1 can Reddi Wip® whipped cream
nutmeg
parchment paper for baking

Instructions: Allow at least 30 minutes of thawing time before you work with the puff pastry. If you use the pastry sheets, take the pastry out of the box and wrap it in a cloth kitchen towel to soak up the moisture that may form as it thaws. If it is still stiff stop unfolding it until it is completely thawed. Unfold it on a lightly floured surface. When it is unfolded, crimp the seams together with your fingertips.

Preheat oven to 400°. Chill 2 pastry sheet pans in the refrigerator.

Peel, core and quarter Granny Smith apples. Use a vegetable peeler or mandolin to cut wafer thin slices, and put them in a small bowl of water with the 4 tablespoons of lemon juice.

After you have crimped the seams of the pastry sheet together, use a floured rolling pin to roll out the pastry sheet to 12"x12" using very, very light pressure on the rolling pin. Using a very sharp knife cut the 12"x12" sheet into 4 sheets of 6"x6". In the center of each 6" square add two tablespoons of the wet apple slices. Wet the top edges of the squares with the lemon water and fold in half over the filling so they resemble triangles. Seal borders well so filling does not escape during cooking. Repeat with a second sheet to make another four triangles. Dust both sides of each pastry with sugar. Place the pastry triangles on one chilled sheet pan and let cool in the refrigerator until ready to bake. **(Avoid all of this work and buy the pre-shaped puff pastry shells and stuff them with the apple slices)** When ready to bake, put parchment paper on second chilled sheet pan. Remove the filled pastry shells from the refrigerator. Flip and transfer the pastry to the sheet pan with parchment paper, spacing evenly. Poke them with a fork to provide an outlet for steam. Dust each pastry once more with sugar and arrange a few apple slices on top of each pastry. Bake on middle rack of oven for 15 to 20 minutes. Poke the crust; if it feels soft it needs more time in the oven. Heat apricot jam in microwave oven. Dab (don't brush) the jam on the hot tarts. Cool tarts at room temperature.

Plating: Use a flat dessert plate. Plate pastry with whipped cream on the side and a sprinkle of nutmeg over both the pastry and whipped cream. Serve.

Grilling from Beginning to End

Grilling from Beginning to End

When we finished the Parsley, Sage, Rosemary and Garlic dinner, my friend, Kenny was so excited he wanted to do another dinner right away. He loves tasty food and already had a plan – to use his new Weber® Grill. He brought his grilling cookbook to the dinner table, and the two of us started leafing through it immediately. Without hesitation I was ready to do it. So I said yes even announced that we would grill every course! Even the soup and salad. As I blurted this out I wondered silently, "hmmm, soup is wet" and "can you grill a salad?" I would find out.

I have been grilling food on the barbecue since I was 10. No gas grills back in those days! Under the watchful eye of my father with a garden hose nearby, I did great slabs of ribs, prime beef, chicken, sausages, chops and pinwheel steaks – what do you mean you never had a pinwheel steak? You haven't lived!

Some consider me quite handy with a fork and tongs in my hands, but I can remember partially melting the siding off of my boss's house one Saturday afternoon after golf. He insisted I take the tongs and work the grill. Ah, "Me, The Expert" let the prime steaks flare-up and get out of hand with nary a water pistol in sight! Six-foot flames. At the start I did think, "Isn't this grill a little close to the house?" Afterwards he quipped, "So what's a little siding damage when we still wound up with perfect steaks." We went inside to join the wives and the rest of our golfing buddies and delivered the steaming platter stacked with delight to the table where one of the other golfers promptly splashed salad dressing all over Loraine's beautiful curtains. He shook the Viva® for his salad with a little too much right hand. Hooked it right into the silk! Funny, but we were never invited back again after golf.

Despite my lifetime grilling achievements, this grilling from beginning to end would be a journey into lands unknown …..grilled soup? ……grilled salad? ……grilled dessert? What had I gotten myself into? My mind harkened back to the old "Honeymooners" TV series with Jackie Gleason (my body double), when he would admit at the end of an episode, "You know what, Alice? I gotta BIG mouth – a BIG MOUTH!" I started my research in the mourning (yes, mourning), and it was my fears, not me, that were quickly laid to rest. Yes, there is grilled soup. YES, YES, there is grilled dessert. YES, YES, YES, there is even grilled salad – how about that!

Lovers of barbecue will love this dinner. It is an adventure at the grill, but even more, in your mouth. Normally, these are restaurant flavors or not in barbecued form at all. The grill champs will also get to sink their teeth and talents into the preparation and cooking of this meal. Sometimes these are the very same characters who bow out of any of this kind of work if it is in a regular kitchen. So you may get full participation from all of the dinner guests with this meal. Enjoy!

Grilling from Beginning to End

5:00 p.m. **Cocktails**

Wine, Beer, Mixed Drinks

Snacks

Grilled Plum-Glazed Chicken Wings
Grilled Garlic-Herb Italian Bread
Caraway Cheese
Stuffed Green Olives

6:30 p.m. **Dinner**

Beverages Water, Wine, Beer and Soda

Soup Grilled Sausage Peperonata Soup

Salad Grilled Radicchio and Romaine Hearts
with Green Pepper, Green Onion, Scallions
and Balsamic Vinaigrette Dressing

Entree Grilled Gyros Roast with Special Sauce

Accompanied by

Grilled Vegetable Kabobs

Grilled Sweet Onions

Grilled Patio Tomatoes

Dessert Grilled Pineapple Bananas Foster with Vanilla Ice Cream
Café and Tea
Liqueur

Grilling from Beginning to End Shopping Lists

Shopper 1

1 large loaf of Italian Bread
1-½ lbs beef round steak
2 lbs Italian sweet sausage
1 large bottle Italian dressing
4 firm bananas
1 can pineapple rings
1 box wheat crackers
2 quarts chicken broth
1 medium jar green olives stuffed with
pimentos, garlic or almonds
½ cup golden raisins
¼ lb butter
½ lb sweet butter
1 pint sour cream
1 lb block Caraway cheese

Shopper 2

1 leg of lamb; boned and filleted to approx.
12"x14" (3-½ lbs); not tied
ask butcher for 6' of string for tying roast

2 cups plum preserves
1 large white onion
3 large sweet onions
3 medium red onions
4 green onions
4 scallions
10 garlic cloves
8 oz grated Parmesan

Shopper 3

3 lbs chicken wings
9 green peppers
7 red peppers
4 small zucchini
4 small yellow squash
3 large Idaho potatoes
8 medium tomatoes
2 medium cucumbers
4 heads of Treviso radicchio
4 Romaine hearts
1 bunch fresh parsley

Shopper 4 (Host)

1 bottle dried basil
2 bottles dried oregano
1 bottle dried Italian seasoning
1 bottle dried dill weed
1 bottle dried thyme
1 bottle garlic powder
salt
ground black pepper
1 bottle cinnamon
¾ cup brown sugar
4 tsp prepared horseradish
1 qt extra virgin olive oil
2 TBSP white wine vinegar
1 cup balsamic vinegar
4 tsp yellow or brown prepared mustard
¼ cup Dijon mustard
1 cup honey
½ gallon premium vanilla ice cream
½ cup dark rum

Preparation Schedule – Grilling from Beginning to End

Teams
1/
2/
3/
4/Hosts

4:00 pm	**1, 2, & 3**- Arrive at **4**'s kitchen. Put on aprons. Stack groceries in a central location. Put steak, sausage, lamb, chicken, romaine, radicchio, sour cream, bananas and pineapple in refrigerator. Put ice cream in freezer. Leave butter and cheeses at room temperature. Have a cocktail.
4:15 pm	**1**- Start Gyros Roast recipe. Season lamb. Work with **2** to roll. **2**- Season beefsteak. Work with **1** to roll and tie roast. Season outside of roast. Cover and place into refrigerator for 1 hour. **3**- Prepare Italian bread for grill, wrap and set aside. **4**- Start Chicken Wing recipe. Put wings on grill by 4:45 pm.
4:45 pm	**1**- Start Sausage Soup recipe. Grill sausages. Cut cooked sausages into ½" pieces for soup retaining juices from cutting. Reserve. **2**- Start Vegetable Kabob recipe. Use 4 green and 4 red peppers for this recipe, leaving some for other recipes. Complete up to marinating vegetables. Marinate for one hour. **3**- Cut Caraway cheese. Plate and serve with olives and crackers. **4**- Place chicken wings on grill over indirect medium heat. Cook 30 minutes with lid down. Prepare plum glaze while wings cook.
5:00 pm	**3**- Grill bread over indirect medium heat for 15 minutes and serve. **4**- Prepare to plate chicken wings at 5:15 pm with plum glaze dipping sauce. Serve on patio at 5:15 pm.
5:15 pm	**Eat Appetizers on Patio Near Grill. Continue eating appetizers while working on next tasks.**
5:30 pm	**1**- Complete Soup recipe. Continue until ready to serve at 6:30 pm. **2**- Make vegetable kabobs and leave in marinade until ready to grill. **4**- Set dinner table. Provide sharp steak knives for roast.
5:45 pm	**3**- Roast Gyros on grill for 75 minutes turning every 15 to 20 minutes. If you have a grill rotisserie, use it.
6:00 pm	**2**- Start Salad Recipe. Refrigerate radicchio and romaine when ready for grill. Prepare vinaigrette salad dressing. Refrigerate. **3**- Turn gyros roast. Cut Patio Tomatoes and brush on marinade. **4**- Start Special Sauce recipe for Gyros Roast and refrigerate.

6:15 pm	**1-** Plate, garnish and serve soup at 6:30 pm. **2-** Slice pepper rings, onions and scallions for salad. Reserve. **3-** Turn gyros roast. Cut sweet onions for grill. Reserve.
6:30 pm	**Eat Soup in Dining Room** **At 6:45 everyone helps clear soup dishes to the kitchen.**
6:45 pm	**2-** Grill salad hearts. Assemble salads, dress and serve at 7:00 pm. **3-** Turn gyros roast. Brush sweet onions with honey Dijon. Reserve. **4-** Complete Special Sauce recipe for Gyros Roast. Assist **2** in plating and serving salad.
7:00 pm	**3-** Remove gyros roast from grill. Let stand covered with foil for 30 minutes before carving.
7:00 pm	**Eat Salad in Dining Room** **At 7:15 everyone helps clear salad dishes to the kitchen.**
7:15 pm	**1-** Grill sweet onions with honey Dijon. **2-** Grill vegetable kabobs. Brush with marinade as they cook. **3-** Coordinate grilling activities of **1, 2** and **4**. **4-** Warm dinner plates. Grill Patio Tomatoes with marinade from kabobs.
7:30 pm	**1-** Assist **3** by plating Grilled Sweet Onions. **2-** Assist **3** by plating Grilled Vegetable Kabobs. **3-** Carve gyros roast into ½" slices. Plate with vegetables. Garnish with Special Sauce. Serve at 7:45 pm. **4-** Assist **3** by plating Grilled Patio Tomatoes.
7:45 pm	**Eat Entree in Dining Room** **At 8:30 everyone helps clear dishes to the kitchen.**
8:30 pm	**2-** Start Bananas Foster recipe. Grill bananas and pineapples. Add to syrup. **3-** Prepare syrup for Bananas Foster. Glaze the fruit when grilled. Flambé!
8:45 pm	**1-** Work with **4** on coffee and tea service. **2-** Plate pineapple rings and ice cream into large bowls for Bananas Foster. **3-** Help **2** plate and serve the Bananas Foster. Serve when ready. **4-** Brew coffee and tea. Serve coffee and tea when ready with liqueurs.
9:00 pm	**Eat Dessert and Have Coffee in Dining Room** **Relax! Job Well Done!**

Caraway Cheese, Stuffed Olives and Crackers

While not grilled, these foods are meant to just get the party going. Get them out fast and whet everyone's appetites for the good things to come later.

Ingredients:

1 lb block of Caraway cheese
1 box wheat crackers; any variety
1 medium jar of Spanish olives with pimientos (alternatives: stuffed with garlic or almonds)
1 bunch fresh parsley

Instructions:

Drain olives well.

Cut Caraway cheese into ¾" cubes.

Plating:

Put half of the bunch of parsley scattered around at one end of a medium size platter (about 1/3 of the platter). Nestle the cubes of cheese in and over the parsley.

Place a medium size bowl on the other end of the platter. Pour the drained olives into the bowl.

Add wheat crackers to center of platter between the cheese and olives.

Garnish the edges of platter with the rest of the bunch of whole parsley.

Serve family style. Put out some napkins and toothpicks next to the platter.

Grilled Garlic-Herb Bread

This will be ready shortly after you serve the cheese and olive platter. Put it out as soon as it is ready while the bread is still warm. The chicken wings will come a little bit after this wonderful toasted bread.

Ingredients:

1 large loaf of Italian bread
½ cup softened butter
1 garlic clove; smashed and minced very fine
¼ cup grated Parmesan cheese
¼ tsp dried basil
¼ tsp dried oregano
a dash of ground black pepper

Instructions:

Mince the garlic clove. If you have a garlic press, it would be even better to squeeze the garlic through the press and only use the precious juices and solids that make it through the grid of holes.

Cream the softened butter in bowl. Thoroughly mix the minced garlic, cheese, basil, oregano and pepper into the softened butter.

Cut the loaf of bread crosswise into 1-inch slices, cutting to but not through the bottom crust. Spread the garlic-herb butter mixture all over the outside of the loaf and inside of all of the cuts. Use all of the butter mix. Wrap the loaf in heavy foil; seal with a double fold on the top and the ends.

Place the wrapped bread in the center of the cooking grate over indirect/medium heat for 15 minutes. Turn the bread three times during the 15 minutes. For crisp crust, loosen the foil on top and at the ends and heat the bread for 5 minutes more, foil-side down.

Plating:

Use a bread basket and napkin that you don't mind getting a little bit of grease on. The buttered outside that make this bread so, so good also stains the things it comes in contact with. You might even consider using a warmed serving platter instead of the bread basket for this loaf. Serve family style next to the olives and cheese when ready.

Plum Glazed Chicken Wings

If you read the Chinese without the WOK story in this book, you already know that having Plum Sauce on chicken dates back 3000 years in China. They probably cooked the chicken right out over the open flame, just like you are doing tonight. I wonder; did they have a Super Bowl back then to go with these Beijing Wings?

Ingredients:

3 lbs chicken wings; tips trimmed off
salt
pepper
garlic powder

Plum Glaze:
2 cups plum preserves
½ cup golden raisins; chopped well
4 TBSP minced white onion
2 garlic cloves; smashed and minced
2 TBSP white wine vinegar
4 tsp prepared mustard
4 tsp prepared horseradish
½ tsp salt

Instructions:

Rinse chicken wings and pat dry. Cut off and discard wing tips. Cut each wing at the joint to make two pieces. Place the wings in a bowl and lightly drizzle them with oil. Toss the wing pieces, like a salad, to distribute oil over all wings. Lightly salt and pepper wings. Lightly garlic powder wings. Toss again to distribute seasonings.

Grill the chicken wing pieces over indirect, medium heat with the grill lid down (technically this is barbecuing since you have the wings over indirect heat). Cook about 30 minutes or until chicken is tender and skin is lightly crisp, turning at least once halfway through the cooking time.

Plum Glaze: While the wings cook on the grill, combine all of the Plum Glaze ingredients in a small saucepan. Cook and stir until well heated. Serve with a spoon or a basting brush or just as a dipping sauce for grilled chicken wings.

Plating:

Use a serving platter. Pour the warm plum sauce into a medium bowl in the center of the platter. Arrange grilled chicken wings around the dipping sauce bowl. Serve family style next to the cheese, olives and grilled bread.

Grilled Sausage Peperonata Soup

For the past 5 years, I have been organizing a summertime family reunion for all of my Italian side. Over the past 50 years, we have grown up, moved away from Brooklyn and raised children who now have children of their own. Since we have been spread out all over the country for most of that time, we only saw pictures of each other in Christmas cards. Boy, did they get old! This summertime reunion thing has been nice and we are growing in numbers each year. Last year we had 65 people hip-to-hip in a small backyard in Levittown, New York. This year, Maplewood, New Jersey. Each year I have successfully communicated with everyone, and the food has always turned out to be varied and plenty. Last year we had a sudden surge of acceptances in the final week leading up to the party. So I just left it up to God and Pot Luck on the last five families. What are the odds of getting five different versions of sausages, peppers and onions? Well here is one that you will love.

Ingredients:

2 lbs sweet Italian sausage

2 quarts chicken stock

Peperonata:

    3 green peppers; sliced
    3 red peppers; sliced
    3 medium red onions; sliced
    2 large garlic cloves; smashed and minced
    ¼ cup olive oil
    1-½ tsp dried basil
    ¾ tsp dried oregano
    salt
    pepper

Instructions:

Mince garlic. Slice peppers and onions.

Do not poke the sausage skin before grilling so as to retain as much of the juices as possible. Place the sausage on the cooking grate over direct medium heat. Grill about 20 to 30 minutes, until sausage is no longer pink in the center. Using tongs, not a fork, turn the sausage several times during cooking to brown all sides and not poke holes. Remove from grill and set aside for 5 minutes on a platter. After the 5 minutes, cut the sausage into ½-inch long rounds in a dish that will retain all of the juices while cutting. Add sausage and juices to soup, see below.

As the sausage is cooking on the grill, sauté the peppers, onions and garlic in oil in large skillet on the stove for 10 minutes; stir in basil, oregano, salt and pepper. Cover and cook over medium-low heat about 30 minutes until peppers are very soft. Add the 2 quarts of chicken stock; raise the heat to high and bring to a boil. Reduce the heat to low-simmer. Add cut sausage with juices, stir and simmer for 5 more minutes.

Plating:

Use large soup bowls. When you ladle the soup, go down to the bottom of the pot and get plenty of sausage, peppers and onions in each serving. Garnish with a dash of Parmesan cheese and a dash of dried basil. Serve.

Grilled Radicchio and Romaine Hearts

Who says all salads have to be chilled? You may be surprised to know that some of the best restaurants around the country are now serving salads - hot off the grill! Undoubtedly, you've experimented with grilled vegetables, and you know that grilling brings out the natural sugars of vegetables. Well even the radicchio and romaine varieties of lettuce hold up on the grill. Radicchio, a red-leafed Italian chicory, makes a wonderful grilled salad. The two radicchio varieties most widely available in the U.S. are Chiogga and Treviso. Either will do fine, but I am recommending the Treviso, if you can find it. Chiogga grows in a small, round head and has burgundy-red leaves with white ribs. You've probably had this one the most. Treviso has narrow and pointed leaves that form a tighter more tapered head. Romaine - well, you know romaine. It's not just for Caesar salad anymore.

Ingredients:
1 cup aged balsamic vinegar
4 TBSP cold water
1 oz dried Italian seasoning
2-¼ cups extra virgin olive oil (2 for vinaigrette, ¼ for brushing hearts)

4 Radicchio di Treviso hearts, sliced in half lengthwise through the core
4 Romaine hearts; sliced in half lengthwise through the core
2 green bell peppers; sliced into rings
4 green onions; chopped fine
4 scallions; sliced

salt
ground black pepper; to taste
½ cup grated Parmesan cheese

Instructions:
Chop green onion fine. Reserve.

Soak radicchio in cold water for 10 minutes.

While radicchio is soaking, whisk together oil, balsamic vinegar, water, Italian seasoning and green onions. Reserve. Seed and slice green bell pepper into rings. Reserve. Slice scallions into small rounds. Reserve.

When the 10-minute soak is up remove the radicchio from the water and pat dry with paper towels. Rinse the Romaine in cool water and pat it dry with paper towels.

Cut each radicchio and Romaine heart in half lengthwise through the core. Keep the cores intact so the leaves remain held together. Brush both sides of the all of the hearts with oil.

Grill the Romaine hearts over a hot fire for about 2 minutes per side and the radicchio hearts for 3 minutes per side.

Plating:
Place a warm Romaine heart in the center of a flat salad plate. Place a warm radicchio heart next to and slightly on top of Romaine heart. Drizzle some vinaigrette over both. Garnish with the sliced green bell pepper rings and scallions. Salt and pepper to taste. Top with grated Parmesan cheese. Serve.

                    168

Grilled Gyros Roast

At first, when you think about rolling a beef steak inside of a leg of lamb you might hesitate, but remember this is only a scaled-down Greek Cowboy version of the famous Paul Prudhomme Turducken (a turkey stuffed with a duck stuffed with a chicken). So it must be okay.

Ingredients:

1 small leg of lamb; boned and filleted to ¾" thick (about 3-½ lbs)
1-½ lbs boneless beef round steak; cut to ½" thick
¼ cup dried oregano leaves
2 tsp dried dill weed
2 tsp garlic powder
½ tsp ground thyme
1-½ tsp salt
1 tsp pepper
olive oil

Instructions:

Pound lamb and beef round steak on both sides with a meat mallet, until each piece of meat measures about 12"x14". Sometimes I have been forced to use a hammer when no mallet was available. If you use a hammer for this step, cover the meat with a layer of plastic wrap.

Combine herbs, salt and pepper, crushing with back of spoon until fine texture, but not powdered. Place lamb on cutting board; brush top lightly with olive oil and sprinkle with 1/3 of the herb mixture. Pound the herbs into the surface of the lamb with the meat mallet. Lay the round steak on top of lamb; brush top lightly with olive oil and sprinkle with ½ of the remaining herb mixture. Pound those herbs into the surface of the beef with the meat mallet. Remove all plastic wrap and then roll up the meats together as tightly as possible, starting at the narrower end. Tie securely in several places with roast string that you obtained from the butcher when you bought the boned lamb. Brush outside of roast lightly with olive oil. Rub remaining herb mixture into the surface of the meat. Place meat on dish and cover with plastic wrap. Place into refrigerator for about an hour to absorb the good flavors of the herbs.

Remove roast from refrigerator and place it in the center of the cooking grate and cook over indirect/medium heat until the internal temperature registers 150°F; about 1-½ hours. Turn roast several times during the cooking. If you have a rotisserie for your grill, it will be easier and better if you use it for this step. The meat will be juicier. After either method, the outside of the meat will become very dark and crusty. Remove it from cooking grate and let it stand for 15 to 30 minutes before slicing. Slice into ½" thick slices.

Plating:

Use large dinner plates. Depending upon appetite, plate 1 or 2 slices of meat, shingling with grilled onions and tomatoes, alternating onion, meat, tomato, meat, onion and tomato. Garnish the layered meat and vegetables with 1 to 2 tablespoons of the Special Sauce. Place the vegetable kabobs still on the skewer next to the layered meat and vegetables.

Special Sauce for Gyros Roast

This is a takeoff on the classic Tzatziki sauce you will find in the Greek Style with Meat dinner in this book. This is a lot easier to prepare and will make a great flavor addition to the gyros meat. Enjoy.

Ingredients:

2 medium cucumbers, peeled, seeded and diced into small cubes (¼")
1 pint of sour cream
1 tsp salt
1 TBSP lemon juice
black pepper
2 cloves garlic; smashed and minced

Instructions:

Peel, seed, dice and salt the cucumber. Wait for half an hour and rinse the cucumber to remove excess salt.

While the cucumber sits, mince the garlic. Then mix the sour cream, lemon juice, minced garlic and pepper. Place the mixture in the refrigerator.

After the cucumber is rinsed, fold it into the sour cream mixture. Refrigerate until ready to garnish the meat.

Grilled Vegetable and Potato Kabobs

Ingredients:

4 large green peppers; cut into 1-inch square pieces
4 large red peppers; cut into 1-inch square pieces
3 large Idaho potatoes; peeled, cut into 1" cubes, blanched, drained and cooled
4 small zucchini; cut into 1" pieces
4 small yellow squash; cut into 1" pieces
1 large bottle of Italian salad dressing; any variety

Instructions:

Put a medium pot of water on high heat to boil.

While waiting for water to boil, wash and cut peppers, zucchini and squash. Peel and cube potatoes.

Blanch cubed potatoes in boiling water for 2 minutes.   Drain and rinse with cold water. Drain again and pat dry.

Place all cut vegetables into a shallow roasting pan. Pour Italian dressing over vegetables and mix thoroughly. Marinate at room temperature for 1 hour. Mix the vegetables and marinade at least once more during the hour. Reserve the excess marinade after skewering vegetables.

Thread vegetables onto eight-8" or longer skewers. Place at least 2 pieces of each (five) vegetables on each skewer. The skewering can be done during the 1 hour marinating time period. Just return the skewered vegetables to the marinating pan. Reserve until ready to grill.

Place the kabobs in center of cooking grate over indirect/medium heat and cook for 10 to 15 minutes turning once, halfway through cooking. Brush the kabobs with marinade, several times while cooking. Reserve at least ¼ cup of the marinade for brushing onto Patio Tomatoes.

Plating:

Plate with Gyros Roast. See Gyros Roast plating instructions.

Grilled Sweet Onions

Ingredients:

3 large sweet onions, sliced ½" thick
¼ cup Dijon mustard
½ cup honey

Instructions:

Slice onions into ½" slices.

Combine honey and Dijon mustard well. Brush on onion slices.

Grill onion slices for 2 to 3 minutes per side until tender and marked with grill marks. Remove from grill and set aside.

Plating:

Plate with Gyros Roast. See Gyros Roast plating instructions.

Grilled Patio Tomatoes

Ingredients:

8 medium tomatoes
Italian salad dressing (from vegetable kabob marinade)
Salt
Pepper
Dried basil leaves

Instructions:

Cut each tomato in half across the tomato. Brush cut surfaces with Italian salad dressing marinade from vegetable kabobs. Sprinkle with salt, fresh ground pepper and basil.

Place cut side up on aluminum foil or greased grill over hot coals about 10 minutes (don't turn) or until heated all the way through.

Plating:

Plate with Gyros Roast. See Gyros Roast plating instructions.

Grilled Pineapple Bananas Foster

We did not serve Bananas Foster in Le Orangerie in New York, but we did flambé Duck L'orange and Crepes Suzette. Ah, the joy of rolling a guéridon up to the customer's table, heating the pan and then having flames shoot 2 or 3 feet high before their glistening eyes was only exceeded by the joy over how much my tip swelled each time I performed the trick. This was true if it was for a young couple in love, 3 or 4 businessmen or 8 matronly customers having a nice lunch before going off to the theatre for a Wednesday matinee on Broadway. Even the people sitting at adjoining tables got a vicarious thrill and paid a little bit extra for the show. The only difficulty as a young waiter was that I was frequently muscled out of the way for the show by a Room Captain, you know those slimy guys in tuxedos who only show up when they can clip a tip for holding a chair, complimenting a lady, popping a champagne cork, or, in those days, lighting a cigar. Once I figured out that all I had to do was guard the guéridon like it was a 5' 6" quarterback who needed extra time in the pocket for a pass, I started making the big bucks! I did outweighed most of those slimy chaps by 50 pounds and was a veteran college football lineman. Your friends probably will not hand you a five-dollar bill for lighting the flambé, so it will just be for the fun of it. Please be careful.

Ingredients:
4 firm bananas
8 slices pineapple; canned and drained
¼ cup dark rum
8 large scoops vanilla ice cream

Syrup:
3/4 cup sweet butter
3/4 cup brown sugar
dash cinnamon

Instructions: Slice the *unpeeled* bananas in half, lengthwise. Grill the banana halves in their peels over a medium-high flame until peel is dark brown (5 min/side). Grill the pineapple slices on a piece of aluminum foil next to the bananas 3 minutes per side.

While the bananas and pineapple slices cook make the syrup. Melt the sweet butter in a large pan on the grill. If you don't have a large grill surface this step can be done on a stove burner in the kitchen. Combine the melted butter, brown sugar and cinnamon in the pan; stir until syrupy. Add the grilled pineapple slices to the syrup. Peel the grilled banana halves and cut each one in half again across the banana. Add them to the bubbling syrup. Baste in syrup, turning until all of the fruit is glazed.

When the fruit is glazed (coated), add the rum and stir slightly. If you want a flambé show, wait for 10 seconds after the rum is poured and gently stirred in. Then gingerly bring a lit match up to the side of the pan and over the edge. Be careful, don't stick your arm over the pan, you may light your clothes on fire. You don't have to flambé to get the rum flavor into the Foster. It really is for show.

Plating: Use large dessert or soup bowls. Keep the ice cream in the freezer up to the last second before plating. Place one hot pineapple slice into each bowl; top the slice with a large scoop of ice cream. Top all with the hot bananas Foster sauce getting two pieces of cut banana in each bowl. Move quickly to serve. The ice cream will begin melting as soon as it hits the grilled pineapple, and it will speed up with the banana sauce on top.

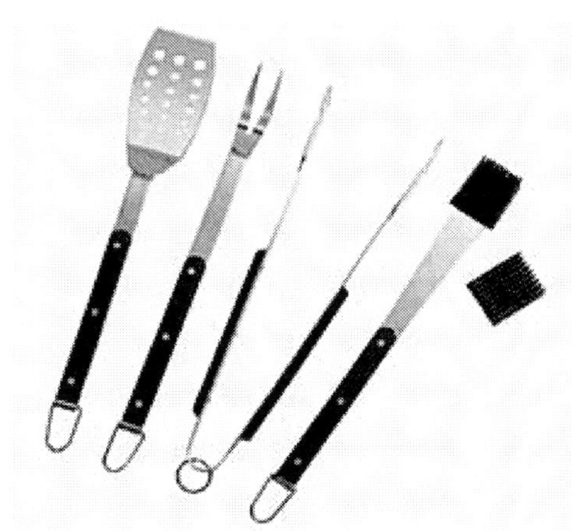

Coriander

A Taste of the East

Coriander, A Taste of the East

Diane and I have had the pleasure of meeting wonderful people during our years in Marriage Encounter. Vinnie and Selma are a great couple originally from the tiny Catholic community of Southwest India. They love our home cooking parties. In fact we staged our very first home cooking party at their house. On that occasion, we had the good fortune of meeting Vinnie's college roommate from 25 years ago, Kinley, who was also visiting for the weekend from his home country of Bhutan. Kinley, a Jesuit priest, was in the USA for just a few weeks to meet with educators and education administrators to share ideas and make observations in a crash course before returning to Bhutan.

While he was born a Buddhist as is everyone in Bhutan, somehow he secretly found his way to Catholicism when he was still very young. Years later after he had completed college and was working at a regular job, he was traveling on business for his employer. He chanced to be on an airplane for many hours sitting next to Mother Teresa. After the two of them talked about life and the state of the poor in the world she said that she thought he should become a priest. Shortly after that chance encounter, he left his job and entered the seminary.

When we met him, he had spent the previous 20 years as a Jesuit priest studying, teaching and leading schools in India and had not been back to Bhutan for over a dozen years because of religious persecution. In the early 1990s, the King of Bhutan had thrown all practicing Catholics out of the country. In 2002, Kinley was invited back by the King to become the principal of a school, but he was clearly instructed that he would not be allowed to evangelize or say mass in public. He would be the only Catholic priest in Bhutan. Kinley accepted. He and his Jesuit Bishop agreed there would be the opportunity to be a key educator of children, and Kinley would bring some presence of his adopted faith back to Bhutan, but before he could do all of that amazing work, he had to chop and cook his way through our home cooking party.

Kinley asked if he could add something to our planned menu. We delightedly accepted and during our prep work, he prepared a spicy Indian appetizer made of cilantro, red onions, chilies, oil, and some richly flavored crispy thin wheat noodles, all tossed together. Spicy but delicious! We eased through the appetizers looking at photographs of Vinnie and Selma's wedding in India. They had 1,000 guests over a 4-day celebration. Yes, I said 1,000! I thought 200 at our wedding was a lot, but noooooo they had 1,000! Vinnie is the youngest of 10 brothers and sisters and Selma also comes from a large family. So it is easy to get to 1,000 when you add all of the in-laws and cousins.

After we finished the dinner, we were all stuffed to the gills. My spring dinner wasn't light, but it was a hit in every other respect, and it was the easiest dinner I had ever prepared for a large dinner party because I had all of the guests working together prior to dinner. They had a ball and the idea for "Home Cooking Parties for™…Eight" was born. By the time we finished dessert, it was pushing 11 o'clock and everyone was ready for bed. The next morning, Vinnie prepared a memorable Indian-inspired breakfast of curried eggs and spiced Indian flatbread. Whew! We sang a few Beatles songs with Vinnie on the guitar and Selma on the drums, and were ready for the road.

We shared many enlightening moments with Kinley, Vinnie, Selma, Ron, Millie, Rich and Sue that weekend while chopping onions and cilantro, cooking, serving each other, sitting, talking and walking through the lovely suburban Philadelphia neighborhood - all surprising and delightful additions to the weekend. That gathering of friends to prepare a Saturday night dinner grew into a complete weekend of stirring memories and proved to be the launching point for Home Cooking Parties. The extra Indian-inspired foods shared by Kinley and Vinnie became the inspiration to create this dinner of Eastern flavors.

Enjoy!

Coriander, A Taste of the East

5:00 p.m.   Cocktails

                            Wine, Beer, Mixed Drinks

          Snacks

                            Cucumber and Cumin Shrimp Spread
With Celery and Wheat Crackers
Curried Crab Fondue

6:00 p.m.   Dinner

          Beverages   Water, Wine, Beer and Soda

          Soup   Fennel & Tomato Soup with Scallops

          Salad   Cool 'n Breezy Fruit Salad

          Entree   Coriander Encrusted Halibut with Papaya Chile Coulis

              Accompanied by

                        Summer Potatoes with Spring Onions
Steamed Asparagus with Lemon Butter

          Dessert   Mumbai Black Coconut Custard
Café and Tea
Liqueur

Coriander, A Taste of the East Shopping Lists

Shopper 1

½ lb small or popcorn shrimp; pre-cooked, peeled (frozen is ok)
12 oz jaggery palm sugar (substitute: dark brown sugar)
1 small bottle rose water (Middle Eastern or Chinese Market)
1 large lemon
3 cups green seedless grapes
2 cups musk melon (substitute: cantaloupe)
1 small to medium watermelon
2-½ cups fresh papaya
24 fresh mint leaves
1 pint extra virgin olive oil

Shopper 2

16 oz cream cheese
6 oz sharp processed cheese spread
6 oz lump crabmeat; canned is ok
1 loaf French baguette
1 package of lady fingers
6 TBSP unsalted butter
1 dozen large eggs
1 quart whole milk
1 pint sour cream
1 pint half and half
12 oz canned coconut milk
18 oz canned evaporated milk
1 can sweetened condensed milk
3 quarts vegetable stock
1 cup toasted unsalted almonds

Shopper 3

16 large scallops
2 lb fennel bulbs
8 medium potatoes
10 medium tomatoes
8 green onions
1 medium yellow onion
8 clove garlic
1 medium cucumber
1 large stalk/bunch celery
1 lb fresh asparagus
1 bunch fresh chives
2 bottles ground coriander

Shopper 4 (Host)

3 lbs halibut fillets; cut into eight 1-½" thick fillets, 6 oz each
4 tsp ground black pepper
10 tsp salt
¾ tsp chili powder
½ tsp paprika
2 tsp cayenne pepper
2 tsp cumin
½ tsp Tabasco® sauce
¼ tsp garlic powder
½ tsp curry powder
½ tsp dried parsley
1-½ tsp ground cardamom
1 tsp cinnamon
1-½ tsp freshly grated nutmeg
¼ tsp ground cloves
1 cup sugar
2 pinches turmeric
1 TBSP ketchup
1 tsp Worcestershire sauce
2 TBSP anise flavored liqueur
1 TBSP dry sherry wine

Preparation Schedule – Coriander, A Taste of the East

Teams
1/
2/
3/
4/Hosts

4:00 pm   **1, 2, & 3**- Arrive at **4**'s kitchen. Put on chef's aprons. Unpack and stack all groceries in a central location. Put shrimp, scallops, halibut, milk, half and half, butter and sour cream in refrigerator. Leave all cheeses at room temperature. Have a cocktail.
2- If shrimp are still frozen, place in a bowl of cool water and stir until thawed.

4:15 pm   **2**- Start Shrimp Spread recipe. Serve when ready.
4- Set table and continue serving drinks.

4:30 pm   **1**- Start Fennel and Tomato Soup recipe. Serve at 6:00 pm.
3- Start Crab Fondue recipe. Serve when ready.
4- Prepare Papaya Coulis from Halibut recipe. Cover and refrigerate when complete.

5:00 pm   **1, 2, 3 & 4**- Eat Shrimp Spread and Crab Fondue in the kitchen as they are ready, and drink cocktails while you merrily work on your other food preparations.
4- Preheat oven to 275°. Start Coconut Custard recipe. Continue through baking, cooling and chilling in refrigerator.

5:15 pm   **2**- Start Halibut recipe. Prepare fish through coating with spice mixture. Cover and refrigerate for cooking later.
3- Start Cool N' Breezy Fruit Salad recipe. Serve at 6:30 pm.

5:30 pm   **4**- Coconut Custard should be in oven by now.

5:45 pm   **1**- Plate soup with garnish and serve with help from **4** at 6:00 pm.
4- Help **1** plate and serve soup.

6:00 pm.   **Eat Soup in Dining Room**
At 6:15 everyone helps clear dishes to the kitchen.

6:15 pm.	**1-** Start Potatoes and Onions recipe. Complete, keep warm and serve with Halibut at 7:30 pm. **2-** Set up sauté pan in preparation for cooking Halibut. **3-** Complete plating of fruit salad. Serve fruit salads with help from **4**. **4-** Check Coconut Custard in oven for doneness. Reset oven to 450° when custard is removed from oven. Help **3** serve fruit salads at 6:30 pm.
6:30 pm	**Eat Fruit Salad in Dining Room** **At 6:45 everyone helps clear dishes to the kitchen.**
6:45 pm	**2-** Cook Halibut according to recipe. Serve at 7:30 pm. **3-** Start Asparagus recipe. Complete, cover to keep warm and serve with Halibut at 7:30 pm. **4-** After Coconut Custard has cooled to room temperature, place in refrigerator to chill.
7:00 pm	**4-** Warm dinner plates.
7:15 pm	**1-** Help **2** plate Potatoes and Onions with Halibut and serve at 7:30 pm. **2-** Plate Halibut with Papaya Coulis, Potatoes and Onions, and Asparagus with help from **1 and 3**. Turn oven off. **3-** Help **2** plate Asparagus and Halibut and serve at 7:30 pm.
7:30 pm	**Eat Entree in Dining Room** **At 8:00 everyone helps clear dishes to the kitchen.**
8:00 pm	**4-** Set up coffee cups, teaspoons and tablespoons for dessert service. Brew coffee and tea.
8:15 pm	**1-** Plate Coconut Custard with ladyfinger with help from **2**. Serve when ready. **2-** Help **1** plate Coconut Custard and ladyfinger. Serve when ready. **3-** Work with **4** on coffee and tea service. **4-** Serve coffee and tea when ready.
8:30 pm	**Eat Dessert and Have Coffee and Tea in Dining Room** **Relax! Job Well Done!**

Cucumber and Cumin Shrimp Spread

Ingredients:

½ lb small or popcorn shrimp; pre-cooked, peeled (frozen is ok)
½ tsp paprika
½ tsp cayenne pepper
½ tsp cumin
½ tsp dried parsley
1 large stalk of celery
8 oz cream cheese; softened
1 clove garlic; smashed and minced
1 medium cucumber; peeled, seeded and diced
½ cup sour cream
3 green onions; finely chopped
1 TBSP ketchup
1 tsp Worcestershire sauce

Instructions:

If shrimp are frozen, place them in a bowl of cool water and stir until thawed.

If you have no food processor, dice the shrimp before seasoning. If you do have a processor, pulse the shrimp 2 or 3 times. Sprinkle the shrimp with paprika, cayenne pepper, cumin and parsley. Toss together well and let stand in a bowl for 10 minutes at room temperature.

While the shrimp marinate, peel and dice cucumber, chop onions, mince garlic. Combine all ingredients except marinating shrimp in a medium bowl and mix well. Use a food processor if you have one by pulsing 5 or 6 times.

When shrimp have marinated 10 minutes, toss the shrimp-marinade mixture into the other mixed ingredients. Fold in well or pulse the food processor 6 times. Refrigerate for 15 minutes to chill.

Wash 8 full stalks of celery. Trim and cut in half to make 16 short stalks.

After chilling the spread, stuff 8 of the short celery stalks.

Plating:

Use a large serving platter. Arrange the 8 stuffed celery stalks on the platter alternating with the additional 8 unstuffed short stalks. Transfer the rest of the shrimp spread into a small bowl and place it in the center of the serving platter. Place the wheat crackers on the other end of the platter. Lightly dust the bowl of spread and stuffed celery with paprika and cumin. Add a light sprinkling of dried parsley around the entire platter for color. Serve family style.

Curried Crab Fondue

Ingredients:

8 oz cream cheese; softened
6 oz sharp processed cheese spread
6 oz lump crabmeat; canned is ok
¼ cup half and half
½ tsp Tabasco® sauce
¼ tsp garlic powder
½ tsp curry powder
1 TBSP dry sherry wine

½ green onion; chopped for garnish

1 loaf French baguette; cut into 1" cubes

Instructions:

Combine cream cheese and cheese spread in 4-cup glass measure. Microwave at medium (50% power). Set for 2-minute intervals and stir after each 2-minute interval. Continue until cheese melts completely. Stir in crabmeat, half-and-half, Tabasco® sauce, curry powder, garlic powder and sherry. Microwave at medium-high (70% power) for 1-minute intervals, until thoroughly heated, stir after each 1-minute intervals.

While the fondue heats, cut the baguette into 1" cubes. Place in a basket lined with a linen or paper napkin. Chop green onion.

Plating:

Pour heated mixture into a fondue pot or chaffing dish. Garnish with green onions and dust with cumin. Cover. Light the pot or dish heater. Serve family style with baguette cubes and dipping forks. (If you do not have a fondue pot or lighted chaffing dish, we have eaten this standing around a pot on the stove over low, low heat.)

Fennel and Tomato Soup with Scallops

Say fennel and most people think of Italy, Florence in particular, but more fennel is grown in India, and it is a favorite flavor in Indian cuisine. The fennel seeds are highly prized as a digestive aid. We have moved the flavor up to the soup course in the meal and are asking you to intensify the level of anise flavor with the use of your favorite anise flavored liqueur such as absinthe, arak, rakı, pastis, ouzo or sambuca. Think about bringing the anise liqueur back out at the end of the meal and dropping a few anise seeds into the glasses, too.

Ingredients:

4 TBSP olive oil
2 lb fennel bulbs; finely sliced (tough stem pieces removed)
10 medium tomatoes; 7 for soup and 3 for garnish
2 stalks celery; finely sliced
2 TBSP anise flavored liqueur
3 quarts vegetable stock
16 large scallops
1 bunch fresh chives
salt
Ground black pepper

Instructions: Boil water for blanching and peeling tomatoes. Set up a bowl of ice water near the boiling water. While water comes to a boil, finely dice 3 of the unpeeled tomatoes and set aside to use as a garnish. Finely chop the chives and reserve for garnish. Finely slice the fennel bulbs and celery for soup.

When the water boils, turn off the heat. Skin the remaining 7 tomatoes by plunging them (2 at a time) into the water for 10 seconds and then transferring them to the bowl of ice-cold water. Peel off all the skins then slice the tomatoes in half and remove and discard the seeds. Chop the tomatoes. Reserve for addition to the cooked vegetables.

Heat 3 tablespoons of olive oil over high heat in a large saucepan and add the finely sliced fennel and celery and sauté until the vegetables are lightly browned, about 4 minutes. Reduce the heat to low, cover the pan and cook the vegetables gently for 20 minutes, or until the vegetables have softened and are a deep golden brown.

Remove the lid and add the anise liqueur, chopped tomatoes and vegetable stock. Stir well, raise the heat to high and bring the soup to a boil. Then reduce the heat to a simmer for 20 more minutes. Add salt and pepper to taste.

While the soup simmers, heat a tablespoon of oil in a small fry pan. Pat dry the scallops with a paper towel and then sear them over a high heat until golden on both sides, about 1 minute per side. Sear only a few at a time. Don't overcrowd the pan. Place the seared scallops aside on a plate. Reserve.

Plating:

Use large soup bowls. Divide the soup between 8 bowls. Add 2 seared scallops to each bowl and garnish generously with the finely diced reserved tomatoes and chopped chives. Serve.

Cool n' Breezy Fruit Salad

Ingredients:

3 cups green seedless grapes
2 cups musk melon; diced or balled (substitute cantaloupe)
3 cups watermelon; diced or balled
¾ cup sweetened condensed milk
¼ cup whole milk
1 tsp cinnamon
1 cup toasted unsalted almonds; coarsely chopped
16 fresh mint leaves; chopped for garnish

Instructions:

Coarsely chop almonds. Reserve.

Peel, seed and dice melons into 1" or smaller cubes. If you have a melon baller, use that instead of peeling and dicing and for improved appearance. Just chop the melons in half, scoop out the seeds, and then scoop out little balls of melon using the balled. No need to peel the skin.

Put grapes and melons in a large salad bowl. Mix the sweetened condensed milk, whole milk and cinnamon powder thoroughly in a separate bowl or measuring cup. Pour the liquid over the fruit and toss gently. Fold in the chopped almonds and mix all, gently. Cover the bowl and refrigerate for 15 minutes.

Coarsely chop mint leaves just before garnishing and serving fruit salad.

Plating:

Use small salad or dessert bowls for plating. Scoop up fruit and some of the liquid for each serving. Garnish with freshly chopped mint leaves.

Coriander Encrusted Halibut with Papaya-Chile Coulis

Halibut, used in this recipe, is a very mild fish. It will pick up the flavorings of the coriander and coulis very well. Even your dinner friends who normally don't order fish in restaurants will like this combination of flavors and textures.

Ingredients:

3 lbs halibut fillets; cut into eight 1-½" thick fillets, 6 oz each

2-½ tsp ground black pepper

8 tsp salt

16 tsp coriander; ground

8 TBSP olive oil, for sauté pan

The Papaya-Chile Coulis:

2-½ TBSP yellow onion; chopped fine

3 garlic cloves, smashed

2-½ cups fresh papaya; diced

¾ tsp chili powder

2 dashes cayenne pepper

5 TBSP extra virgin olive oil

sugar; for coulis, use sparingly to taste, if needed

Instructions: Pre-heat oven to 450°.

Thoroughly mix the coriander, salt and ground pepper in a small bowl. Crush together with the bowl of a large spoon to grind these dry ingredients together. Reserve.

Leaving any skin on the halibut steaks, but skinless is okay, too. Pat the steaks dry with a paper towel to remove any excess moisture. Coat each piece of fish on all sides with the dry ingredients and press slightly into the flesh. Set the pieces on a plate, ready for sautéing. If there is any delay in sautéing, cover and place the coated fish steaks in the refrigerator until ready to sauté.

Preheat a sauté pan (non-stick if you have it) over medium-high heat. Add the olive oil to the heated pan and when the oil is hot, just below the smoking point, add 2 or 3 of the halibut steaks leaving space all around each steak. Sear the steaks in the hot oil, being careful not to over cook, 3 minutes per side, turning once. Remove the fish to a baking sheet and hold until the rest of the steaks are seared. Finish on the middle rack of a 450° oven for about 6 minutes for 1-½" fillets. Thinner fillets (1" or less) may not need to be finished in the oven. You want up to a total of 8 minutes per inch or 12 minutes in our 1-½" thick case. Keep baking sheet on stove when total cooking time is reached.

Papaya Coulis: This can be made ahead of time and refrigerated. If it is not prepared earlier in the preparation period, prepare the coulis while the fish sears and bakes. Chop onion, dice papaya and smash and peel garlic. Place all of the ingredients except the oil and sugar in a blender (or food processor) and purée until smooth, scraping the sides of the blender often. With the blender on, slowly add the oil until uniformly smooth. The flavor should be slightly sweet. Add sugar sparingly until the taste is pleasing to your palate. Season with salt and pepper if needed.

Plating: Use large flat dinner plates. Place one halibut steak in the center of the plate. Place 4 to 6 tablespoons of papaya coulis in the center of the halibut and overflowing off of the steak to one side. Plate the potatoes and onions to the dry side of the steak. Plate the asparagus on the coulis side of the steak. After all asparagus is plated, spoon some of the residual lemon butter sauce on the asparagus.

Steamed Asparagus with Lemon Butter

Ingredients:
1 lb fresh asparagus
salt
6 TBSP unsalted butter
zest of 1 large lemon
2 TBSP lemon juice

Instructions:

In a large skillet, bring about ½ inch of water to a rapid boil.

While waiting for water come to a boil, wash asparagus and trim or break off tough bottoms of stems. To break off bottoms, gently hold the asparagus with both hands about 1/3 of the way in from each end and gently bend. Wherever the asparagus breaks, use the skinny end and discard the tough bottoms. (You can use these bottoms for asparagus soup on another day if you want to save them.)

Zest one large lemon. Reserve. Squeeze the lemon and reserve the juice.

Season the water with salt and add the asparagus. Cook the asparagus for 2 minutes or until bright green and just tender.

Drain and temporarily aside the asparagus to a plate. Discard the cooking water. Add butter to the skillet and melt over medium-low heat. When the butter is melted, stir in the lemon zest and juice. Return the drained asparagus to the skillet and toss to coat. Turn off the heat, cover with foil or skillet cover and let the asparagus sit in the lemon butter sauce until ready to plate.

Plating:
Plate with halibut and potatoes. See Halibut plating instructions.

Summer Potatoes with Spring Onions

Ingredients:

8 medium potatoes
2-½ cups green onion, chopped
2 TBSP olive oil
1-½ tsp cumin powder
1-½ tsp salt
1-½ tsp ground black pepper
2 pinches turmeric

Instructions:

Peel potatoes, cut in half and place directly into a pot of salted, cold water as they are peeled and cut in half.

Bring the pot to a boil and continue boiling potatoes for 15 more minutes. Drain and plate to cool slightly before dicing.

Coarsely chop green onions while potatoes boil.

Heat oil in a large skillet (on medium heat). When oil is hot add chopped onions. Sauté chopped onions for 1 minute and then add all the spices and 1-½ teaspoons of salt. Continue to sauté spiced onions for 5 more minutes.

After cooling them enough to not burn your hands, dice the potatoes into 1" to 1-½" bite size pieces.

Add diced potatoes to the skillet and sauté gently on medium heat for about 5 more minutes. Toss all of the ingredients in the skillet after every 30 seconds.

Plating:

Plate with halibut and asparagus. See Halibut plating instructions.

Mumbai Black Coconut Custard

If you can find dark brown jaggery when you shop for the rosewater, use it in place of the dark brown sugar for a more authentic flavoring of this very interesting custard.

Ingredients:

12 oz jaggery palm sugar (substitute dark brown sugar)
9 eggs
12 oz canned coconut milk
18 oz canned evaporated milk
1-½ tsp ground cardamom
1-½ tsp freshly grated nutmeg
¼ tsp ground cloves
3 TBSP rose water (Middle Eastern or Chinese Market)
8 fresh mint leaves
1 package of lady fingers (or biscotti or similar long cookies)

Instructions:

Preheat oven to 275°.

Chop jaggery palm sugar into small pieces and put into a small heavy saucepan with 1-¼ cups water. Dissolve over low heat. If you cannot find jaggery, use dark brown sugar. Allow sugar water to cool to room temperature. Stir to hasten cooling but do not chill. Add coconut milk and ¾ cup water.

Beat eggs until well mixed but not frothy, add palm sugar and coconut milk mixture slowly while you beat the eggs. Mix well. Strain the mixture through a fine strainer into a large bowl. Discard anything caught in the strainer. Stir in evaporated milk, spices and rose water or rose essence.

Pour into individual ovenproof custard cups placed in a baking dish (bain marie). Add hot water to the baking dish to surround and come half way up sides of the custard cups and bake at 275° until set (about 1 hour). After 45 minutes of baking, jiggle one or two of the cups to see if the pudding is set. If the centers are very loose let it bake some more. If they just jiggle in the center 1" of the cups take them out of the oven and move them onto a cookie sheet or tray to cool to room temperature. Then chill in refrigerator. It is okay to eat this pudding warm, so if you don't get to the chilling, it's okay.

Plating:

Use a flat dessert plate. Place a doily on the plate. Put a custard cup on the doily. Place a fresh mint leaf on the custard. Place one ladyfinger on the dessert plate. Serve.

PEDRO XIII
Cardenal Cisneros
Coffee

A French Meal

Inspired by

Ossau-Iraty
Tomatoes
And
Pumpkins

A French Meal
Inspired by Ossau-Iraty, Tomatoes and Pumpkins

Inspiration for this meal was simple – fall – ripe tomatoes, pumpkins, sheep's milk cheese and two friends who I can't say no to asking for a French dinner. Besides this menu being a wonderful fall menu, it is full of the flavors of Provence. For those who really don't like pumpkin pie, there are other ways to use pumpkin. My favorite is this dessert, Pumpkin Crème Brulée. Get really ripe tomatoes, if you can, for the fresh Tomato Soup Provençal. You will love this recipe for braised Pork Chops and Fennel in Pastis. The chops are marinated and then braised in the pastis, which adds a wonderful dimension to the dish. I have left out snacks before the meal, since there is a cheese course between the main course and dessert. Use your discretion if you would like to put something out as a snack or munchies before the meal begins.

Running Wild with a French Pumpkin Inspiration

When we did this dinner with friends, I had a funny experience that I thought might help you to stay calm if it ever happens to you.

Diane and I arrived around 2:30 pm. just as we all had agreed since there was a football game on TV that the men insisted had to be seen until the 4:00 pm. scheduled finish (really 4:15). The plan was to watch the second half of the football game and start the preparation and cooking schedule at 4:30. Our friend, Dorothy, who was hosting had put out some great picking foods, cucumber slices with bleu and cream cheese piped topping, a spinach and artichoke dip to go along with phenomenal home made tortilla chips from Linda and olives and other chutney items. None of these were on the menu; they were just treats to go along with the football.

So I settled right down with a glass of wine and the other guys to watch the Eagles get embarrassed again; this time losing their quarterback for the season with a devastating injury, but there was always hope, and hope kept us glued to the TV. On this particular Sunday, hope wasn't enough. I checked with the cooking team who was responsible for starting the pork marinade, since this would take a couple of hours longer than the 4:30 starting time would allow. They had gone to work immediately at 2:30 and had the marinating pork chops heading to the refrigerator in a jiffy. I was at peace and decided to go back to the game.

About 3:30 I took a moment to look in the kitchen and what did I find? Instead of enjoying an aperitif and some snacks the women were all RUNNING WILD in the kitchen getting way ahead of the preparation schedule. They had decided that the good French chef (me) who had supplied the recipe for the Tomato Soup Provencal didn't know a tomato or leek from a hole in the ground (that part is true). They all wanted the soup to simmer longer than the recipe called for, so they sprinted on ahead of the prep clock. They also decided that if they were doing that they might as well run ahead of the Taboulé and tomato salad schedules as well. So here I was with a full-fledged kitchen revolt by my sous chefs! What was I to do? Easy, I went back to the TV and the rest of the game, waiting for the true 4:30 starting time to arrive. Hmmm, how about another glass of wine?

Well, I must admit, when we started the meal with the soup, it was phenomenal! I suspect when you do it without sprinting ahead of the schedule, the layers of flavor and richness of the ingredients will provide just as startling a beginning to your French Inspiration meal, as well, sans revolt. Above all else, if you experience a similar sous revolt and insurrection during this or any of the meal plans in this book, just go with the flow. Everyone is there to have a good time. Let them have that good time, and the food will always taste better.

I am sure your eyes will also sparkle when you bite into the Red Onion and Ossau Iraty Tart like all of ours did. That cheese is worth the search and the cost, but shop well for the Ossau-Iraty. I wound up paying half the price at Trader Joe's® versus a local supermarket with a good cheese department. When you serve the cheese course make sure the cheese is at room temperature. It will make your eyes bulge from its richness. You will also learn that God did have a plan for dry bulgur wheat, and it wasn't just as a breakfast food. The pistou (pesto) raises this ancient food to a sparkling complement in the main course. I have since found that the leftover pistou Taboulé adds great body to a salad. Try it. You will love it!

I have suggested in the ingredients that you use a fattier cut of pork (shoulder) for the chops. Our pork came from the loin and while the fennel and stock flavored it magnificently, the combination of frying, boiling and oven braising left it a bit chewy. The less lean cut will remedy this while maintaining the magnificent pickup of the flavorings. Braising is a method typically used to tenderize cheaper cuts of meat anyway. Serve the au jus from the braising on the side. I also recommend that the host buy the chops and the marinating ingredients to provide the opportunity to marinate them overnight for more tenderness, rather than just the few hours shown in the recipe.

On this particular night, the crowd oooohed and ahhhhed all the way from the start to the crowning ending – the Pumpkin Crème Brulée! Enjoy this French Inspiration dinner with your best friends. They will love it and you even more! You might decide to do just as I did this year. I replaced the usual Thanksgiving pumpkin pie with this fantastic Pumpkin Crème Brulée. None of our guests complained.

Enjoy!

For those of you, who may speak a wee-bit of French; have fun with this…...

et les recettes:

L'Entrée – **Soupe de Tomate Provencal**

A tomato soup made with a combination of fresh and canned tomatoes and brightened with the addition of orange juice.

La Salade - **Salade de Tomates et d'Olives**

The salty olives and tangy lemon bring out the tomato flavor even more.

Le Plat – **Cotelettes de Porc Braise et Fenouil**

Pork chops marinated in pastis and then braised with fennel accompanied by Taboulé and a cheese and onion tart.

      Plat Lateral -   **Taboulé Provençal**
      Plat Lateral -   **Ossau-Iraty Tourte de Fromage et Oignon**

Le Fromage – **L'Ossau-Iraty**

A sheep's milk cheese from the Basque region

Le Dessert – **Citrouille Crème Brulee**

A French Meal
Inspired by Ossau-Iraty, Tomatoes and Pumpkins

5:00 p.m.   **Cocktails**

                Wine, Beer, Mixed Drinks

          Snacks

                Optional, As You Please

6:00 p.m.   **Dinner**

      Beverages   Water, Wine, Beer and Soda

      Soup   Tomato Soup Provencal

      Salad   Tomato and Olive Salad

      Entree   Braised Pork Chops and Fennel

            Accompanied by

                Bulgar with Pesto
                Cheese and Onion Tart

      Cheese Course   Ossau-Iraty and Fruit

      Dessert   Pumpkin Crème Brulee
                Café and Tea
                Liqueur

French Pumpkin Inspiration Shopping Lists

Shopper 1

1 pint olive oil
2 cans plum tomatoes (28 oz.)
3 quarts chicken stock
8 oz Niçoise black olives, pitted
1 pre-made plain pie crust (10")
1 cup solid pack pumpkin puree
½ cup packed brown sugar
½ tsp cinnamon
2 cups sugar
2 cups walnuts (pieces are okay)
1 vanilla bean
2 loaves of French baguette

Shopper 2

20 ripe medium to large tomatoes
3 leeks
3 carrots
4 cloves garlic
8 scallions
3 lbs. red onions
4 fennel bulbs with leaves
4 shallots
2 lemons
1 orange
1 lb red seedless grapes
8 oz blueberries or raspberries
3 Gala apples
1 bunch fresh basil
1 bunch fresh parsley

Shopper 3

1-½ cups dry bulgar wheat
4 TBSP pistou (pre-made pesto in a jar ok)
1 pint orange juice
1 lb butter
1 doz eggs
2 cups whipping cream
1-½ lbs L'Ossau-Iraty: Ewe's milk cheese (expensive)

Shopper 4 (Host)

3 oz pine nuts
6 oz sun-dried tomatoes
2 TBSP fresh oregano
3 tsp dried thyme
1 tsp fennel seeds
1 tsp kosher or sea salt
1 TBSP pumpkin pie spice
8 1" thick pork chops; shoulder cut
table salt
freshly ground black pepper
3 TBSP Cointreau
1 cup pastis (Pernod or Ricard) licorice flavored liqueur made with star anise

Preparation Schedule – French Pumpkin Inspiration

Teams
1/
2/
3/
4/Hosts

2:00 pm.	**4-** Marinate pork in refrigerator. Turn pork every 30 minutes for 2 hours. If this can be started during the previous night, all the better.
4:00 pm	**1, 2, & 3-** Arrive at **4**'s; Unpack; Put on chef's aprons. Unpack and stack all groceries in a central location. Put whipping cream, berries, grapes and eggs in refrigerator. Leave butter, cheeses, orange juice, apples, and French bread at room temperature. Have a cocktail.
4:15 pm	**2-** Pre-heat oven to 350°. Prepare Pumpkin Crème Brulée according to recipe. Place in refrigerator to chill after cooling on counter. **4-** Set table and continue serving drinks.
4:30 pm	**1-** Follow Taboulé recipe. Steep bulgar on counter to allow swelling. Chop and prepare other ingredients and set aside. **3-** Prepare pastry shell for onion tart. While shell bakes prepare tart filling. Remove baked shell from oven. Reserve. **4-** Soak chopped leeks to remove sand. Chop vegetables for soup.
5:00 pm	**1-** Prepare Taboulé according to recipe up. Do not add lemon juice at this time. Set aside on counter. **4-** Cook soup according to recipe. Simmer until serving time.
5:30 pm	**1-** Start salad recipe. Assemble according to recipe. Set aside to marinate at room temperature until ready to serve. **2-** Remove baked crème Brulee from oven and set out to cool. Leave oven at 350°. Start Pork Chop recipe cooking. Break to eat soup during cooking. Put pork into oven to braise when it is ready. **3-** Fill tart shell and bake for 8 minutes. Remove tart from oven, set on counter and break to eat salad.
5:45 pm.	**4-** Plate soup with basil garnish and serve with baguette at 6:00 pm. **1-** Warm baguette in oven 5 minutes. Help **4** plate and serve soup.
6:00 pm	**Eat Soup in Dining Room** **At 6:15 everyone helps clear soup dishes to the kitchen.**

| 6:15 pm | **1-** Drizzle oil on tomato salad, toss to recombine all ingredients. Plate and serve at 6:30 pm. |

1- Drizzle oil on tomato salad, toss to recombine all ingredients. Plate and serve at 6:30 pm.
2- Turn pork chops over, top off liquid with water and recover casserole. Continue braising. Move crème Brulée into refrigerator to chill. Help **1** plate and serve salad.

6:30 pm

Eat Salad in Dining Room
At 6:30 everyone helps clear salad dishes to the kitchen.

6:45 pm

1- Slice cheese and apples for Cheese Course. Set cheese on counter and cover and refrigerate apples slices.
2- Continue pork braising steps.
3- Wash grapes, plate and chill for Cheese Course.
4- Provide assistance to **2** during pork preparation.

7:00 pm

3- Put onion tart back in oven for 5 minutes to heat up, then remove.
4- Remove pork from oven, place on stovetop. Keep casserole covered so juices will absorb back into meat. Warm dinner plates.

7:15 pm

1- Add lemon juice to Taboulé and toss. Plate entrée with **4**.
2- Slice bread. Heat bread for 5 minutes in oven. Place in basket, cover with a cloth napkin and set on table. Serve with butter.
3- Cut onion tart wedges. Plate separately. Garnish with oregano sprigs. Serve at 7:30 pm with entrée.
4- Plate pork slightly stacked on Taboule. Pour a small amount of remaining juices over each piece of pork. Pass to **3** for tart.

7:30 pm

Eat Entree in Dining Room
At 8:00 everyone helps clear dishes to the kitchen.

8:00 pm

1 & 2 – Prepare cheese, grapes, berries, apples and sliced bread. Serve when ready.

8:15 pm

Eat Cheese and Fruit Wherever You Favor

8:30 pm

1- Caramelize tops of crème Brulée. Plate and serve.
2- Help **1** plate and serve crème Brulée when ready.
3- Brew coffee and tea.
4- Set up coffee cups, dessert plates, spoons and forks for service. Assist **1** with crème Brulée.

8:45 pm

Eat Dessert and Have Coffee and Tea in Dining Room
Relax! Job Well Done!

Tomato Soup Provençal

This tomato soup recipe from Provence is made from both fresh and canned tomatoes and has a surprise ingredient ~ orange juice. You will have and will want leftovers of this soup!

Ingredients:

¼ cup olive oil
3 leeks; thoroughly cleaned and then minced
3 carrots; peeled and minced
1 medium red onion; chopped
4 cloves garlic; smashed and minced
grated zest of 1 orange
2 tsp dried thyme
1 tsp fennel seeds
8 ripe tomatoes; seeded and diced
2 cans plum tomatoes (28 oz.) undrained
1-½ quarts chicken stock
¾ cup orange juice
salt
freshly ground pepper

1 French baguette; sliced
1 cup julienned basil; for garnish

Instructions:

Soak leeks in cold water for 5 minutes to clean thoroughly. While the leeks soak, cut, chop and mince vegetables according to directions, above. Then rinse, drain and mince the leeks last.

Heat the oil in a large stockpot over medium-high heat and add the leeks, carrots, onion and garlic and cook for 15 minutes. Stir several times during this cooking. After 15 minutes, add the orange zest, fennel seeds, dried thyme and cook, stirring frequently for 3 minutes. Add all the tomatoes, stock and orange juice and stir to combine. Cover the stockpot and simmer over medium-low heat for 30 minutes.

Remove from heat. Purée the soup using a hand food processor (food mill). Work in batches if you must use a standard food processor or blender. Season with the salt and pepper.

Strain the soup back into the stockpot to remove any chunky material and bring it to a simmer. Hold at low-simmer until ready to serve.

Heat baguette in oven 5 minutes before serving soup.

Plating:

Use medium or large soup bowls. Just before serving, julienne basil and use as a garnish for soup. Serve hot soup with warm baguette and butter.

Tomato and Olive Salad - Salade de Tomates et d'Olives

This salad should be made with well-ripened tomatoes. The salty olives and tangy lemon bring out their flavor even more. There is no lettuce in the salad.

Ingredients:

8 ripe tomatoes
8 oz Niçoise or other black olives; pitted
4 shallots; peeled and very thinly sliced
1 lemon; zested and squeezed
olive oil
fresh parsley; chopped

Instructions:

Smash and pit the olives. Cut them in half. Thinly slice shallots.

Chop the tomatoes and place them in a bowl Leave the tomato seeds in the salad. Toss in the shallots. Zest the lemon.

Squeeze the lemon juice into the bowl with the tomatoes.

Add the olives, lemon zest and parsley to the bowl and toss to combine.

Allow to rest at room temperature for about 15 minutes.

Plating:

Use flat salad plates. Just before plating toss the salad again to distribute liquids. Divide tossed salad among 8 plates. Drizzle on some olive oil and serve.

Pork Chops with Fennel

Try to get a pork chop that is not too lean. Bone-in, shoulder cut may prove to cook up more tenderly in this preparation process. If a lean cut chop is used, buy with bone-in and serve extra marinade jus for guests to further moisten chop as they consume it.

Ingredients:
8 1" pork chops; shoulder cut
4 fennel bulbs; sliced lengthwise into chunky 1" x 1-½" strips
8 sprigs of fennel leaves (cut the from the above bulbs)
1 cup pastis (Pernod or Ricard)
6 TBSP olive oil
5 cups chicken stock
1 tsp kosher or sea salt for marinating
salt
freshly ground black pepper

Instructions:

Marinate the pork chops: In a shallow glass baking dish, large enough to hold the chops in a single layer, place the sprigs of fennel leaves. Place a chop on top of a fennel sprig and sprinkle the pastis over the chops. Add 1 teaspoon of kosher or sea salt to marinade to tenderize pork chops. Season chops with freshly ground pepper. Cover with plastic wrap and marinate 2 to 3 hours in the refrigerator, turn chops over every ½ hour. If you can set this up the night before and allow the chops to marinate in the refrigerator overnight, even better.

Preheat oven to 350°F.

In a large flameproof casserole, heat the oil over medium-high heat. Remove the chops from the marinade. Set the fennel aside on a plate. Also reserve the rest of the marinade. Pat the chops gently dry, then sauté in the oil about 3 minutes per side. Adjust the heat as necessary, so that the oil does not burn but the chops brown well. Transfer the chops to a plate. Pour the marinade into the casserole and increase heat again to med-high. Add the stock and the chops. The liquid level should be most of the way up the sides of the chops with the chops just peeking above the liquid. Bring to a boil. Transfer the casserole to the oven and braise at 350°F, covered, 25 minutes, turning the meat once.

Remove the casserole from the oven and remove the chops once more. Add the fennel and stir to coat with the liquid. Place the chops back in the casserole on top of the fennel, but nestle the chops down so that they are also in the liquid. Top off with more chicken stock so the liquid level is again most of the way up the sides of the chops with the chops just peeking above the liquid. Cover the casserole and continue braising another 20 minutes, basting often. The chops and fennel should be tender and the liquid reduced.

Plating:

Plate the Taboule in the center of the plate in a mound and the chop slightly off-center on the Taboulé. Spoon the fennel over the chop. Pour a small amount pan juices over the fennel Eand the pork and serve. Serve extra pan juices as "au jus" in a gravy boat on the side.

Bulgar with Pistou (Pesto) - Taboulé Provençal

Ingredients:

1-½ cups bulgar
4 TBSP pistou (use pre-made pesto in a jar)
4 tomatoes, seeds removed and diced
4 scallions, sliced
juice of 1 lemon

Instructions:

Rinse the bulgar in a colander. Place in a large bowl.

Bring 1-½ cups of water to a boil and pour over the bulgar. Let the bulgar set at least 30 minutes to swell and become soft.

There shouldn't be any water remaining but if there is drain it off. Mix in the pistou/pesto, chopped tomatoes, and scallions. Fold together.

Add the lemon juice and toss. Allow to sit at room temperature until ready to serve.

Plating:

Use a flat dinner plate. See plating instructions in Pork Chops with Fennel recipe.

Ossau-Iraty & Red Onion Tart

Ingredients:

1 pie crust recipe (10") (pre-made plain pie crust is okay, but NOT graham!)
2 lbs red onions, peeled & sliced
3 oz pine nuts, toasted
6 oz sun-dried tomatoes, chopped
2 TBSP fresh oregano, chopped + a few sprigs for garnish
8 oz Ossau-Iraty, cubed (if camembert is used, discard rind before cubing)
½ cup olive oil

Instructions:

Preheat oven to 400°F.

Pre-bake pie crust. Line the bottom with some crumpled waxed paper and pie weights or dry beans to keep crust flat. Blind bake (no filling) for 15 minutes. Remove the beans & paper and bake an additional 5 minutes.

While the tarts are baking, heat the olive oil and cook the onions over low heat for about 20 minutes, stirring occasionally. In a separate dry pan, toast the pine nuts (watch carefully and pour out of pan into a bowl as soon as the nut brown lightly). Remove onions from heat, stir in the toasted pine nuts, chopped sun-dried tomatoes, oregano and the cheese cubes. Spoon the onion mixture into the tart (baked pie crust) and return to the oven. Cook for about 8 minutes to warm through. Set aside.

Return to the oven for 5 minutes, just before slicing and serving.

Plating:

Use a small flat plate. Garnish with the oregano sprigs and serve warm on the side of the main course.

Cheese Course

L'ossau-iraty is an AOC cheese from the Basque region of France. This cheese is actually a "combined" cheese, having been developed in two distinct regions, Béarn and the Basque region of France. Ossau was produced in Béarn and Iraty in the Basque country. The two provinces joined forces to create this "marriage" and the cheese was granted AOC status in 1980.

This delicious ewe's milk cheese is made by shepherds who still tend their flocks in the high pastures during the summer. Romantic thought, isn't it! I wonder if the shepherds think so, too. The cheese belongs to the family of uncooked, pressed cheeses. After being pressed, it is kept in a cool room where it is turned every day for 3 weeks. It is then aged from 2 to 5 months. The best of this cheese is still made by shepherds living in their mountain cabins during the summer months.

Ingredients:

1 lb L'Ossau-Iraty: ewe's milk cheese
1 lb red seedless grapes
8 oz blueberries/raspberries
3 gala apples; washed and sliced
1 baguette; sliced

Instructions and Plating:

Use a large, decorative serving platter.

L'ossau-iraty is a large round of cheese with a diameter of about 10 inches and is 6 inches high. It can weigh up to 11 pounds. You will have a wedge from one of these rounds. Allow the cheese to come to room temperature before cutting. Use 1 pound of cheese cut into bite size pieces arranged on half of the platter.

Wash and slice apples and place on platter. Add grapes, raspberries and blueberries to fruit side of platter. Sprinkle some of the berries among the pieces of cheese.

Serve family style with slices of French bread on the side in a basket and your favorite wine. Provide small bread and butter size plates and knives.

Pumpkin Crème Brulée

A perfect alternative to Pumpkin Pie.

Ingredients:

2 cups whipping cream
1 vanilla bean, split
8 egg yolks
10 TBSP granulated sugar
1 TBSP pumpkin pie spice
1 cup solid pack pumpkin
2 TBSP Cointreau
1 cup packed brown sugar
½ tsp cinnamon

Instructions:

Bring cream to a boil, remove from heat and add vanilla bean. Allow to steep 25-30 minutes; remove vanilla bean after steeping.

Preheat oven to 350°F.

The following steps can be done using an electric mixer.

Whisk together the egg yolks, granulated sugar and pumpkin pie spice. Add pumpkin and Cointreau and mix until smooth. Whisk in steeped cream. Divide mixture among 8 half-cup ramekins (oven-proof cups). Arrange the ramekins in one or two baking pans (bain marie) and add enough hot water to come halfway up the ramekins' sides.

Bake in bain marie about 20 to 30 minutes in 350° oven on middle rack. The sides should be set but the centers should still move slightly when shaken. Remove from bain marie and allow to cool to room temperature.

When cool, place in refrigerator for at least one hour to chill.

Plating:

Preheat broiler. Place cups of custard on a baking sheet. Sift the brown sugar and cinnamon into a small bowl, then sprinkle over the custards. Broil about 30 seconds, until sugar begins to melt and brown slightly. Be careful here. The sugar can blacken quickly, so watch it. If you have a blow torch for desserts, it can be used here in place of the oven broiler. Transfer each cup of custard onto an individual large dessert plate. If you have doilies place them under the custard cups. Serve.

A Low Country Boil

With All the Fixins

A Low Country Boil with All the Fixins

I sat next to Lorraine in school for over a dozen years. Her last name started with Pa, mine with Pe. We were always friendly in our seats, but we ran with different crowds. In late-June 1965 we graduated from Massapequa High School, and the last time we saw each other was alphabetically in the row of chairs on the football field at graduation. She went her way; I went mine.

Thirty-five years later I was in my reunions phase of life – family, fraternity, school chums, etc. – and went onto Classmates.com to try to organize a reunion dinner at Dick and Dora's, a school haunt back in the old hometown. That started a lot of chatter amongst people who had been out of contact for almost four decades. Whole lives had been changed, changed again, and again. There was a lot to catch up on and a feeling of picking up where we left off between people who had shared the same space year after year in the 1950s and 60s. Lorraine "from one seat over" answered via e-mail. She had become a schoolmarm, a head mistress, in Atlanta running a small private school she created after years in the teaching ranks. One thing, she was no longer Lorraine, just plain Rain. She had gotten the nickname shortly after high school when she moved to Hawaii. I guess it fit – tropical forest – sarong - Rain. Her flowers for the age of Flower Power were orchids. After several years of that life Rain came home to that other tropical island paradise, Long Island, met Ron and rode off on his Harley down Jericho Turnpike into the sunset. Thirty years later they still ride off to the Great Smokey Mountains each summer on his Harley (a new one) and enjoy romping in fields of flowers – I have pictures! You can take the girl out of Hawaii and the '60s, but not the other way 'round.

As we corresponded, we found we had a great passion in common, cooking. Not just cooking, but cooking big for friends and family. You can't get around people with Italian heritage. Sooner or later we all venture into the kitchen and renew the demands of our DNA. Rain and I started swapping recipes, and when I started doing Home Cooking Parties, she was enthralled. Each time I would put on a dinner, she wanted all of the details – so I wrote. Story after story of what happened; who I met; what menu I created. Quite a few of the stories in this book came from my e-mails to Rain. Thanks, R.

Rain introduced me to an exciting one-pot dish that comes from the Gullah and Geechees traditions in the Low Country, the coastal marshlands of South Carolina and Georgia. The Low Country Boil is a really spicy and delicious combination of seafood, meat and vegetables like a New England Clambake, only without the clams, crabs, lobsters and seaweed. Well, it's sorta like a New England Clambake. It's boiled in a pot and spiced with African, Spanish and Caribbean influences, it has romantic local names like St. Helena Island Stew, Capt'n Fuskie's Boil and Frogmore Stew and as many variations as its distant Creole cousin from Louisiana, gumbo. It has been made for over 400 years in the Low Country and each family has its own secret recipe.

I prepared this dish with friends not knowing what to expect, and when we sat down and ate it the spices seemed mild upon first bite, but in 5 minutes some of us had tears and were sweating! I have dialed down the spices in this version of the recipe to give you a slightly milder experience. I also dialed up the flavor by adding vegetable stock. My take on Rain's recipe is still full of flavor and zing, but with less mouth and lip-burn. I guess I have joined the ranks of families with their own secret boil recipes. Have fun with The Boil and other Gullah treats of Low Country Cooking.

Enjoy!

A Low Country Boil with All the Fixins

5:00 p.m.	Cocktails	
		Wine, Beer, Mixed Drinks
	Snack	
		Low Country Crab Ball Bites
6:00 p.m.	Dinner	
	Beverages	Water, Wine, Beer and Soda
	Appetizer	Spicy Shrimp over Summer Greens with Mango Dressing
	Soup	Geechees Okra and Red Rice Soup
	Entree	Rain's Secret Low Country Boil

Accompanied by

Heartfelt L-C Cornbread
Zingy Cole Slaw

Dessert   Everyone's Favorite Fresh Fruit Tart
Gullah Benne Wafers
Café and Tea
Liqueur

A Low Country Boil with All the Fixins Shopping Lists

Shopper 1

3 lbs smoked sausage; kielbasa or any variety
1 quart chicken stock
1 quart vegetable stock
5 lemons
2 limes
1 mango
1-½ cups pineapple chunks (canned okay)
2 lb strawberries, raspberries & blueberries (buy the berries that are in season)
2 kiwi fruit
1 lb red or green seedless grapes
¼ cup sesame seeds

Shopper 2

1 lb medium raw shrimp (24 to 30 count); peeled and deveined, frozen okay
1 lb lump (or claw) crabmeat
1 cup mayonnaise
1 cup corn, frozen is okay
¾ cup stone ground cornmeal
½ cup apricot preserves (substitute peach)
3 cups coarse unflavored bread crumbs
1 cup olive oil
½ lb butter
8 oz 10X powdered sugar
½ cup brown sugar
2-¼ cups uncooked rice

Shopper 3

½ lb bacon
1 jar cocktail sauce
2 green onions
1 lb young Okra pods
6 large tomatoes
1 large package spring mix lettuce
1 red onion
3 medium sweet onions
16 small onions
16 small new or red-skin potatoes
4 ears of corn
8 large carrots
5 green bell peppers
1 large head of cabbage (substitute 1 bag pre-shredded cole slaw)
1 bunch fresh parsley
1 can (16 oz) diced tomatoes
1 (8 oz) package cream cheese
¼ cup sour cream
¼ cup half and half
1 doz eggs
1 cup buttermilk
1 Keebler Ready Crust® Graham

Shopper 4 (Host)

2 lbs large raw shrimp in shell; 16 to 20 count per pound, frozen is okay
3 TBSP Tabasco® or Crystal® Hot Sauce
2 TBSP Worcestershire sauce
½ tsp dried thyme
coarse salt, sea or kosher
salt
ground black pepper
1 tsp chili powder
1 tsp cayenne
1 tsp whole cloves
2 tsp garlic powder
1 tsp garlic salt
4 bay leaves
1 tsp Old Bay® seasoning
2 cups sugar
3 TBSP yellow mustard
2 TBSP ketchup
1 TBSP red wine vinegar
paprika
1 cup flour
3 tsp baking powder
¼ tsp baking soda
2 TBSP vanilla extract
1 TBSP Crisco® or 2-½ TBSP bacon fat

Preparation Schedule – A Low Country Boil with All the Fixins

Teams
1/
2/
3/
4/Hosts

4:00 pm	**1, 2, & 3**- Arrive at **4**'s kitchen. Put on chef's aprons. Unpack and stack all groceries in a central location. Put smoked sausage, kielbasa, lump crabmeat, sour cream, half and half, buttermilk and eggs in refrigerator. Leave frozen corn, bacon, butter and cream cheese at room temperature. If shrimp are frozen, put in a pot of cool water at room temperature. Keep peeled and unpeeled shrimp separate. Have a cocktail.
4:15 pm	**1**- Set oven to 350°. Start Fruit Tart recipe. Refrigerate by 5:45 pm. **2**- Start Crab Ball Bites recipe. Serve when ready. **3**- Start Spicy Shrimp recipe. Serve at 6:00 pm. **4**- Set table and continue serving drinks. Start chopping vegetables and slicing meats for Red Rice recipe.
4:30 pm	**4**- Start Okra Soup recipe and continue until ready to serve. Continue with cooking in Red Rice recipe. Serve at 6:30 pm.
5:00 pm	**1, 2, 3 & 4**- Eat Crab Ball Bites in the kitchen as they are ready, and drink cocktails while you merrily work on your other food preparations. **2**- Start Zingy Cole Slaw recipe. Serve at 7:30 pm with The Boil.
5:45 pm	**1**- Refrigerate Fruit Tart. Turn oven off. **2**- Refrigerate cole slaw. Help **3** plate and serve Spicy Shrimp. **3**- Plate Spicy Shrimp and serve with help from **2** at 6:00 pm.
6:00 pm.	**Eat Spicy Shrimp in Dining Room** **At 6:15 everyone helps clear dishes to the kitchen.**
6:15 pm.	**1**- Start Rain's Secret Low Country Boil recipe. Serve at 7:30 pm. **2**- Help **4** plate Okra and Red Rice Soup. Serve at 7:30 pm. **3**- Set oven to 375°. Put pan of water on bottom of oven. Start Heartfelt Cornbread recipe. Serve at 7:30 pm with The Boil. **4**- Plate Okra and Red Rice Soup with garnish and serve with help from **2** at 6:30 pm.

6:30 pm   **Eat Okra and Red Rice Soup in Dining Room**
At 6:45 everyone helps clear soup dishes to the kitchen.

6:45 pm   4- Warm dinner plates. Put butter on the table to go with cornbread.

7:00 pm   4- Start Benne Wafer recipe. Change oven to 325° and carefully remove pan of hot water (discard) from oven 5 minutes before putting in wafers. Continue until wafers are out of oven and cooling.

7:15 pm   1- Plate The Boil. Serve at 7:30 pm.
2- Plate Zingy Cole Slaw. Serve at 7:30 pm.
3- Plate Heartfelt Cornbread. Serve at 7:30 pm.
4- Keep an eye on the Benne Wafers. Remove them from the oven to cool as soon as they are golden brown. Turn oven off.

7:30 pm   **Eat Entree in Dining Room**
At 8:00 everyone helps clear dishes to the kitchen.

8:00 pm   4- Set up coffee cups, teaspoons and tablespoons for dessert service. Brew coffee and tea.

8:15 pm   1- Plate Fruit Tart and serve with help from **2**. Serve when ready.
2- Help **1** plate Fruit Tart and Benne Wafers. Serve when ready.
3- Work with **4** on coffee and tea service.
4- Serve coffee and tea when ready.

8:30 pm   **Eat Dessert and Have Coffee and Tea in Dining Room**

                   Relax! Job Well Done!

      214

Low Country Crab Ball Bites

Ingredients:

Crab Ball Filling:
1 lb lump (or claw) crabmeat; chopped/minced
½ cup mayonnaise
1 egg; beaten
2 green onions, chopped fine
½ tsp Tabasco® or Crystal® Hot Sauce
1 dash of Worcestershire sauce
¾ cup coarse unflavored bread crumbs
½ lemon for juice
½ tsp dried thyme

Breading:
2 eggs; for egg wash
¼ cup half and half, for egg wash
2 cups coarse unflavored bread crumbs

¾ cup olive oil
coarse salt; for dusting, sea or kosher
ground black pepper; for dusting
1 bunch fresh parsley
1 jar cocktail sauce
1-½ lemons; sliced into eighths (12 pieces)

Instructions:

Filling: Finely chop green onions and crab. Use a medium size bowl. Beat egg in bowl and then combine all remaining filling ingredients into the beaten egg and thoroughly fold them together by hand until mix is uniform. Form into 1" balls and put them on a plate. Use just enough force to hold the ball together. Don't over compress. The balls will be a bit loose.

Breading: Make an egg wash of eggs and half and half in a small bowl. Put 2 cups of bread crumbs in a shallow dish. Dip crab balls in egg mixture, and then roll in bread crumbs. Cover all sides of the crab ball. Pick up and reform into a ball, if necessary. Set on a plate until all of the crab balls have been breaded. Refrigerate while you heat up the cooking oil.

Put olive oil in a small enough sauté pan to allow a bit of oil depth in the pan. Heat pan and oil over medium heat. When oil is hot sauté/deep fry small groups of crab balls until golden brown. Roll them over in the oil to cook on top and bottom. Drain on paper towels on a plate. Dust with coarse salt and freshly ground pepper and keep plate on top of stove to keep crab balls warm.

Plating:

Use a medium size serving platter. Pour cocktail sauce into a small dipping bowl. Place in center of platter. Distribute fresh parsley around the dipping bowl on the platter. Place fried crab ball bites on parsley surrounding dipping bowl. Slice the remaining 1-½ lemons into eighths. Distribute the lemon slices all around the outer border of the platter around the crab balls. Serve family style with toothpicks or forks, small plates and cocktail napkins.

Spicy Shrimp over Summer Greens with Mango Dressing

Do yourself a favor and buy already peeled and deveined shrimp. Frozen, cleaned shrimp are okay.

Ingredients:

1 mango; peeled, pitted and pureed
2 tsp lime juice

1 lb large shrimp (24 to 30 count); uncooked, peeled and deveined
2 tsp chicken stock (from 1 quart of stock for Okra Soup recipe)
1 tsp chili powder
1 tsp hot sauce (Tabasco® or Crystal® Hot Sauce)
1-½ cups pineapple chunks; drained and diced (canned are okay)
1 cup tomato; seeded and diced
1 red onion; thinly sliced

1 large package spring mix lettuce

Instructions:

Slice red onion. Seed and dice tomato. Drain and dice pineapple chunks. Reserve.

In a large sauce pan, combine peeled and deveined shrimp, chicken stock, chili and hot sauce. Turn on heat to medium. Cook and stir until the shrimp are just cooked through.

Remove from heat; add tomatoes, pineapple and onion. Stir well and let sit for a minute. Transfer to a bowl, cover and cool for 10 minutes. Refrigerate the shrimp mixture and chill for 30 minutes.

Puree peeled mango in a blender or food processor with lime juice for dressing. Reserve.

Plating:

Use a large flat salad plate. Divide the spring mix equally among the eight plates centering on plate in a small pile. Use a slotted spoon to toss the shrimp mixture and to arrange mixture around the slopes of the lettuce with an opening at the peak. Leave the loose marinade liquids in the bowl. Spoon the mango dressing directly on the center of the lettuce over the peak. Serve.

Geechees Okra and Red Rice Soup

This delicious soup is served in true Geechees tradition over red rice for a soup with abundant flavor. Enjoy this.

Ingredients:

1 lb young Okra pods; sliced into ¼" rounds
2 large tomatoes; skinned, seeded and diced
1 cup corn (frozen is okay)
1 quart chicken stock (reserve 2 tsp of this stock for Spicy Shrimp recipe)
2 slices bacon; sliced to 1" pieces
1 lemon; for zest and juice
salt for seasoning to taste
ground black pepper for seasoning to taste

(see separate recipe for red rice)

Instructions:

Put a pot of water on to boil for skinning tomatoes. Set up a bowl of ice water next to the boiling water.

While waiting for the water to boil, cut off the ends of the okra pods. Discard ends. Slice the pods into approximately ¼" thick rounds. Reserve.

When the water boils, submerge the tomatoes into the boiling water and leave for about 60 seconds. Remove from boiling water and submerge in ice water. Leave water boiling for use with corn. After 15 seconds remove tomatoes from the ice water and peel the skin off the tomatoes. Seed and dice the tomatoes. Reserve.

Use the boiling water from the tomatoes for boiling the corn. Season the boiling water with a pinch of salt. Add the corn and boil until it is soft and tender. Drain and reserve.
While the corn boils, slice the bacon into 1" pieces. Use a large sauce pan with a lid. Fry the sliced bacon over medium-high heat until it is crispy. Do not drain the fat. Keep it. It is part of the soup. When the bacon is crispy, place the chicken stock, sliced okra, boiled corn, diced tomato, lemon zest, lemon juice into the large sauce pan with the bacon and bacon grease. Bring to a boil. Stir well and cover the pan. Reduce the heat to low and simmer for about 15 minutes, until the okra is tender. Test it. Plate soup over the red rice as soon as the okra is tender.

Plating:

Use large soup bowls. Plate ½ to ¾ cup of Red Rice in the center of the bowl. Ladle the Okra Soup on top of the Red Rice. When you ladle dig down to the bottom of the soup pot on the first ladle to get all of the good ingredients of the soup. After you have placed a first ladle into each soup bowl, go around again and top off with more soup liquid. Serve. No other garnishes are necessary.

Red Rice for Okra Soup

Some Low Country residents prefer their red rice drier. We are using that approach with our ingredient proportions because this rice will be underneath when we plate our Okra Soup. Frying the uncooked rice along with the bacon intensifies the flavor rice.

Ingredients:

4 slices bacon, sliced into 1" pieces
2-¼ cups uncooked rice
1 medium onion, chopped
1 can (16 oz.) diced tomatoes
1 lb smoked sausage; diced into very small pieces
1 green bell pepper; chopped finely
salt to taste
ground black pepper to taste
dash of sugar

Instructions:

Chop onion. Chop green pepper. Dice smoked sausage. Slice bacon into 1" pieces. Reserve.

Use a large sauté pan that has a tight-fitting cover. Over medium heat fry the bacon until brown (do not drain the bacon fat). When the bacon is mostly rendered, add the dry rice. Stir well coating all of the rice with bacon grease and continue to cook and stir until bacon crisps.

Push the rice and bacon to the edge of the pan and fry the chopped onion in the center of the pan. Stir frequently until the onion is transparent (about 5 minutes).

Add the canned tomatoes, diced sausage and chopped green pepper to the pan. Bring to a boil. Stir well and cover the pan with the tight-fitting lid. Reduce heat to lowest setting and simmer for 20 minutes until rice is done. In true Low Country fashion, do not stir or otherwise disturb the rice during the 20 minutes of simmering. Transfer cooked rice to a large bowl and reserve for plating with Okra Soup.

Plating:

Plate with Okra Soup. See Okra Soup plating instructions.

Rain's Secret Low Country Boil

Use your favorite brand of smoked sausage for this recipe. Kielbasa keeps it tame, andouille raises the stakes! If you can get deveined shrimp with shells, do it. If your choice is between deveined without shells or not deveined with shells, pick the shells for this particular dish. Peeling the cooked shrimp is part of the friendliness of this dish.

Ingredients:

2 lbs smoked sausage; kielbasa or any variety, cut to 3" lengths
2 lbs large raw shrimp in shell; 16 to 20 count per pound, frozen is okay (thaw before using)
16 small new or red-skin potatoes
4 ears of corn; cut in half
16 small onions; peeled but not cut
8 carrots; cut into quarters

Seasoning Ingredients:
1 quart vegetable stock
1 tsp cayenne
1 tsp whole cloves
2 tsp garlic powder
4 bay leaves
1 tsp Old Bay® seasoning
½ tsp ground black pepper
1 tsp Tabasco® or Crystal® Hot Sauce
1 lemon; juiced plus peel

Instructions:

Thaw shrimp in cool water. While shrimp thaw, fill your largest pot or kettle one-third of the way up with water and put it over high heat to boil. When you first put the pot on the heat, immediately add the vegetable stock and seasoning ingredients shown above. Squeeze in the juice of one lemon and toss in the complete lemon peels, too. Remember this is a dialed down recipe version to moderate the spiciness. If you want to play with the seasoning measures, no one is looking over your shoulder. Go ahead.

While waiting for the water to boil, prepare the meats and vegetables for cooking. Cut 2 lbs smoked sausage into 3" lengths. Peel onions, but leave them whole. Peel and cut the carrots into quarters. Wash, but do not peel the potatoes. Cut ears of corn in half.

When water is at a rolling boil, add the potatoes, carrots, smoked sausage and onions. Bring back to a boil and continue boiling until potatoes are almost tender (about 15 minutes). Add the corn-on-the cob and boil for 5 minutes longer. Finally, reduce the heat to low and add the raw shrimp in shells and simmer for 3 to 4 minutes more, or until shrimp are just cooked. Remove from heat and plate immediately to avoid rubberizing the shrimp. If there is a delay in plating, strain out the shrimp to a separate plate until ready to serve.

Plating:

Use a large soup or pasta bowl for each serving. Each plate should get at least 1 or 2 pieces of every item depending upon appetite. Ladle some of the boil broth into each bowl. Sprinkle 3 or 4 shrimp on top. Serve cornbread and coleslaw on the side in separate dishes.

Zingy Coleslaw

Ingredients:

4 green bell peppers; sliced
2 medium sweet onions; shredded
1 large head of cabbage; shredded (substitute 1 bag of pre-shredded cole slaw)

Dressing:
½ cup mayonnaise
3 TBSP yellow mustard
1 tsp hot sauce (Tabasco® or Crystal® Hot Sauce)
2 TBSP ketchup
2 TBSP olive oil
1 TBSP red wine vinegar
1 tsp garlic salt
1 TBSP Worcestershire sauce
1 medium lemon; juiced
3 tsp salt (to taste)

paprika; for garnish

Instructions:

Slice bell peppers. Reserve. Peel and shred onions, using the large holes on a grater. You want the shredded onion soft and wet from shredding. Reserve. Mince any big pieces of onion left over. Shred cabbage or cut to medium fine slices no longer than 4". Reserve.

Dressing: Put mayonnaise and mustard in a bowl large enough to hold complete mixture of all ingredients. Beat mayonnaise and mustard until well combined. Continue beating the mixture during all of the following steps. Add the olive oil slowly to the mix. Beat until mixture has returned to the thickness of original mayonnaise. Add hot sauce. Add ketchup. Add the garlic salt and 2 teaspoons of the salt. Add wine vinegar (this will thin the sauce down). Beat this thoroughly. Add the lemon juice. Stop beating and taste for salt and pepper. Add these to your taste.

Place shredded cabbage, peppers, and onions in a large salad bowl. Pour dressing over and toss well. Cover and refrigerate for about an hour before serving.

Plating:

Use a small dessert bowl. Remove coleslaw from refrigerator just before serving and toss again, rewetting all parts of the slaw. Place a generous amount of slaw in each dessert bowl. Spoon on some extra dressing. Dust the dressed slaw with a pinch of paprika for garnish. Serve on the side of the entrée.

Heartfelt L-C Cornbread

We borrow a page from our friends the Cajuns in the way they make their cornbread for this heartfelt Low Country treat, by putting a pan of water right on the bottom of the oven (not the bottom rack – put it on the floor of the oven) to moisten the hot air in the oven while we bake the bread. This is a low rising, hearty cornbread which stands up well with the entrée.

Ingredients:

2-½ TBSP melted fat; half Crisco®/half butter; but rendered bacon fat is a better choice

Dry Ingredients:
¾ cup whole-kernel stone ground cornmeal
¼ cup wheat flour
1 tsp salt
2 tsp baking powder
¼ tsp baking soda
2 TBSP sugar

Wet Ingredients:
1 egg
¾ to 1 cup buttermilk

Instructions:

Pre-heat oven to 375°. Place an extra skillet or metal baking pan half-filled with water on bottom of oven. This will keep the oven air moist while it is baking the cornbread.

Melt 1 tablespoon of Crisco® and 1- ½ tablespoons of butter in a 9" cast iron skillet or heavy 9" by 9" baking pan over medium-low heat on the stove to get grease for cornbread and to season the pan. Turn off heat and keep pan warm on stove. If you have bacon fat, use it in place of the Crisco® and butter mixture. It will be more authentic.

Thoroughly mix the dry ingredients together in a bowl.

Mix in the egg. Then slowly mix in the buttermilk until you make a goopy, sloppy mix. Pour the slop into the slightly warm skillet and fat. Don't stir this into the grease. Just let the grease form a barrier between the slop and the pan.

Bake for 15 minutes, until a toothpick or metal knife stuck in the center comes out clean.

Allow at least 10 minutes cooling before cutting the cornbread. If you used a skillet, cut the cornbread into 8 equal wedges. If you use a square pan, cut the cornbread into nine 3" by 3" pieces.

Plating:

Use a flat butter dish. Place one wedge of cornbread onto butter dish. If you used a square pan, serve the 8 outer pieces to assure everyone of getting some crust on their slices. It is okay to serve the cornbread at room temperature if it cools off. Serve on the side of the entrée.

Everyone's Favorite Fresh Fruit Tart

The original recipe for this called for a rice pudding crust made of 3 cups of cooked rice, ¼ cup of sugar and 2 beaten eggs thoroughly mixed, pressed into the tart pan and baked for 15 minutes. I thought it was great being a big Greek rice pudding fan, but my guests thought it too strange for general consumption, so I substituted a Keebler crust to make an elfin Gullah.

Ingredients:

Crust:
1 Keebler Ready Crust® Graham
1 egg yolk beaten

Filling:
1 (8-ounce) package cream cheese, softened
¼ cup sour cream
¼ cup 10X powdered sugar
1 tsp vanilla extract

Topping:
½ cup apricot preserves (substitute: peach preserves)
3 cups fresh fruit (sliced strawberries, raspberries, blueberries, sliced kiwi fruit, and red or green seedless grape halves)
10X powdered sugar; for dusting tart

Instructions:

Crust:
Preheat oven to 350°. Brush bottom and sides of crust with 1 egg yolk. Place on baking sheet. Bake at 350°F for 5 minutes. Cool to room temperature.

Filling: After you remove the crust from the oven and start it cooling, beat the cream cheese and sour cream in medium bowl until light and fluffy. Add sugar and vanilla; beat until well blended. When the crust is room temperature, spread the filling over the crust.

Topping: Heat the apricot preserves with 1 tablespoon of water in a small saucepan over low heat. Strain into a cup squeezing as much liquid as possible through the strainer into the cup. This is your glaze. Discard the remaining pulp from the apricot. Cool the glaze for a couple of minutes. While the glaze is cooling, slice the strawberries and kiwi fruit and cut the seedless grapes in half. Reserve. When the glaze is not hot (it can be a little warm), brush half of the glaze over the filling. Arrange the fruit attractively over crust, starting at the outer edge with the sliced strawberries and kiwi fruit. Alternate one slice of each and continue until you have gone around the pie completely. Working your way in toward center of the tart. Try to make a complete ring of one kind of fruit before switching the next fruit. After making a ring of strawberries and kiwi, use the blueberries, then the grapes, then raspberries and finally return to the strawberries and kiwi, etc. until you reach the center of the tart.
Brush remaining glaze evenly over fruit. Refrigerate for at least 1 hour before serving.

Plating:

Use a large flat dessert dish or flat salad plate. Cut the tart into 8 generous slices. Carefully remove the first slice. That is never easy. Place each piece slightly off-center on the dish. Dust the tart with 10X powdered sugar. Garnish the plate with 2 or 3 benne wafers. Serve.

Low Country Benne Wafers

Benne Wafers have been a Low Country favorite for hundreds of years. Benne is sesame in the West African Bantu language. These tiny Gullah cookies can be found all over the South Carolina coastal area, especially in Charleston. West African slaves introduced sesame seeds to America, and the name, "benne," stuck. I suspect these cookies may well find their way into your next cookie exchange, so the recipe below will yield 2 to 2-½ dozen wafers for tonight's dinner. Multiply the amounts of ingredients, as needed, for bigger batches.

Ingredients:

¼ cup butter; softened
½ cup brown sugar
1 medium/large egg
½ cup flour
¼ cup sesame (benne) seeds; toasted
1/3 teaspoon vanilla
1/8 teaspoon baking powder

Instructions:

Preheat oven to 325°.

Toast sesame seeds in a dry wide pan on medium-high heat for just a minute or two. Watch them carefully and shake them around the pan to keep from burning. When they brown slightly and become fragrant they are toasted. Pour them out of the pan onto a plate.

Cream softened butter and sugar together in a large bowl.

Mix in other ingredients in the order given. Add egg and mix. Add flour and mix. Add toasted sesame seeds and mix. Add vanilla and mix. Add baking powder and mix.

Drop with a teaspoon onto a well-greased cookie pan, far enough apart to allow spreading while baking. You can use a non-stick pan or parchment paper in place of greasing the pan.

Bake in a 325° F oven for 7-10 minutes.

Plating:

Plate 2 to 3 cookies on each dessert plate on the side of the fruit tart.

Mexican Gourmet

Mexican Gourmet

I studied Spanish for five years in Junior High and High School. I was known as "Juan Peredeth" (slight Castilian accent). For some reason we stayed on verb conjugation for all of those years and never got to conversational Spanish. Forty-five years later I asked for the check in a Colombian restaurant near my home in South Florida and found out I had asked the waitress for a dance. That would have been fine with me since I love the Salsa, Merengue, Mambo and Cha Cha Cha, but I found out the owner wanted to be paid in cash. My charm offensive was ended abruptly!

During my college years, I worked as a waiter in New York City in a wonderful French restaurant, Le Orangerie (The Orange Grove). The waiters and bus boys were fed before every shift, but we never ate from the menu, nothing French was allowed. One of the sous chefs would always be assigned to prepare a "help meal." The head chef was Swiss. Nearly all of the sous were Puerto Rican. It was at the Le Orangerie where I developed my great affection for "Arroz con Pollo" (chicken and rice). While it is not on tonight's menu, don't shy away from this peasant meal when you see it on a restaurant menu. It is economical, and it usually is an explosion of great flavors in one simple dish.

I expect you will not have tasted most of the recommendations for this meal (comida), except for the fast, easy snacks I have suggested to go with your cocktails. While the meal is based in Mexican tradition, there are some fusion elements present to make them somewhat familiar to your palate. I also have been careful to stay away from heat as much as possible in the various dishes to please most guest palates. Many of my friends seem to have very limited taste for capsaicin and the sparkle that the heat component of the pepper brings to your eyes, tongue, throat, and sinus cavity. Where hot peppers are included be careful to trim away the seeds, stems and rib core. Those parts hold the most heat. Roasting (pan or oven) and removal of the skin further reduces the heat and raises the flavorful nature of the chili. Working with just the meat of the chili reduces the heat to a minimum impact. Remember, drink milk or eat a wad of peanut butter if you are ever overwhelmed by the heat of a pepper. The fat cuts the burn. I guess chocolate would work too. I'll have to try that one.

You're going to love the dessert. The creamy sweet goodness highlighted by the flavoring of the toasted pine nuts will linger on your mind the morning after the big dinner. Get some good Mexican beer and wine. The Mexican wine industry got its start in the 1500s thanks to Cortez, so you should be able to find a good vintage if you try. Remember the Kahlua or Tia Maria for after dinner. Maybe a drop or two in your coffee. Enjoy!

Mexican Gourmet

4:30 p.m. **Cocktails**

Wine, Beer, Mixed Drinks

Snacks

Guacamole with Breadsticks
Salsa with White Corn Tortilla Chips

5:30 p.m. **Dinner**

Beverages   Water, Wine, Beer and Soda

Appetizer   Mexican Shrimp Cocktail

Soup   Tortilla Soup with Sausage

Salad   Ensalada Fresca con Queso Frito

Entree   Raspberry-Chipolte Pork Cutlets

Accompanied by

Stuffed Poblano Chiles with Walnut Sauce
White Rice Pilaf with Corn and Roasted Chiles

Dessert   Crema de Pino Encarcelada (Pine Nut Cream)
Café and Tea
Liqueur - Kahlua

Mexican Gourmet Shopping Lists

Shopper 1

2 lbs large shrimp; 16 to 24 count, deveined, cooked, peeled (frozen are okay)
1 large bag of white corn tortilla chips
1 medium bag blue corn tortilla chips
7 well-ripened tomato
1 cup grape tomatoes
6 cups spring mix salad (mesclun)
1 head romaine lettuce
2 lemons
3 fresh limes
1 bottle ranch dressing
2 cups long grain rice
2 cups thawed, frozen-corn (or kernels cut and removed from 3 cobs of corn)
1 lb cream cheese
1 pint sour cream
2 quarts whole milk

Shopper 2

4 full heads garlic cloves
4 large white onion
1 medium red onion
1 bunch scallions
3 bunches fresh cilantro
8 sprigs of mint
1 bunch fresh Italian parsley
3 small green or other cooking apples
5 ripe, firm peaches
3 small ripe plantains
1 pomegranate
3 avocados, ripe and Hass preferred
4 chipotles chilies, canned in adobo spice
3 jalapeno chiles
10 large poblano chiles
2 large jars of medium salsa

Shopper 3

4 links Italian sweet sausage
1 French baguette
8 tortillas, either corn or flour
1 package crispy breadsticks
24 ladyfingers, soft spongy kind
3 quarts chicken broth or stock
16 ounces tomato/clam juice cocktail (Mott's Clamato or 8 oz tomato juice and 8 oz clam juice)
½ cup shredded Monterey Jack cheese
1 lb block of Monterey Jack cheese
1 pint sour cream
8 oz (2 cups) pine nuts
3 cups toasted walnuts
6 TBSP preserved citron
8 TBSP golden raisins
2 cups seedless raspberry spreadable fruit jam (no sugar added)
1 quart extra virgin olive oil

Shopper 4 (Host)

4 lbs pork tenderloin, cut to 1-½ " slices; pounded out to ¾ " cutlets
Salt
3 cups granulated sugar
¼ cup ketchup
1 teaspoon hot pepper sauce
¼ cup prepared horseradish
1 tsp cumin
½ tsp dried chili pepper
3 TBSP Adobo seasoning
3 tsp ground cinnamon
1 cinnamon stick
2 TBSP raspberry vinegar
1 cup dry sherry
½ cup brandy or rum
2-½ TBSP cornstarch
1 cup 10X powdered sugar
3 eggs
1 quart canola oil

Preparation Schedule – Mexican Gourmet

Teams
1/
2/
3/
4/Hosts

4:00 pm   **1, 2, & 3**- Arrive at **4**'s kitchen. Put on chef's aprons. Unpack and stack all groceries in a central location. Leave all cheeses at room temperature. Put meat, eggs and sour cream in refrigerator. If shrimp are frozen, place in a bowl of cool water to thaw. Have a cocktail.

4:15 pm   **1**- Serve salsa in a bowl. Add a spoon for scooping salsa onto chips. Serve with white corn tortilla chips on the side.
2- Start Guacamole recipe and serve when ready.
3- Start Mexican Shrimp Cocktail recipe. Place marinating shrimp in refrigerator by 4:45 pm. or earlier. Serve at 5:30 pm.
4- Put raisins in 1 cup of dry sherry to soften. Set table and continue serving drinks. Preheat oven to 350°. Oven toast 3 cups of walnuts for Chile en Nogada and Pork Cutlet recipes. Watch carefully to avoid burning. Chop nuts, coarsely. Divide nuts into 2-cup and 1-cup portions.

4:30 pm   **1, 2, 3 & 4**- Eat salsa and guacamole as they are ready, and drink cocktails while you merrily work on your other food preparations.
1- Start Tortilla Soup recipe. Serve at 6 pm.
2- Prepare dressing for salad. Chop onion and cilantro for salad.
4- Start Chiles en Nogada recipe. Use sherry from softening raisins for Nogada Sauce preparations. Complete sauce and chiles recipes up to plating. Should be complete and ready for plating by 7 pm.

5:15 pm   **3**- Plate Mexican Shrimp Cocktail. Serve at 5:30 pm.
2- Help **3** plate, garnish and serve shrimp cocktail.

5:30 pm.   **Eat Shrimp Cocktail in Dining Room**
At 5:45 everyone helps clear dishes to the kitchen.

5:45 pm.   **1**- Plate Tortilla Soup, garnish and serve.
2- Continue recipe for salad and plate. Fry cheese and dress salad after soup course is complete.
3- Start Raspberry-Chipotle Pork Cutlets recipe. Continue until ready for plating. Serve at 7:30 pm.

6:00 pm   **Eat Soup in Dining Room**
At 6:15 everyone helps clear soup dishes to the kitchen.

6:15 pm   **1-** Start Rice Pilaf recipe. Continue until ready for plating.
2- Fry cheese for salad. Complete salad plating. Dress and serve.

6:30 pm   **Eat Salad in Dining Room**
At 6:45 everyone helps clear salad dishes to the kitchen.

6:45 pm   **2-** Start Crema de Pino recipe. Complete just prior to entrée service. Leave custard in bowls on counter to cool to room temperature. Add garnishes after entrée course is complete.

7:00 pm   **4-** Warm dinner plates.

7:15 pm   **1-** Plate rice pilaf. Work with **3 and 4** in plating entrée.
3- Plate pork cutlets with **1 and 4.**
4- Plate Chiles en Nogada. Work with **1 and 3.**

7:30 pm   **Eat Entrée in Dining Room**
At 8:00 everyone helps clear dishes to the kitchen.

8:00 pm   **4-** Set up coffee cups, dessert plates, spoons and forks for service.

8:15 pm   **1-** Work with **4** on coffee and tea service.
2- Final plating of dessert. Add pine nuts and cinnamon.
3- Work with **2** on plating dessert. Dust with powdered sugar. Add mint sprig.
4- Brew coffee and tea.

8:30 pm   **Eat Dessert and Have Coffee in Dining Room**

                 Relax! Job Well Done!

Guacamole

This is a chunky sauce made primarily of avocado with various additions depending on the region of Mexico where the guacamole is made. The avocado is a fruit (pear family) and has the highest fat content of any fruit. The Hass avocado is generally recognized as the best for making guacamole. While there are many variations, traditional Mexican guacamole has only a few ingredients, the avocado, onions, chiles, fresh tomatoes, cilantro and salt. Lime juice helps preserve the color of the guacamole for a short period of time but it can overwhelm the balance of the other flavors, so we won't be using it here. Just make your guacamole and eat it right away, and jazz it up with surprise ingredients if you are creative. Guacamole dates back to the Aztecs and their ingredients were the same as those used today.

Ingredients:

2 avocados; ripe, Hass preferred
6 TBSP onion; finely chopped
2 tsp jalapeno chile; chopped and seeded
3 tsp chopped cilantro; chop finely
4 TBSP well-ripened tomato; seeded and chopped (discard juice and seeds)
salt to taste
breadsticks
white corn tortilla chips

Instructions:

Chop onions and cilantro. Remove seeds, stems and ribs from jalapenos and chop. Combine about (don't worry about being exact) half of the chopped onions, chopped jalapeno and cilantro with 1 teaspoon of salt in a food processor. Reserve the other half of the ingredients to be added later. Process these ingredients into a spice paste. This releases the juices of these ingredients. If you don't have a food processor, mash them together in a bowl with a wooden spoon.

There is a single large seed in the center of the avocado. Cut both avocados in half by running the knife completely around the seed and twisting the halves apart. The seed will remain in one of the halves. Place the half with the seed on the counter or a cutting board with the seed up. Keep your hand away. Using a sharp, heavy knife gently tap the seed with the sharp edge of the knife blade. The blade will sink slightly into the seed. Pick up the seed and avocado half with the knife still in the seed, and gently twist the avocado with your other hand. The seed should release from the avocado and remain stuck on the knife blade. Discard the seed. Remove the seed from the second avocado. Discard the seed. Use a tablespoon to separate the avocado meat from the skin. It should slide out of the skin in one piece with a single scoop of the spoon. Repeat with all avocado halves and discard the skins.

Slice all of the avocado halves lengthwise in about ¼ inch strips, and then across, forming a grid of small chunks. Place in a large bowl. Add the spice paste. Fold to combine thoroughly. Add the chopped tomato and other half of the reserved chopped onions and cilantro, folding gently, taking care not to mash the guacamole. Leave it a bit chunky. Taste and add more salt and some of the remaining jalapenos to taste. Transfer the finished guacamole into a serving bowl. Serve family style with breadsticks and white corn tortillas chips. Put a spoon in the guacamole so it can be spooned onto the chips.

Cóctel de Gambas (Mexican Shrimp Cocktail)

You may not find this recipe served in a Mexican restaurant, but it is the product of cunning and experimentation. It will make your tongue dance a happy step.

Ingredients:

2 lbs large cooked frozen shrimp; 16 to 24 count, peeled (tails left on arc okay) and deveined (thaw in refrigerator overnight or more quickly in a bowl of cool water on the counter)
1 TBSP crushed garlic and minced
½ cup finely chopped red onion
¼ cup fresh cilantro; chopped well
2 cups tomato/clam juice cocktail (substitute 1 cup each clam and tomato juices)
¼ cup ketchup
3 fresh limes; juiced
1 tsp hot pepper sauce
¼ cup prepared horseradish
salt to taste

cumin for dusting avocado
1 ripe avocado; peeled, pitted and chopped, not mashed
1 head romaine lettuce.
2 lemons; sliced in quarters

Instructions:

Mince garlic. Chop onion and cilantro.

Place the thawed, cooked shrimp in a large bowl.

In a separate bowl, combine garlic, red onion, cilantro and ½ teaspoon of salt. Mash these herbs and spices together slightly with a wooden spoon to release some of their juices. Mix in tomato/clam juice cocktail, ketchup, lime juice, hot pepper sauce, and horseradish. Season with additional salt, to taste. Stir to thoroughly combine. Pour over shrimp, toss shrimp, cover, and marinate in refrigerator for 30 minutes or more if time allows.

When the shrimp are marinated and you are about ready to plate and serve. Chop the avocado.

Plating:

Place the leafy half of one piece of romaine lettuce in a large soup bowl. If you have a large stemmed cocktail glass, the presentation will be improved, but use a much smaller piece of the lettuce so it does not protrude too far out of the glass. Place 4 to 6 marinated large shrimp into each bowl/glass. Ladle a small amount of the marinade onto the shrimp. Use a slotted spoon or one with holes so you don't drown the shrimp, but make sure you get some of the small chunky pieces of the marinade on the shrimp. Top with one tablespoon of chopped avocado. Garnish with a slice of lemon on the side. Dust entire dish with a small pinch of cumin. Serve.

Sopa de Tortilla con Salchicha (Tortilla Soup with Sausage)

The focus in this dish is the fried tortillas and the flavoring offered by the chili pepper and cilantro. You can use corn or flour tortillas based on your taste. The Italian sausage adds a bit of special flavor to the dish that will be familiar to most of the dinner party guests.

Ingredients:

4 links Italian sweet sausage; skinned
8 tortillas cut into ¾" strips and 2" lengths; either corn or flour tortillas are okay
8 cups of chicken broth or stock
2 tomatoes; seeded and chopped finely
2 cloves of garlic; smashed and minced
¼ onion; chopped finely
1 cilantro sprig; whole
½ tsp dried chili pepper
3 TBSP extra virgin olive oil
salt; to taste

¼ cup cilantro; chopped coarsely
½ cup of shredded Monterey Jack cheese
1 pint sour cream

Instructions:

Use a heavy bottom sauce pan big enough to hold all of the soup ingredients (5 quarts or larger). Skin and fry the meat from the sausages over medium high heat until lightly browned. While sausage browns chop tortillas, tomatoes, garlic and onions.

Remove meat to a paper towel to drain grease from the sausage. Drain most of the liquid fat from the sauce pan. Leave about 2 tablespoons of the liquid fat and all of the caramelized sausage bits stuck to the bottom of the pan. Add about 3 tablespoons of extra virgin olive oil and heat.

Add one teaspoon of dried ancho chili pepper to hot oil and fry the tortillas in the oil and fat mixture until golden brown. Remove the tortillas to a paper towel to drain. Drain off excess grease from the pan, but preserve in the pan a coating of grease and any bits of sausage and tortilla still clinging to the pan bottom or sides. Add the chopped onion and minced garlic to the pan. Continue to fry for 5 minutes while stirring. Add tomatoes and smash down the tomatoes to liquefy. Cook 5 more minutes while continuing to smash down tomatoes. Add the chicken broth, fried tortillas, cooked sausage, and the sprig of cilantro. Boil for 10 minutes and serve hot. Add salt to taste (the chicken broth may be salty enough for you). While soup boils shred Monterey Jack cheese and chop cilantro.

Plating:

Ladle the soup into individual bowls. Be sure to dig down into the pot to scoop up some sausage and tortillas into each bowl. Sprinkle on Monterey Jack cheese. Add a garnish of chopped cilantro overall. When all of the soup bowls have been filled and garnished, place a dollop of sour cream in the center of the bowl and serve immediately so the sour cream remains somewhat intact in the center of the presentation.

Ensalada Fresca con Queso Frito (Fresh Salad with Fried Cheese)

This meatless fresh salad has a delightful twist, fried Monterey Jack cheese.

Queso Frito:

1 lb block of Monterey Jack cheese
½ cup canola oil

Queso Frito Instructions:

See salad preparation instructions, below for instructions on when to fry the cheese.

Heat oil in frying pan over medium-high heat.

Slice cheese into 2" to 3" strips ½" x ½". Place on plate slightly separated. Perform the next steps when you are ready to plate and serve the salad.

Place cheese strips in freezer for one minute. Remove from freezer and place strips in heated oil for 10 seconds. Flip to other side for 10 more seconds. Turn off heat and immediately place fried cheese strips on a paper towel for 30 seconds. Don't leave them on the towel too long or the cheese won't be runny. Place cheese strips on salad according to plating instructions.

Salad Ingredients:

6 cups spring mix salad (mesclun)
¼ cup scallion; chopped
1 cup fresh cilantro; stemmed and chopped (half for salad mix; half for garnish)
¾ cup crushed blue corn tortilla chips (regular tortilla chips will also work)

1 cup grape tomatoes

½ cup sour cream
1 cup medium salsa (half for dressing; half for topping)
1 cup ranch dressing

Salad Preparation and Plating:

Blend ½ cup of salsa with ½ cup sour cream and 1 cup ranch dressing. Maintain at room temperature while you assemble salad and fry the cheese.

Chop scallion and cilantro. Crush corn chips.

Toss spring mix, cilantro, crushed tortilla chips and scallion in a bowl. Divide equally among salad plates. Top each plate with grape tomatoes.

Fry cheese (see directions above). When the fried cheese has drained on the paper towel for about 30 seconds, drizzle salad dressing over all salads. Top each salad with fried cheese and 1 more tablespoon of salsa. Garnish with a sprinkle of chopped cilantro over all.

Serve immediately.

Raspberry-Chipotle Pork Cutlets

Adobo Seasoning Paste/Rub:
8 cloves garlic; smashed
3 TBSP Adobo seasoning
1-½ tsp salt
Grind all ingredients together in a mortar and pestle or food processor to make into a paste.

Cutlets:
4 lbs pork tenderloin, cut into 1-½" slices and pounded out to ¾" thick cutlets
4 TBSP olive oil, or more as needed for sautéing

Raspberry Sauce:
2 cups seedless raspberry spreadable fruit jam (no sugar added)
6 cloves garlic, chopped
2 cups loosely packed cilantro leaves stripped from stems
4 chipotles chilies, canned or jarred in adobo
2 TBSP raspberry vinegar

Garnish:
1 cup toasted walnuts; chopped coarsely

Instructions:
Heat oven to 350°. Prepare adobo seasoning paste.

Ask butcher to prepare the tenderloin by trimming any visible fat and removing the silvery membrane, or do it yourself with a small, sharp knife. Cut tenderloin into slices about 1-½" thick. Pound slices between 2 sheets of plastic wrap, into cutlets about half the original thickness. Rub both sides of each cutlet with adobo paste, recover with plastic wrap and set aside on counter for 30 minutes to marinate.

While pork is marinating, toast shelled walnuts in oven for 5 to 8 minutes until skin is flaking off. Toast enough walnuts for this recipe and Chiles en Nogada recipe. Do not burn. When walnuts are slightly cooled, coarsely chop all nuts and set aside in 1-cup and 2-cup portions.

Prepare sauce. Pull stems and seeds from chipotle chilies to reduce heat of sauce. Puree all the sauce ingredients in a food processor or blender.

Heat oil in 2 large skillets over medium-high heat. Sauté cutlets about 3 minutes on each side or until almost done. Pour sauce over cutlets, cover, and simmer another 3 minutes, or until the cutlets are cooked through and sauce is hot and bubbly.

Plating:
Use the largest dinner plates you have. Spoon 2 tablespoons of raspberry sauce onto 1/3 of the plate. Place one or two cutlets, depending upon appetite, on plate over the sauce. If two, lay the second cutlet about one-third over the first. Before transferring the cutlets to the plate allow the excess sauce to drip off each cutlet slightly back into the pan. You will add a bit more sauce to each plate when the chiles and rice pilaf have been added to the plate. Plate the rice pilaf. Plate the Chile en Nogada. Try to keep the chile and rice pilaf separate on the plate. Add 2 tablespoons of walnut sauce over the chile. Add a small amount of additional raspberry sauce over one edge moving toward the center of the cutlet(s). Sprinkle chopped, toasted walnuts as a garnish on cutlet(s) and sides of plate next to cutlet(s).

Chiles en Nogada (Stuffed Poblano Chiles with Walnut Sauce)

This dish adds excitement to any Mexican entrée. It is traditionally served in season in the late summer months when walnuts and pomegranates are being harvested. The poblano chile is most often used in chile relleno and is on most Mexican restaurant menus. In this recipe it has a sautéed fruit filling, a perfect compliment for the pork cutlet.

The poblano varies in heat, sometimes up to very intense. In this recipe you will be stripping the chile of its stem, seeds, ribs and skin. You will soak them for a short period of time in salt water to lessen the heat and then proceed with the roasting and peeling. When shopping for fresh poblanos, you may find them labeled pasilla. This is a misnomer, but they are routinely mislabeled that way.

Ingredients:

10 large poblano chiles (2 will be used in the rice pilaf recipe)
canola oil for frying

4 medium ripe tomatoes (About 2 pounds)
3 small green or other cooking apples; peeled and cut into ½" cubes
5 ripe, firm peaches; peeled or ½ cup dried, diced
3 small ripe plantains; skin removed, diced
6 TBSP preserved citron; diced
8 TBSP golden raisins; softened in 1 cup dry sherry

2 garlic cloves; smashed and minced
2 medium onions; finely diced
1 tsp cinnamon

1 pomegranate; use seeds for garnish
50 (approx) Italian parsley leaves stripped from stems

Nogada - Walnut Sauce:

2 cups toasted walnuts; ground finely
1 lb cream cheese, softened
1 cup whole milk for sauce
2 cups whole milk for soaking French baguette
2 slices of French baguette, each slice 3" long and diced
2/3 cup dried sherry (use sherry from softening raisins)
¼ tsp cinnamon
1 TBSP sugar
pinch of salt

Prepare the walnut sauce after poblanos are soaking in salt water. Soak the slices of French baguette in 2 cups of whole milk for 15 minutes. While bread soaks, grind 2 cups of toasted walnuts in a food processor or blender until they are a fine powder. Squeeze out liquid from bread, discard the soaking liquid and rough chop the bread. Add the chopped bread, cream cheese, 1 cup milk, sherry (from soaking raisins, save the raisins for fruit filling), cinnamon, sugar and salt. Process or blend until sauce is smooth. Maintain at room temperature while preparing stuffed poblano.

                    235

Fruit Filling and Poblano Chiles Preparation:

Put poblano chiles into a large bowl with a teaspoon of salt. Fill bowl with water, covering the chiles. Put a plate on top if need be to "sink" the chiles and hold them under water. Prepare Nogada Sauce (above).

Dice and peel fresh fruit. Dice dried fruit.

Wash and thoroughly dry the tomatoes. Heat a heavy cast-iron skillet or griddle over high heat until a drop of water sizzles on contact. Dry pan-roast the tomatoes, turning several times, until blistered on all sides. Slight blackening of the skin is to be expected. Let tomatoes cool until just cool enough to handle. Peel the tomatoes, remove the seeds and chop finely. Set aside.

After at least 15 minutes (more is better), remove the poblano chiles from the salt water soak and thoroughly dry. Make one small lengthwise slit (1 to 1-½" long) in each chile. Pour oil into large heavy skillet to a depth of about ½" and heat over high heat until very hot but not quite smoking. Fry the chiles, 4 at a time, turning once or twice, until they puff up and take on an olive-beige color. Remove from pan to a paper towel for excess oil draining and repeat until all chiles are done. Discard oil. Allow chilies to cool slightly, and then carefully peel chiles under cold running water. Using a small spoon, very gently pull out seeds and as much of the ribs as possible through the slit in each chile. Avoid tearing the flesh. If less heat is required from the chile, carefully remove the stem. Do this gently because you want the chile to be intact for stuffing and baking. Set aside.

Pre-heat oven to 350°.

In large skillet, heat 1 cup of fresh canola oil over medium heat until very hot. Add the diced onion and smashed garlic and sauté for 3 minutes. Add the peeled tomatoes, fresh fruit, soaked raisins and dried fruit. Stir and sauté for 3 more minutes. Add the cinnamon and cook 2 more minutes. Stir frequently. Season with salt, and pepper to taste. Carefully fill the mixture into the chiles through the slit in each. Bake on greased baking sheet or shallow pan for 5 minutes at 350°. While the stuffed chile is baking, score and split open the pomegranate in a bowl of water. Loosen the seeds. The seeds will drop to the bottom of the bow of water while the pith and skin will float to the top of the bowl.

Plating:

Use a spatula to carefully place one stuffed chile on the plate with the slit side down. Dress the top of the chile with the nogada sauce and sprinkle with pomegranate seeds and a few leaves of Italian parsley. Chiles should be served warm, but can be at room temperature.

White Rice Pilaf with Corn and Roasted Chiles

For this recipe you will use a small amount of the roasted poblano chiles prepared for the other side dish, Chiles en Nogada. The chiles in this case are more for the color than the flavor since they will pale against the backdrop flavor of the other side dish.

Ingredients:

3 TBSP vegetable oil
2 cups long or medium-grain rice
1 large white onion; finely diced
3-½ cups chicken broth or stock
salt (1 tsp if using salted broth or 2 tsp if unsalted broth)
2 large fresh poblano chiles; roasted, peeled, seeded and sliced into short thin strips
2 cups thawed, frozen-corn (or kernels cut and removed from 3 cobs of corn)
parsley springs for garnish

Instructions:

Start the rice about 40 minutes before you want serve.

Combine the oil, rice, and onion in a saucepan over medium heat. Stir frequently for about 7 minutes until the onion is translucent but not browned. Meanwhile, add the salt to the broth and bring to a simmer.

Get two roasted chiles from Chiles En Nogada prep work. Peel, seed and slice into short strips.

Add the broth to the rice mixture along with the sliced, roasted chiles and corn, stir well, scrape down the side of the pan, cover and simmer over medium-low heat for 15 minutes.

When the rice has cooked 15 minutes, let it stand off the fire, covered for 5 to 10 minutes until the grains are tender but not flowered open. Fluff the rice.

Plating:

Plate with entrée and garnish with parsley. See plating instructions with pork cutlets.

Crema de Pino Encarcelada (Pine Nut Cream Custard)

A dessert of Spanish origin traditionally uses pine nuts but pecans can be substituted as well. The egg yolks help thicken the mixture. For best flavor the dessert should be served at room temperature. Any leftovers should be refrigerated.

Ingredients:
4 cups whole milk
4" piece of cinnamon stick; roughly broken up into a few large pieces
1 cup granulated sugar (¼ cup to grind with pine nuts, ¾ cup to cook in custard)
2-½ TBSP cornstarch
8 oz pine nuts; toasted (reserve ¼ cup of toasted nuts for garnish)
3 egg yolks; well beaten
½ cup brandy or rum
24 ladyfingers; soft spongy kind, roughly broken up
10X powdered sugar
8 sprigs of mint (substitute dried mint)
ground cinnamon for garnish

Instructions:
Bring milk up to the boiling point in a saucepan, but do not scald. While milk heats up, pan toast pine nuts in a dry pan for a few minutes. When the nuts begin to brown, pour them out of the pan onto a plate. Allow the nuts to cool. Set ¼ cup of nuts aside for plate garnish. When cool, finely grind the rest of the nuts with ¼ cup of sugar in a food processor.

Add the cinnamon stick pieces to nearly boiled milk, and stir in ¾ cup of sugar. Lower the flame to medium and stir until the sugar is melted. Stir ¼ cup of the warmed milk into the cornstarch and work to a smooth paste. Stir this into the milk and sugar mixture and continue cooking, stirring all the time, until it thickens slightly. Stir the ground pine nut and sugar mixture into the boiling milk mixture. Cook until it has reduced and thickened - about 20 minutes. Stir frequently. Fish out the cinnamon stick pieces and discard.

While cooking the milk mixture, beat the egg yolks. After you fish out the cinnamon sticks, slowly add about 1 cup of the hot mixture to the egg yolks as you beat them well. Pour the egg mixture slowly into the saucepan while stirring rapidly and continue to cook, stirring and scraping the bottom of the pan constantly, until the mixture thickens. It should coat the back of a wooden spoon thickly. Stir in about two-thirds of the brandy. Keep stirring over heat for one more minute and remove from heat.

Set up 8 empty dessert bowls. Break up a ladyfinger and place it in the bottom of the bowl. Pour or spoon the mixture (still hot) partially up into each bowl until the first ladyfinger is covered. Break up 2 more lady fingers and place them on the first layer of cream, sprinkle these 2 lady fingers in all bowls with the rest of the brandy and cover with the remaining cream. Set aside to cool off to room temperature before serving. This dessert is best at room temperature or warm, but it is still good chilled.

Plating:
Decorate the top of each bowl with the whole nuts and a light dusting of cinnamon. Dust each bowl with 10X powdered sugar and a sprig of fresh mint or pinch of dried mint. Serve.

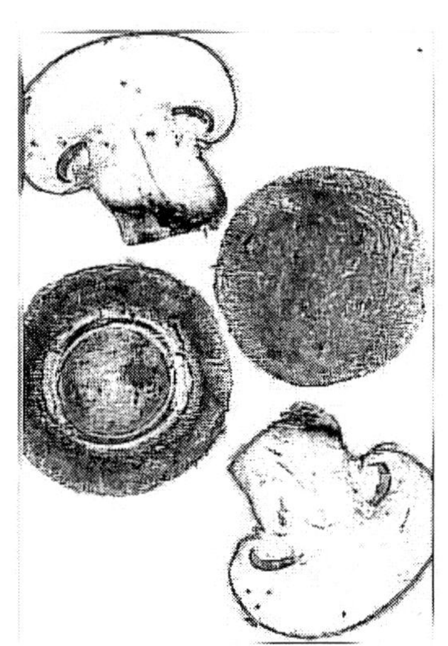

Way Down Yonder

In

New Orleans

Way Down Yonder in New Orleans

Where else could a world renowned chef get away with serving rat? Where else could a banana be the centerpiece of much sought after adult dessert? Where else do visitors from out of town rush to make a donut shop their first stop?

The answer to all of these is the same, New Orleans.

Paul Prudhomme, the intrepid inventor of turducken (a turkey stuffed with a duck stuffed with a chicken), put his blackening technique for steak and fish to its ultimate test when he applied it to nutria, the famous South American rat relative that had infested Louisiana in the 1990s. He did it as a service to the state which was looking for a way to reduce the burgeoning population of nutria. He even appeared on the Today Show to promote the idea. While Chef Paul did serve some nutria, in the long run the idea of having people eat them did not fly, but an original New Orleans restaurant creation that did fly way beyond the borders of the establishment where it was created is Bananas Foster. Nearly fifty years before Paul Prudhomme's nutria experiment, the well established Brennan family and their top chef Paul Blange discovered that by drowning a fried banana with rum and banana liqueur tossing in butter, sugar, cinnamon and vanilla ice cream (What's not to like?) you could get adults to flock in to get their potassium. Ah, Bananas Foster, a health food!

But what about a donut institution? Nearly 150 years ago a modest coffee stand was set up in the French market. Their specialty in addition to great coffee was the beignet (bin-yay!). This square fritter is sold only in threes with a winterscape covering of beautiful white powdered sugar. Three is okay; you can't eat just one, anyway. Naturally, I would say that because of my lifelong love of Greek Kourabiedes. This is the French version of the famous "choking snack" offered in many cultures. Those of us who have breathed in and choked on powdered sugar understand our deep attraction to these perilous foods. Once you have sat in the French Market location of the Café Du Monde and eaten a "plate of three" a powerful imprint is inscribed in your brain calling you back each time you return to the Big Easy. This is why so many flock right on down to the French Market anytime, day or night to get their New Orleans starter food, the Du Monde beignet!

Food is as important in New Orleans as the Mardi Gras. I might say, it is as important as music. Well truth be told, it is more important than anything else. This food adulation includes the cooking that goes on in even the most modest households, where every family has their own version of gumbo, all the way to some of the oldest continually operating restaurants in the country and on to the most current celebrity chef venues. It's all good. So let's have a dinner party with our friends and celebrate the great food of this great city. Enjoy!

Way Down Yonder in New Orleans

5:00 p.m.   Cocktails

Wine, Beer, Mixed Drinks

Snacks

Cajun Pork Fingers
Cajun Cheese Straws

6:00 p.m.   Dinner

Beverages   Water, Wine, Beer and Soda

Appetizer   Shrimp Remoulade

Soup   Creole Onion Soup

Salad   Creole Tomato and Onion Salad

Entree   New Orleans Jambalaya with Color

Accompanied by
Homemade Creole Cornbread

Dessert   Brennan's® Bananas Foster
Café and Tea
Liqueur

Way Down Yonder in New Orleans Shopping Lists

Shopper 1

3 boneless pork chops, ¾" thick
1 lb andouille smoked sausage
2 lbs boneless white chicken meat
1 bottle of Emcril's Essence®
1 bottle Worcestershire sauce
1 bottle Crystal® Hot Sauce or Tabasco®
1 bottle ketchup
1 bottle real mayonnaise
2 cups light brown sugar
3 cups medium-grain white rice
6 cups chicken stock
8 cups beef stock

Shopper 2

1 lb puff pastry
2 cups parmesan; grated
1lb butter
½ lb unsalted butter
1 jar Dijon mustard
1 bunch fresh Italian flat leaf parsley
2 bunches fresh thyme
1 bunch fresh chives
6 ripe large tomatoes, Heirloom preferred
6 bell peppers; red, yellow and green
3 TBSP fresh mint

Shopper 3

½ cup Creole mustard (substitute Dijon, ok)
8 artichoke hearts, bottled
10 bay leaves
15 large Spanish onions
1 large sweet onion, Vidalia preferred
2 full heads of garlic
2 bunches scallions
1 bunch celery
1 head of romaine lettuce
8 large bananas
3 lemons
12 oz heavy cream
½ gal premium vanilla ice cream
1 French baguette

Shopper 4 (Host)

2 lbs shrimp, 16/lb, raw, peeled and deveined
1 cup sugar
2 cups flour
1 cup yellow corn meal
½ cup extra virgin olive oil
1 cup red wine vinegar
1 pint canola oil
2 tsp brown mustard
salt
black pepper
1 TBSP cayenne pepper
1 TBSP ground white pepper
4 tsp baking powder
1/3 tsp allspice
1 tsp cinnamon
2 large eggs
1 cup whole milk
1 cup red wine
½ cup banana liqueur
½ cup dark rum
parchment paper for baking

Preparation Schedule – Way Down Yonder in New Orleans

Teams
1/
2/
3/
4/Hosts

4:00 pm	**1, 2, & 3**- Arrive at **4**'s kitchen. Put on chef's aprons. Unpack and stack groceries in a central location. Put meat in refrigerator and ice cream in freezer. Leave butter and puff pastry at room temperature. Have a cocktail.
4:15 pm	**1**- Start Creole Onion Soup recipe. Continue through to serving at 6:30 pm. **2**- Start Cajun Pork Fingers recipe. Serve when ready. **3**- Pre-heat oven to 400°. Start Cajun Cheese Straws recipe. Serve when ready. Reduce oven heat to 250° when straws are removed from oven. **4**- Set table and continue serving drinks.
4:30 pm	**4**- Prepare sauce for Shrimp Remoulade recipe and refrigerate.
5:00 pm	**1, 2, 3 & 4**- Eat Cajun Pork Fingers and Cheese Straws in the kitchen as they are ready, and drink cocktails while you merrily work on your other food preparations. **1**- Continue soup recipe. **2**- Chop onions and macerate in vinegar for Creole Tomato Onion salad recipe. Slice salad tomatoes spice and set aside at room temperature. **3**- Start New Orleans Jambalaya recipe. Serve at 7:30 pm. **4**- Cook shrimp for Shrimp Remoulade recipe and refrigerate. Wash and dry romaine lettuce for Shrimp Remoulade recipe.
5:15 pm	**1**- Pre-heat oven to 250°. Prepare Baguette slice croutons for soup recipe. When slices are golden brown remove from oven and set aside. Leave oven on at 250°.
5:45 pm	**1**- Continue soup recipe. **2**- Help **4** plate and serve Shrimp Remoulade. **3**- Continue Jambalaya recipe. **4**- Plate Shrimp Remoulade and serve with help from **2** at 6 pm.
6:00 pm.	**Eat Shrimp Remoulade Appetizer in Dining Room** **At 6:15 everyone helps clear dishes to the kitchen.**
6:15 pm.	**1**- Plate soup with croutons and garnish and serve with help from **2** at 6:30 pm. **2**- Help **1** serve soup. **3**- Continue Jambalaya recipe.

                244

4- Adjust oven temperature and pre-heat oven to 425°. Place a baking pan or heavy skillet 2/3 filled with water on the floor of the oven. Start Creole Cornbread recipe. When ready, place pan with cornbread batter on the middle shelf of the oven above, not in, the pan with water. When cornbread is baked, remove from oven and set on stovetop to cool. Turn oven off.

6:30 pm   **Eat Soup in Dining Room**
At 6:45 everyone helps clear soup dishes to the kitchen.

6:45 pm   **1-** Cut bananas according to recipe for Bananas Foster. Place the pieces in two bowls, cover with plastic wrap and leave on counter at room temperature.
2- Prepare salad vinaigrette dressing using vinegar from macerated sliced onions. Complete assembly and plating of salad. Dress and serve salads with help from **4**.
3- Continue Jambalaya recipe.
4- Warm dinner plates. Cut remaining half of baguette into 8 to 10 slices. Place on table with butter for salad course. Help **2** serve salads.

7:00 pm   **Eat Salad in Dining Room**
At 7:15 everyone helps clear salad dishes to the kitchen.

7:15 pm   **2-** Place 8 large dessert bowls in refrigerator to chill.
3- Plate Jambalaya and cornbread with **4**.
4- Cut cornbread and help **3** plate and serve Jambalaya.

7:30 pm   **Eat Entree in Dining Room**
At 8:00 everyone helps clear dishes to the kitchen.

8:00 pm   **1-** Begin the cooking part of Bananas Foster recipe, complete and serve with help from **2**. Serve when ready.
4- Set up coffee cups, teaspoons and tablespoons for dessert service. Brew coffee and tea.

8:15 pm   **2-** Remove vanilla ice cream from freezer and set on counter. Set up the chilled dessert bowls for plating the Bananas Foster. When **1** starts the flambé, divide the half-gallon of ice cream into 8 large portions and scoop into chilled bowls. Help **1** plate and serve the Bananas Foster. Serve when ready.
3- Work with **4** on coffee and tea service.
4- Serve coffee and tea when ready.

8:30 pm   **Eat Dessert and Have Coffee and Tea in Dining Room**
Relax! Job Well Done!

Cajun Pork Fingers

While this quick cooking snack carries the name Cajun, it is not firey hot. It has some spiciness to it, but you will find it to be a highly flavored starter that will leave a slight tingle on your tongue. Stay with this as it cooks so you don't overcook and toughen the pork fingers. After you remove the pork, thicken the sauce to a point where it won't drip all over the counter when you dip the fingers into it - the pork fingers that is, not your own.

Ingredients:

3 boneless pork chops, ¾" thick
1 TBSP of Cajun spice; Emeril's Essence®, Paul Prudhomme's Magic® Spice for Pork, etc.

1 cup ketchup
2 tsp brown mustard
4 TBSP light brown sugar
2 tsp vinegar; white or red
2 TBSP Worcestershire sauce
1 TBSP Crystal® Hot Sauce or Tabasco® Sauce

½ cup red wine

Instructions:

Trim any excess fat from the boneless pork chops, and cut each chop into strips (fingers), approximately 2"x ¾"x ½". Place strips in a bowl. Sprinkle with Cajun spice. Toss and mix the spice and strips well. Cover and let sit at room temperature while you make the sauce.

Mix all sauce ingredients in another bowl, except pork fingers and wine. Stir well until all ingredients are combined and you have a smooth sauce.

Start with a cool pan. Put sauce into pan. Put pork into pan while it is still cool. Start with medium-high heat. Bring pan to a slow bubbling boil. Immediately turn down the heat to low. Stir briefly, place lid on pan and continue simmering on low heat for about 10 minutes. Turn the pork fingers over once at the 5 minute mark. Place the lid back on the pan.

After the 10 minutes are up, check a piece of pork to be sure it is cooked through but still tender. Remove pork fingers to a plate, shaking most of the sauce back into the pan. Pile the fingers on the plate to retain most of the heat in the meat. Cover the pile with a piece of aluminum foil, shiny side down.

Return the heat to medium-high and add the wine to the sauce. With the lid off bring the sauce to a boil, stirring constantly. Cook the sauce down a few minutes until it thickens. It should coat a wooden spoon without dripping. This is your dipping sauce.

Plating:

Serve this as a group snack. Pour the sauce into a heat-resistant dipping bowl. Center that bowl on a large platter. Pile pork fingers on the platter around the dipping bowl. Garnish just around the outside of the dipping bowl, between the bowl and the pork fingers with a few sprigs of parsley. Stick toothpicks in the pork fingers and serve immediately.

Cajun Cheese Straws

Crispy and delicious with a Cajun parmesan filling. Get these out of the oven just as they turn a light golden brown.

Ingredients:

1 pound puff pastry; thawed
flour for dusting puff pastry

1 large egg; beaten for brushing pastry

1 cup parmesan; grated
1 stick butter; softened
1 TBSP Cajun spice; Emeril's Essence®, etc.

Directions:

Pre-heat oven to 400°.

Soften butter. Cream butter well with cheese and Cajun spice.

Beat egg well with a pinch of Cajun spice.

Line a large baking pan or cookie sheet with parchment paper.

Dust the pastry, rolling pin and rolling surface lightly with flour to prevent sticking when rolling out. Using light pressure, roll out puff pastry into a rectangle, 24" x 12". Spread the Cajun parmesan butter evenly over the dough.   Fold the dough in half crosswise into 12" x 12" with butter to the inside. Roll out again to 24" x 12". Fold again to 12" x 12" and lightly roll to fuse the layers, but do not roll out. Leave dough at folded size of 12" x 12".

The use of a very sharp knife in this next step is important so you don't fuse the edges of the pastry. That would reduce the puffing of the pastry during baking. Cut the dough into twenty-four ½" strips. Take each strip by its end and twist 2 or 3 times until evenly corkscrewed. Lay the twists of dough on the parchment paper on the cookie sheet, arranged so they are just touching each other; this will prevent untwisting. Brush top sides of all twists well with beaten egg.

Set the baking sheet on the middle rack of the preheated 400° oven and bake until the straws are crisp, puffed and a light golden brown, 12 to 15 minutes. Keep an eye on this at the 12 minute mark.

Remove from the oven, cool for 5 minutes, then cut apart with a sharp knife. Finish cooling the straws on a rack, until serving time.

Plating:

Place the Cajun cheese straws on a platter and serve next to the Cajun pork fingers.

Shrimp Remoulade

It was the summer of 1966. The brand new Fountain Café was about to open in Central Park (NYC). Somehow I had landed a waiter's job, and the owners did something unusual. They let us taste the menu food so we could honestly recommend it to customers. At 18 years of age, my experience with appetizers basically was those I helped my mother prepare about a dozen times a year when she entertained BIG! Those were canapés of meat and cheese, but rarely – no, never – seafood. Both of my parents were allergic to seafood. Oh, tuna salad on a Ritz was okay because "tuna wasn't seafood," it was just what my sister and I ate every Friday our entire childhood. Well there I was, 18 years old and about to have my first taste of shrimp remoulade. Freshly cooked chilled shrimp in a creamy delight of a sauce over an artichoke heart. I suddenly realized there was a whole other cuisine world outside of Massapequa, Long Island! At the time I had no idea that shrimp remoulade was the 100+ year old signature dish of a great New Orleans chef, Count Arnaud, but now you do. Enjoy and don't worry, the mayonnaise will protect you from the hot sauce in this recipe.

Ingredients:

2 cups heavy-duty real mayonnaise (no substitutes!)
½ cup Creole mustard; (if you can't find the real stuff it is okay to substitute ½ cup Dijon mustard, 1 tsp hot pepper sauce and 1 tsp Worcestershire)
1-½ TBSP Worcestershire sauce (in addition to any used above)
1 tsp hot pepper sauce (Tabasco® Sauce or Crystal® Hot Sauce) (in addition to any used above)
½ cup scallions; finely minced
½ cup celery; finely diced
2 TBSP garlic; smashed and minced
¼ cup parsley; finely chopped
1 TBSP lemon juice
8 artichoke hearts; sliced in quarters
salt and cracked black pepper to taste

2 lbs large shrimp; 16/lb, peeled and deveined
1 lemon; juiced (for shrimp pot)
2 bay leaves (for shrimp pot)
1 medium onion; quartered (for shrimp pot)
1 tsp salt
½ tsp ground pepper

1 head of romaine lettuce for plate garnish

Instructions:

Prepare sauce. In a large mixing bowl, combine all of the above ingredients, except shrimp, whisking well to incorporate the seasonings. Once blended, cover and place in the refrigerator, for as long as time will allow so the flavor will develop more. When you are ready to plate the shrimp, remove the sauce from the refrigerator and season to taste with salt and pepper.

Cooking the shrimp. I am recommending that you buy fresh raw shrimp and boil it yourself for this recipe since that is the best way to achieve the crunchy mouth feel with the shrimp that this dish deserves. In order to save time during the preparation of the meal, buy fresh already-peeled and deveined shrimp that are roughly 16-count to the pound. Add salt, pepper, bay leaves, cut onion and the juice of one lemon to a large pot of cold water. Bring to a boil and continue boiling for 5 minutes. Strain out the bay leaves and onion pieces and discard. Add the shrimp. When the water returns to the boil, boil shrimp for an additional 2 minutes. Then remove, drain and douse the shrimp with cold water to stop the cooking. When cool, transfer shrimp into a bowl, cover and refrigerate until ready to plate.

While shrimp chill, wash the romaine lettuce and dry very thoroughly.

Plating:

Pile four shrimp in the center of a leaf of romaine lettuce and spoon a generous serving of remoulade sauce on top of the shrimp. Serve immediately. Do not sauce the shrimp prior to service, as they will lose the firm texture you have worked so hard to achieve.

Creole Onion Soup Recipe

The Creole of this onion soup is created by making a roux and using cayenne pepper in the recipe. Classic onion soup typically would have you making your own stock and simmering the soup for much longer periods of time, but the use of prepared beef broth provides a rich background for the soup in far less time. The roux adds depth and the cayenne, piquant. It is true, the longer this soup cooks or ages the better it gets, so you might want to bulk up some of the ingredients (onions/broth) to ensure leftovers. If so, refrigerate and enjoy the next day.

Ingredients:
½ lb unsalted butter (2 sticks)
10 large Spanish onions; cut and thinly sliced into 1" - 2" length pieces
5 tsp sugar
3 TBSP garlic; smashed and minced
8 TBSP flour
6 oz. dry red wine
8 cups beef stock
5 TBSP Worcestershire sauce
8 sprigs fresh thyme
5 fresh bay leaves
½ tsp cayenne pepper
½ tsp ground white pepper
12 oz heavy cream
salt to taste
ground black pepper to taste
1 French baguette; for croutons
½ stick salted butter; for croutons
½ cup parmesan cheese; for garnish

Instructions:

Chop and thinly slice onions. Smash and mince garlic. Cut ½ baguette into thin slices (about ¼"). Let the slices sit out on the counter to stiffen a bit. Close the other half of the baguette up in the original package to serve with salad.

Melt the butter over medium heat in a heavy bottomed Dutch oven or the heaviest big pot you have. Add the sliced onions and sugar, raise the heat to high until the onions are transparent, stirring often, about 4-5 minutes. Lower the heat to medium and cook the onions, stirring occasionally, for about 15 minutes or until the onions are nicely caramelized. This is an important step because the deep brown caramelized onions will give the soup much of its rich flavor. Add the minced garlic and cook for 2 minutes.

Roux. Push the onions and garlic to the sides of the pot. Sprinkle in flour slowly 1 tablespoon at a time, stirring constantly into liquids in bottom of the pan until well incorporated and smooth, about 2 minutes. Allow this roux to gain the tan color of sandpaper and then stir the onions and garlic into the roux. Immediately begin to whisk in the wine and then the beef stock, pouring each slowly into the roux to keep the liquid in the pot smooth. Raise the heat to high and bring to a boil. Reduce the heat to a simmer, add the fresh thyme, bay leaves, Worcestershire sauce, cayenne, white Pepper, a few pinches of salt and few twists of ground black pepper. Cover the pot and simmer this for about 1-½ hours.

Croutons. While the soup is simmering prepare the croutons. Melt ½ stick salted butter in a small pan. Add ¼ cup olive oil and one clove of smashed and minced garlic to pan mix together and keep over low heat while you prepare to brush the croutons. Place the thin sliced baguette, cut earlier, in a single layer on a baking sheet. Brush the tops of the slices with the butter-oil mixture. Bake in a 250° F oven until crisp and lightly browned, about 25 to 30 minutes. Remove from oven and leave on counter at room temperature.

Just before serving the soup, fish out the bay leaves and herb sprigs if you can find them and discard. Turn the heat to low and whisk in the heavy cream, taste the soup and add salt and pepper to taste.

Plating:

Ladle the soup into heavy bowls. Place the bowls on service plates to ease of handling as you deliver to the table. Toss one or two baguette croutons onto soup browned side up. Shave or grate parmesan on top of croutons and soup. Place a sprig of thyme on the service plate and serve.

Creole Tomato and Onion Salad

This simple salad will set up your taste buds well for the lively nature of the next course – the Jambalaya!

Ingredients:

For the salad:

6 ripe large tomatoes; Heirloom preferred
1 large sweet onion; Vidalia preferred
3 TBSP fresh mint; thinly sliced
½ cup fresh chives; chopped
1 TBSP Cajun spice; Emeril's Essence®, etc. for dusting plated salad

For the Vinaigrette:

½ cup extra virgin olive oil
½ cup red wine vinegar; used for macerating sliced onion, too
4 tsp Dijon mustard
2 tsp garlic; smashed and minced

Instructions:

Keep all ingredients at room temperature.

Cut the Vidalia (hopefully) onion into thin slices and shake apart into loose rings. Place in a shallow bowl. Pour on the red wine vinegar. Add a pinch of salt. Allow to macerate at room temperature for at least 10 minutes. Toss halfway through to rewet onions.

While onions macerate, chop chives and mint.

Cut tomatoes into ¼" slices and place all slices on a large platter. Discard the small end pieces. Sprinkle tomato slices with chopped chives and mint. Allow to sit for at least 10 minutes at room temperature.

While tomatoes sit, prepare vinaigrette. If onions have macerated for at least 10 minutes, pour vinegar from macerating onions into a jar. Add oil, mustard and garlic to the jar. Cover and shake vigorously.

Plating:

Arrange alternating layers of tomatoes and onions on each salad plate. Shake vinaigrette once more just before adding to salad. Drizzle a small amount of vinaigrette onto each salad. Sprinkle with a few chopped chives and mint. Dust each plate with a pinch of Cajun spice (Emeril's Essence®, etc.). Serve immediately.

New Orleans Jambalaya with Color

This is truly a southern Louisiana dish and is the brown variety rather than a lot of the tomato based jambalayas you will see in New Orleans. This dish will come out a bit milder than some you have had in restaurants, but it will have zip.

Ingredients:

½ cup canola oil
2 tsp salt
3 cups yellow onions, chopped
3 cups bell peppers; red, yellow and green; chopped
½ tsp cayenne pepper
1 lb andouille smoked sausage; cut diagonally in ½" slices
2 lbs boneless white chicken meat; cut into 1" cubes
2 bay leaves
3 cups medium-grain white rice
6 cups chicken stock
½ tsp hot pepper sauce (Tabasco® Sauce or Crystal® Hot Sauce)
1 cup scallions; chopped
1 bunch fresh Italian flat leaf parsley
1 bunch fresh thyme

Instructions:

Chop the bell peppers and onion.

Use the heaviest bottomed, big pot that you have with a cover.

Heat the canola oil in the heavy pot over medium heat. Add all of the chopped bell peppers, chopped yellow onions, 1 teaspoon salt, and ½ teaspoon cayenne. Stirring often, brown the vegetables for about 20 minutes, or until they are caramelized and dark brown in color. Use a wooden spoon to scrape the bottom and sides of the pot to loosen any browned particles. These and all of the other brown bits created as you cook are very important to the intensity of flavor of the final dish.

While the vegetables cook, slice the sausage, and cut the chicken into cubes. Keep chicken and sausage in separate plates. Season the chicken with 1 teaspoon salt and ½ teaspoon cayenne.

When the vegetables are dark brown (caramelized), add the sausage and cook for 10 to 15 minutes. Stir often and scrape the bottom and sides of the pot to loosen those good browned bits.

After the sausage is browned, push the vegetables and sausage to the sides of the pot opening a center hole in the middle of the pot. Toss the seasoned chicken into the pot in that center hole. Toss the bay leaves into the pot on the chicken. Brown the chicken for 8 to 10 minutes. Use the wooden spoon and keep up the scraping. After the chicken browns stir it together with the sausage and vegetables in the pot.

Add the rice and turn the ingredients in the pot together. Don't overturn the ingredients because over-stirring tends to break up the rice grains. Just make sure to coat the rice with the good oils and liquids in the pot. Add the chicken stock and the hot pepper sauce, turn once or twice again to combine. Bring to a rolling boil and cover. Reduce heat to medium-low. Continue cooking over medium-low heat for 25 minutes, without stirring. Take a peek after the 25 minutes are up, if the loose liquid has been absorbed, remove the pot from the heat and let it stand, covered, for 10 minutes more. If the loose liquid has not been absorbed when you peek, recover and check again after 5 more minutes. Remove from the heat, no matter what at this point. Let it stand, covered, for 10 more minutes.

While the rice is cooking, chop fresh parsley and thyme for garnish.

Fish out the bay leaves when ready to serve (if you can find them).

Stir in the scallions onions thoroughly and evenly just before serving.

Plating:

Jambalaya rightfully belongs in a big, big bowl. This has to be the largest individual bowls you have for soup or pasta. If you do not have large individual bowls, spoon it onto a large flat plate (oh, I hope not). Keep piling it up in the center of the dish. Garnish with mix of chopped fresh Italian parsley and chopped fresh thyme on top of the mound of jambalaya.

Serve with a wedge of cornbread lying askance on the side of the jambalaya mound.

Homemade Creole Cornbread

We are a nation of cornbread eaters. This delectable item serves in this meal as a side to the beautiful jambalaya entrée, but it can stand on its own as a morning or afternoon meal. Remember to put the pan of water on the floor of the oven when you are pre-heating, and leave it there while the cornbread cooks. This is an old Creole trick for keeping baked bread super moist. Our ingredients here are classic and simple, but they produce cornbread just as it is meant to be. Put a glob of butter on it while it is still hot and enjoy.

Ingredients:

1 cup yellow corn meal
1 cup flour
1 TBSP sugar
4 tsp baking powder
1 tsp Cajun spice; Emeril's Essence®
½ tsp allspice
¼ tsp ground white pepper
1 large egg
1 cup milk
¼ cup vegetable shortening (substitute: butter)

Instructions:

Pre-heat oven to 425°. Place a baking pan 2/3 filled with water on the floor of the oven. This will humidify the oven and keep the finished cornbread very moist.

Sift the dry ingredients together into a large mixing bowl. Add the egg, milk, and ¼ cup shortening and beat with a wooden spoon or spatula until smooth, about 1 minute.

Grease an 8- or 9-inch iron skillet (or a heavy 8-inch square baking pan) with the shortening, pour in the batter, and bake in a preheated 425°F oven for 25 to 30 minutes, until light golden brown on top.

Plating:

Plate with jambalaya. Cut out of skillet into wedges and lay one wedge on the side of the mound of jambalaya. If you used a square baking pan, cut the cornbread into 9 squares. Lay one on the side of the jambalaya mound.

Brennan's® Bananas Foster

Chef Paul Blange invented this New Orleans banana split back in the 1950s in response to a challenge from Owen Brennan to look for scrumptious ways of included the imported fruit in the menu at Brennan's. They agreed to name the dessert after a regular customer and good friend of Owen, Richard Foster. The first time I had this desert was in the warm glow of the burning fountain in the courtyard seating area of Brennan's. When you wrap your lips around your first bite of this gift from heaven you have to stop in mid-bite and look up at those you are with to be reassured that this much pleasure is permissible in public. Then you are free to resume chewing. I think you will like this dessert.

Ingredients:

½ cup (1 stick) butter; halved
2 cups brown sugar; halved
1 tsp cinnamon; halved
½ cup banana liqueur; halved
8 bananas; cut in half lengthwise, then halved again (32 pieces)
½ cup dark rum; halved
8 large scoops premium vanilla ice cream

Instructions:

Since you will have 32 pieces of banana to heat in the sauce, use two large pans for the sauce preparation and flambé. Divide all ingredients to use in 2 pans.

Combine the butter, sugar, and cinnamon in each flambé pan or skillet. Place the pans over low heat and cook, stirring, until the sugar dissolves. In the next steps, if you are a little heavy-handed with the banana liqueur and rum, don't worry, the alcohol will cook off.

Stir in ¼ cup of banana liqueur into each pan; then place half of the bananas in each pan.

When the banana sections soften and begin to brown, carefully add ¼ cup of rum to each pan. Continue to cook the sauce until the rum is hot, then if you are cooking over gas and flame, tip the pan slightly to ignite the rum, otherwise light with a match (watch your arm and shirt sleeve). Let the flames go out before you plate. If you get no flame, don't worry it will taste just as good.

Plating:

Use a chilled large soup bowl so you don't lose any of the goodness about to be plated. Flat plates just don't give you enough scoop-ability when you are eating this and trying to spoon out the sauce and melted ice cream. Put one large scoop of vanilla ice cream in the center of each chilled bowl.

When the flames subside, lift the bananas out of the pan and place four pieces over each portion of ice cream. Try to make a teepee out of the banana pieces, but don't fret if they slide down. Leave them be. Use a spoon to drizzle the warm sauce over the top of the ice cream and serve immediately. When you have plated all 8 portions, you should go back and spoon some more sauce on each plate making sure you have left no sauce in the pan. Serve immediately. Use soup spoons or tablespoons to eat this dessert.

Extra Tips and Ideas You Really Don't Need to Use This Guide but They May Be Helpful

Invitations and Reminders

Sample Invitation
Asking a Couple to a Home Cooking Party for Eight

Dear Ken and Chris,

I would like to ask you to a special dinner on Saturday, November 16. I hope you can make it. Let me tell you about it. I bought a book called Home Cooking Parties for Eight. The idea of the book and the dinner is that eight people, in our case four couples, share in buying the food, working together to prepare the meal, cooking together and then eating the meal together. Your responsibility is 25% of the food budget, 25 % of the work and 100% of the pleasure. I have staged several of these dinners and they have turned out to be great evenings.

*I have a menu from soup to nuts, recipes for each dish, the shopping list split four ways, and a preparation schedule for everyone. We will gather in our kitchen promptly at 4 pm on Saturday, and with no advance preparation we follow the prep schedule, talk, laugh, chop, cook, and have a jolly good time on our way to a complete meal of foods few of us ever try at home. The menu I have selected for the evening of November 16 is called **A Calabrian Festival of Food.** I have attached the menu and the shopping list for your reading enjoyment. You will be Team 1. Just buy and bring the items on the shopping list under Shopper 1.*

You two are so much fun, I couldn't think of a better couple to add some fun and spice to our mix on that evening. I hope you are free and can make it.
John

Sample Couple Reminder
Sent a Few Days before the Home Cooking Party

Ken and Chris,

*The shopping list for our dinner, **A Calabrian Festival of Food**, is attached. Remember, you are Team 1 and Shopper 1. The list is divided so that each team is purchasing approximately one-quarter worth of the groceries. The measures shown on the list are meant to clue you in on how much to buy and bring. There is no need* to pre-measure or precut the items. Just bring enough and we will prepare it, cut it or measure it right there at the gathering. The host and hostess supply the beverages, so there is no need to bring anything extra. Bring a couple of knives for chopping and a cutting board.

I have a preparation schedule that we all follow that tells us exactly what to do and makes the work easy as pie. Please arrive at 4 pm or a few minutes early, if you would like. Dress for the evening is casual. Remember to bring an apron for each of you. We will all be wearing them while we prepare and cook. Expect to have fun!

John

Sample Invitation
Asking a Single to a Home Cooking Party for Eight

Dear Ann,

I would like to ask you to a special dinner on Saturday, November 16. I hope you can make it. Let me tell you about it. I bought a book called Home Cooking Parties for Eight. The idea of the book and the dinner is that eight people share in buying the food, working together to prepare the meal, cooking together and then eating the meal together. Since you will be teamed up with another person when you arrive, your team's responsibility is 25% of the food budget, 25 % of the work and 100% of the pleasure. I have staged several of these dinners and they have turned out to be great evenings.

I have a menu from soup to nuts, recipes for each dish, the shopping list split four ways, and a preparation schedule for everyone. We will gather in my kitchen promptly at 4 pm on Saturday, and with no advance preparation we will form teams, follow the prep schedule, talk, laugh, chop, cook, and have a jolly good time on our way to a complete meal of foods few of us ever try at home. The menu I have selected for the evening of November 16 is called **A Calabrian Festival of Food.** I have attached the menu and the shopping list for your reading enjoyment. You will be on Team 1. Just buy and bring the items on the shopping list under Shopper 1 and we will balance off all the costs when we are together.

You are so much fun, I couldn't think of a better person to add some fun and spice to our mix on that evening. I hope you are free and can make it.

John

Sample Single Reminder
Sent a Few Days before the Home Cooking Party

Ann,

*The shopping list for our dinner, A **Calabrian Festival of Food**, is attached. Remember, you are on Team 1 and are Shopper 1. The list is divided so that each team is purchasing approximately one-quarter worth of the groceries, but we will even that off when we get together. The measures shown on the list are meant to clue you in on how much to buy and bring. There is no need to pre-measure or precut the items. Just bring enough and we will prepare it, cut it or measure it right there at the gathering. The host supplies the beverages, so there is no need to bring anything extra. Bring a knife for chopping and a cutting board.*

I have a preparation schedule that we all follow that tells us exactly what to do and makes the work easy as pie. Please arrive at 4 pm or a few minutes early, if you would like. Dress for the evening is casual. Remember to bring an apron. We will all be wearing them while we prepare and cook. Expect to have fun!

John

Asking a Friend to Host

Asking a Couple to Host a Home Cooking Party for Eight

Dear Michele and Jeff,

How would you feel about hosting a Home Cooking Party for Eight in November or early December? It would be under the format I explained to you where everyone shares the grocery shopping, costs, preparation, cooking, eating and cleanup. It is a real party and great get-together experience.

*Since you have that lovely and spacious kitchen and very pretty dining room I could not think of a friendlier, happier place to try out the **Way Down Yonder in New Orleans** menu. I'll send you a copy of the menu. The commitment is actually easier than throwing a normal dinner party for fewer people. You would select one other couple that is willing to participate in the Home Cooking Party for Eight and we would select one. They could be people we already know in common or people from other walks of life who might bring a new mix to our experience. When you invite them, they just need to know they are involved equally in the shopping, preparing, cooking and eating.*

If you have soup bowls, appetizer plates, dinner plates, dessert plates, coffee cups and eight chairs, you have everything we need for the night. I encourage everyone to bring a couple of chopping knives, a cutting board and aprons with them, so your prep equipment should not be overwhelmed. Your other commitment is to supply beverages for the night, within your realm of comfort. This could be alcoholic or non-alcoholic. While the menu may call for some specific beverages, this can be immediately over-ruled by you as the host without notice to the participants.

If you agree to do this, we have any of the following Saturday evenings open (I do recommend a Saturday or a Sunday for your first experience of a meal like this since we ask everyone to be at the host's house around 3:30 to 4 p.m. for preparation) 11/16, 11/30, or 12/7. After I know your response I will distribute the menu and shopping lists, so everyone knows exactly what to expect.

I truly hope this is agreeable to you, I can't think of anyone we would rather share one of these experiences with.

John

Asking a Single to Host a Home Cooking Party for Eight

Dear Marilyn,

It was so much fun seeing you again on Saturday. It's been a while. I was overjoyed when you expressed such enthusiasm about hosting a Home Cooking Party for Eight. The first thing we need to do is pick a date. It should be a Saturday or Sunday because we will be gathering some time between 3:30 and 4 p.m. The date should be just far enough off to give everyone good notice and ensure more acceptances of your invitations. Naturally, I will be one of the eight and there to share in the work and cost of the groceries. You will need to find six other people. The preparation guide and recipes in the book really are enough to get everyone through the evening. You won't need any extra instructions from me. Even rookie cooks will do fine. When we get to your kitchen we will form up four teams of two. As soon as you get acceptances from people to attend, you will pick three people along with yourself to do the shopping. The shopping list is divided four ways, and while four people do the shopping, all eight people will share equally in the cost of the groceries. We can settle that up when we all get together in your kitchen, before we begin. Just pick three people who you think will be comfortable in a grocery store. They don't have to shop together.

When you form the 2-person teams, the team members don't have to know each other. In fact, it's better if you partner people who don't know each other. It makes for a more interesting evening. The teams don't have to be married couples. They could be all-girl teams or all-guy teams, however you think it will be the most fun. If you have any trouble coming up with 6 people, let me know and I will get the rest. People who have done this before always seem willing to jump right in.

If you have soup bowls, appetizer plates, dinner plates, dessert plates, coffee cups and eight chairs, you have everything we need for the night. I usually encourage everyone to bring a chopping knife, a cutting board and apron with them, so your prep equipment should not be overwhelmed. Your other commitment is to supply beverages for the night, within your realm of comfort. This could be alcoholic or non-alcoholic. While the menu may call for some specific beverages, this can be immediately over-ruled by you as the host without notice to the participants.

So here you go! Pick a date and let me know (January 11 is the only bad date for me). Then start picking people for the dinner party. Once you pick a date, we can go over the menus in the Home Cooking Parties for Eight book. I will send you a copy of the one you pick along with the shopping lists. This will be a great evening.

John

Dinner for Twenty? More?
You Asked for a Team Building Event!

During my professional career in engineering and project management, I have worked and consulted for some of the largest companies in the land. A while back, a Director of one such client decided to take me along with her team to a company-owned farm for a two-day planning meeting. The site is on the Eastern Shore of Maryland right next to the Chesapeake Bay – a serene, pastoral setting replete with ducks, geese, cormorants, loons, deer and a Pepsi machine.

A few weeks before we went on the trip, the Director came to me, knowing some of my history with Home Cooking Parties, and asked if I would be willing to orchestrate a big cooking event and dinner party for the entire team. She wanted the cooking experience to be a team building exercise. Now, the farm does have a three-person professional cheffing team that cooks all of the meals for farm guests, so I contacted them and let them know that our team would be doing all of the cooking for our dinner meal on the night of our stay. In fact, I told them that I would plan the menu, work up the shopping list and direct the entire group of twenty. All the chefs would have to do is buy the groceries, stand-by, show us where the pots and pans were and join us for dinner. They were delighted. So there was me, sixteen of my working associates and the three chefs, 20 in all. A Home Cooking Party for Twenty was about to be born.

The first thing I did was have the chefs take pictures of their kitchen and dining rooms and e-mail them to me. They had a professional sized cook top, but only one oven so special planning would be necessary to rotate the various items through the baking and roasting parts of the event in a timely fashion. I decided to use the **Parsley, Sage, Rosemary & Garlic** Home Cooking Party for Four plan as a starting point. The shopping list was the easiest thing to change. I just multiplied everything by 5 and there I had it, food for 20. I e-mailed that to the pro chefs turned Shopping Team and they said that they would take care of it all. The farm also has a bar so we selected the option for cocktails, wine and liqueur all the way from cocktail hour to the end of the night. That was easy.

Next I had to decide how I was going to use the other sixteen people on my team. They could not all fit into the kitchen. It was an old farmhouse kitchen from the turn of the century (19th to 20th) with only a few professional upgrades. Hip room was not one of them. In fact the pros were afraid that we would overwhelm their little country kitchen. We would have, so I decided to segregate the team. Eight of them would be sous chefs working under my direction. Six of them would be waiters working under my direction. The remaining two would be sommeliers working under my direction. Since I did a three year stint as a waiter in New York City when I was in college, I knew how to direct the wait staff part of the team. I made my own wine, beer and liqueur in the 1970s and drank a lot from 1965 through 1995, so I was completely comfortable with the sommeliers. The good fortune of this arrangement was that I did not have to change my meal preparation plan from a timing standpoint. I had noticed over many of my Home Cooking Parties for Eight that the four two-person chef teams always seemed to have plenty of time to complete their cutting and cooking jobs, so I went on the hunch that increasing the workload from 8 to 20 portions would not be that much more work. I was almost right. Boy oh boy, some of them worked like dogs in the kitchen, but I kept telling them to have faith and confidence and it would all work out okay.

My plan was that once the sous chef teams were launched on their first courses I would show the waiters how to set the dining rooms (we needed two rooms in the small farm house for the large crowd). We had two very long tables, one in each dining room, and a small side table for the three professional chefs who wanted to eat but said they would be more comfortable not encroaching on our party. The wait team was divided into two groups of three, one team for each dining room. We did some social engineering experimentation, as well. We assigned all of the waiters to eat in one dining room with one sommelier serving them, and all of the chefs in the larger dining room with the other sommelier serving in there. Interestingly enough there was a huge esprit de'corp among the chefs and a similarly robust one among the waiters. The teaming experience worked well from that standpoint.

The first lesson for the wait team was the place setting. We needed wine glasses, water glasses, soup bowls, salad plates and dinner plates. The dessert plates and coffee cups were kept on a sideboard until after the main course. It was a good break that one of my sous chefs was also an expert napkin folder, so she took a break from cooking and trained the wait team in several folding techniques. They wound up choosing the one they could do 20 times in a row. We had a marvelous menu and would be serving everything banquet style with arm service. I showed them how to carry up to four plates at a crack in their arms. Consensus was reached quickly by the slightly tipsy team that each of them would handle no more that one plate in each hand at a time. They were greatly relieved.

Since the sommeliers were mixing cocktails and serving wine like champs I spent almost no time with them. They were both sauced, so additional training would not have stuck.

The sous chefs were magnificent, especially when you consider the fact that they did not have any idea what they would be doing right up to 15 minutes before they started.

That afternoon, when we finished our last business meeting of the day, I was given the floor by the Director. I handed out hats which the sous chefs wore with bills front, the waiters wore them with the bills back, and the sommeliers wore them with the bills right or left, their choice. Everyone of the team received a booklet with the prep instructions and recipes for the meal. I told them to meet me in the kitchen in 15 minutes and we would start with our first cocktail and I would give out a few other instructions.

Everyone showed up in the kitchen on time and proved that 17 of us plus the three pros would have never fit. We did put our aprons on. Sous got to wear them straight up. Waiters and sommeliers folded them down to the waist and wore them French café style. I told the waiters to go into the bar room, drink and wait (makes sense). The sous chefs were instructed to open their booklets and see who each was partnered with. The pros armed the sous with knives and cutting boards and the work began. Each team simply followed the prep plan and recipes and was focused on a different task. Some cut baguettes, some chopped vegetables, others strained lentils, others chopped fresh herbs and still others prepared tart fillings. They turned to me whenever they were not sure how something should look or feel, but for the most part they worked merrily along until there was a dispute.

Two of the teams quickly turned out the Antipasto, so at least the booze was being accompanied by something, but the dispute was between the other two teams. One of the sous (an engineer) insisted he was supposed to finish the soup because he started it. The plan really called for him and his partner to make the base soup, while another team was in the plan to make the roux, finish the mint infused butter and plate the final soup. It took all of my might to convince him he did not have to finish every item he started, only the parts the instructions said to finish; besides he had to jump onto the deep fried vegetables preparation. He relented, even though he didn't buy in completely, and did a great job on the vegetables.

The steak cooking was a trip! The waiters took orders from everyone whether they wanted their filets rare, medium rare, medium, medium well or well-done. Have you ever worked with someone who has only cooked a little bit for himself, has not been married and never threw a dinner party? Fortunately he was an engineer, understood process and how to read instructions. He followed the directions explicitly and my subtle nurturing. You know what? Everyone got a steak exactly as it was ordered. He seared, ovened, also set some steaks on the top shelf of the stove to achieve varying degrees of doneness. That night he was superb.

The courses were served in perfect order, just 20 to 30 minutes late each — it's okay to not be perfect! The confluence of flavors and doneness was magnificent. Everyone had a great meal, and they were stuffed. They could barely move by the time we finished the main course, so we put off dessert for an extra thirty minutes and went on the front porch of the farmhouse for cigars and brandy. Even a few of the women smoked stogies. It was a riot. When we went back in for dessert, they were floored by the creamy and lightly sweet creation. Since the Director had worked on the dessert, they were all very complimentary. She deserved it. The tart was really good.

Thus ended my first try at a Home Cooking Party for Twenty. What I learned from that night was that any of you could run such an experience for a large crowd like this simply by splitting the jobs like I did. I also learned that the size of your kitchen won't matter much, so if you have enough dining space in a private home with a large kitchen you might not have to rent a banquet facility. In my Team Building Plan for 20, which can be found on my website, www.homecookingparties.com, I have revised the shopping lists and menus and even made a few changes in the Preparation and Service Plan to balance the work properly. You can even vary the group size up or down a bit. Good luck if you ever try it. I promise you will thrill 16, 20 or 24 people with a classy, arm-service sit-down dinner.

Friends, Cooks and Chefs

Thanks to these friends, cooks and chefs with providing inspiration in the kitchen and for menu and recipe ideas. I would have included George Washington as the Father of Our Country, but I don't recall any stories about him cooking....

Steve Perides	Assunta Perides	Teresa Malvetti
Margaret Casey	Mary Razzetti	Frances Tabeek
Anastasia Bilello	Larry Abbomonte	Neil Oculato
Rachael Ray	Mario Batali	Rick Bayless
Nicholas Tselementes	Sarah Moulton	Ina Garten
Zarela Martinez	Tyler Florence	Rain Ross
Bobby Flay	Giada De Laurentiis	Paula Dean
Paul Prudhomme	Emeril Lagasse	Paul Blange
Dorothy VonHoltum	Count Arnaud	Paolo Villoresi
Sandra Lee	Kenneth Domzalski	Ming Tsai
Martin Yan	Vinod Menezes	Kinley Tshering

Home Cooking Parties for™ . . . Eight

This easy to follow guide for home cooking parties includes everything you need to hold a cooking party for eight friends tonight. Best of all you share the cost and all of the work equally. You only need to invite them and tell them what to buy and bring. The rest is taken care of by this guide. So start the fun tonight. Included in this guide

Complete Menus for
15 Different International Meals

Shopping Lists for Each Friend

Recipes for Every Item

Preparation Plans Down to the Minute

Including . . . Who chops
. . . Who cooks
. . . Who plates and serves
. . . When to start
. . . When to serve
. . . Which pot or pan to use
. . . Which plate to use
. . . How to dress the plate

Enjoy!

You can order other menu plans or editions of Home Cooking Parties for ™ by visiting

www.HomeCookingParties.com